Tell me the
TRUTH
ABOUT
LOSS

Tell me the

TRUTH
ABOUT
LOSS

A PSYCHOLOGIST'S PERSONAL STORY
OF LOSS, GRIEF AND FINDING HOPE

NIAMH
FITZPATRICK

GILL BOOKS

Gill Books
Hume Avenue
Park West
Dublin 12
www.gillbooks.ie

Gill Books is an imprint of M.H. Gill and Co.

© Niamh Fitzpatrick 2020
978 07171 8384 5

Original design by www.grahamthew.com
Edited by Rachel Pierce
Proofread by Jane Rogers
Printed by CPI Group (UK) Ltd, Croydon, CRO 4YY

The author and publishers gratefully acknowledge permission to
reprint copyright material in this book as follows:
'Run'
Words and music by Gary Lightbody, Jonathan Quinn, Mark
McClelland, Nathan Connolly and Iain Archer
© Copyright 2003 Kobalt Music Services Limited
Kobalt Music Publishing Limited/Universal Music Publishing BL
Limited
All rights reserved. International copyright secured.
Used by permission of Hal Leonard Europe Limited.

This book is typeset in Sabon.
The paper used in this book comes from the wood pulp of
managed forests. For every tree felled, at least one tree is planted,
thereby renewing natural resources.

5 4 3

This book is dedicated to the men and women of both the Search and Rescue and Emergency Services, who cross land, sea and air to go to the aid of strangers.

And to the heartbroken loved ones left behind when they don't come home.

Go Mairidís Beo
(THAT OTHERS MAY LIVE)

A donation from the proceeds of this book will go to The Irish Hospice Foundation, the national charity dedicated to death, dying and bereavement. In telling my own story of loss, it feels fitting to help continue their important work of supporting those who are dying and those who carry the pain of loss when they are gone.

ABOUT THE AUTHOR

Niamh Fitzpatrick has a BA in psychology, an MA in clinical psychology and an MSc in sport management, specialising in sport psychology. For 28 years she has worked with clients seeking to achieve optimal mental health, as well as with clients aiming for optimal performance in sport, business or life.

CONTENTS

INTRODUCTION

A STORY OF LOSS AND HOPE

have learned an important truth: grief is not just about death, it's about change and what we lose when things change. It's the old life that we knew gone for ever and a new one in its place. We can encounter grief in many different situations and it's important to give ourselves permission to grieve for all such losses, to accept the necessity of grief as part of the healing and recovery process. There are many different types of loss throughout life. Perhaps your loss is the death of someone you love, maybe it's the end of a relationship or the realisation that you'll never be a parent. It could be a life-altering medical condition, a miscarriage or an accident that sees you having to say goodbye to the life you once knew or to the hopes you had for the future. Whatever it is, any loss can be a cause of grief. I've experienced the loss of my sister, the loss of my marriage and the loss of my plan to be a mother.

These losses all occured within a relatively short period of time: the failure of IVF was followed only a few years later by the end of my marriage, which happened at the same time as the devastating loss of my sister. Dara died on 14 March 2017 while piloting the Irish Coast Guard helicopter Rescue 116 over Blacksod Bay in County Mayo. Her death was sudden, it was shocking, it was far too soon. Death had visited my family in the middle of the night as we lay sleeping in our beds. I was overwhelmed by grief. Shaken to the core. Already reeling from my sister's death, I would have said that it wasn't possible to feel any more sorrow than I was already experiencing, it felt like that cup was filled to the brim. I thought that I was all cried out, to be honest. I was wrong. When my marriage ended, waves of grief came crashing over me. It was sadness layered on top of sadness, loss on top of loss. It has changed me for ever.

Up close, I have found grief to be nothing like I imagined it to be. I'm a psychologist, but what I knew from a professional perspective didn't come close to covering what it has been like actually living with grief. I've now seen loss from the inside, a different viewpoint I suppose, one that obviously I wish I didn't have.

Grievers are the same; we know that death means emotions all over the place for a very long time. It means anger like you never knew you were capable of feeling, often expressed in the wrong place and at the wrong time and directed at the wrong source. It means not being able to concentrate enough to read a newspaper and being absentminded to the point of putting your cup in the fridge instead of the dishwasher. It means mourning the loss of the person who died and the life they had yet to live, and the loss of the life you had with them in it. Grief means spending too much money in shops on random stuff you don't need, yet not having a pint of milk in the house when people call over. It means eating too much or too little, or not being able to get out of bed in the morning even though you stared at the ceiling most of the night with no interest in sleep. It means some people avoiding you because they don't know what to say, and others smothering you because they think you need saving (we don't). Grieving means not being able to stop the tears streaming down your face when you hear a song that reminds you of your sister, even though you're standing in the queue to pay for your T-shirts at Marks & Spencer. It means snapping at people who don't deserve it and not being properly there for your friends when they have things going on in their own lives. Grieving means resenting those who have what you have lost and connecting with those who have lost too. Grieving means a magnification of existing troubles or situations. Grief means you can feel like living only for the moment, throwing caution to the wind, yet you're the same person who sometimes doesn't want to put your two feet on the floor each morning and start a new day. Grieving means wrestling with emotions that you don't understand when your mind eventually begins to start to accept the loss. Grief means physical, mental, emotional and spiritual exhaustion. Then, one day, grief means hope. That somehow you may be able to remember the person you love and at the same time live your life. Grievers come to know this in time and so the community of those who are bereaved is a tightknit group that can be a lifeline for many. There's healing in that togetherness.

Like everyone else, I wasn't ready for loss. You can't prepare for a sudden death, of course, but you also can't prepare for the slow erosion of your future as you watch the family you thought you were going to have evaporate in front of your eyes. There is no way to be ready for loss. All you can do is front up to it, feel the feelings it brings and try to get through to the other side – and to keep believing that there is another side, that there is a life after loss. It's a horribly difficult challenge, but it also throws up important lessons and important realisations about yourself and what exactly you're capable of doing. It is a hard teacher.

This time of loss and grief has tested me in every way and pushed me to what seemed like the furthest corners of my limits. It would be a magnificent understatement to say that it has been a tough few years and there were times when it all got too much for me and the constant struggle to be hopeful felt like a mountain too high to climb. It felt like a mental and emotional battle that was relentless. Beforehand, I would have said that I couldn't cope with it, but I did cope, I did go on and now, three years after my sister died and my marriage ended, I am learning to live with the losses in my life and doing okay in that regard.

I wanted to write this book because of what I have learned from these personal experiences of loss. I believe lived experience has a value when it comes to the learnings that we can extract. In the same way that there is value in the personal account of the oncologist who is living with cancer, or the neurologist who has suffered a stroke, the personal perspective of a psychologist living through trauma, shock, loss and grief also has value. I didn't feel any responsibility to write this book. I don't have any need to ride in on a white horse and save the day, so responsibility is too strong a word for it. But as a psychologist it feels as though it would be a missed opportunity not to share a perspective of loss from the inside.

Ever since I qualified as a psychologist back in the early 1990s, I have regularly dipped in and out of attending sessions as a client myself. Throughout my career, working with different therapists, I have been in the client's chair, although for the most part I am in the therapist's chair. When my sister died and my marriage ended, I was the one who needed help rather than being the one who was helping. That lived experience of trauma, shock, loss and grief meant that I got a look at them all from the other chair, as a client. Most important, I got to see coping from a different side. Paired with my psychology background, it provides an interesting perspective that may yield useful reflections.

I have learned, for example, that there are many myths around grief and grieving and they can be very unhelpful for those living through it. There are inaccurate beliefs that many of us hold before grief lands on our own doorstep and shows us different. Some people think that grief is about sadness and tears. That's not true. As an understanding of grief that's not nearly enough. Grief is complex and layered and involves a wide range of emotions and states. Anger. Rage. Bewilderment. Loneliness. Numbness. Guilt. Confusion. Exhaustion. Intense, bone-deep sorrow. They're all in there, along with a host of other feelings that show up along the way.

Personal experience also tells me that grief is not about doing well or badly, there's no rating scale or progress chart with grief; the aim is to live through it and with it, not to do well at it. The notion that someone can be 'strong' or 'indulgent' in grief is so wrong. This idea can make things harder because as time goes on society expects those of us grieving to 'be okay' or some version of 'okay'. No one wants to be around that sad person all the time. And most times now I am okay, or some version of it, but sometimes I'm not and I just put on a happy face and get on with it because I feel that's expected of me. Inside, I want to scream. That's why talking and writing about grief is so important to me – hopefully, it helps to set people free from these narrow ideas and permits us to be authentic in our grief.

The other idea that's not helpful is the popular belief that grief has stages that you move through on the way to some sort of 'not-grief'. As a psychologist I knew this was a myth, a misinterpretation of the work of psychiatrist Elisabeth Kübler-Ross, who was actually seeking to understand the mental and emotional experiences of people living with terminal illness and facing their own death when she first proposed 'five stages of grief'. Over time, the stages evolved and Kübler-Ross later wrote about them as applied to the grief of the bereaved. However, grief isn't neat and linear, and Kübler-Ross never meant to imply that it was. Rather, she wanted to outline some observed responses to loss in order to help people understand the landscape of loss. Sure enough, from my own experience I know that grief is messy and unstructured, a journey that's more of a lurching from one emotional state to another and back again many times over. It's unpredictable and unavoidable and not something that can or should be expected to happen along a defined process.

We often describe grief as a journey, but the important thing to realise is that it has no endpoint, no final destination, no time when the grieving is all over and there is no pain. When you love someone and they die, you'll always feel their loss in some way, I think. I imagine I will feel Dara's loss until the day I take my own last breath. Indeed, I think that I *want* to feel her loss until that day; that sits right with me, it's as it should be. I'm not saying, however, that when we grieve we will feel that high-level pain for ever. The feelings of grief do change as time marches on. I can't say that it gets better or easier, but it does get different. There's hope in that thought. My experience is that grief becomes an ongoing part of your life, something you grapple with until you learn to live with it. This means grief isn't about being strong, staying strong or being resilient or, the worst one of all, 'getting over it'. It's not about 'moving on'. It's not about 'closure'. Never any of those.

The truth is that grief is in many ways initially about survival, pure and simple. It's about getting through, just one day at a time, each day bringing you to another day, then another day. Then in time it becomes about finding new ways to relate to the person who has died, finding ways to express the love you have for them, because that doesn't die when they die. People say to me, 'You loved your sister.' No, I didn't. It's not past tense. I LOVE her. She's just not here to feel that love.

At base, grief is about change, about figuring out how to live this new life when you were perfectly happy with your old life and you just want it back, with everyone you love still in it. You are a different person with a new life after a loss and you have only one real option, which is to somehow accept, adapt and adjust to the loss you have experienced. That's quite a task, so a big truth about loss is that dealing with it requires work, consciously or subconsciously. What I mean by that is that grief doesn't feel to me like a passive experience, where we just sit and wait to emerge from it on some miraculous day. Navigating grief feels more like a journey in which I am an active participant, a driver rather than a passenger. Figuring out how to cope with the emotions around grief has been the steepest learning curve of my life and it's a journey that I am still on to this day.

It was for all these reasons that I agreed to write this book and share my story, in order to impart some of the observations and learnings on my journey in grief. Writing a book like this feels a bit like doing a therapy session in public, letting others in to the thoughts and feelings that I would normally keep to myself, but I wanted to pass on my truth about loss in the hope that it might be of use to someone else trying to figure out their own experience of loss and grief. While all our journeys are different, sometimes hearing from those at a different place along the path of grief can illuminate the way for others, shining a light on some of the ground they are about to tread. This won't make anyone's grief journey easier, because it won't eliminate the pain, but it may help some people feel less alone and perhaps feel less blindsided by some of the experiences along the way. That's what this book is about.

It's important to say that this is not a self-help book nor an 'everything there is to know about grief' book. There will be things that I will know but leave out and things that I will not have experienced at the time of writing but may experience when I'm further down the road of grief. Grief is like a fingerprint: it is personal, it is individual and it is different for everyone. We all feel and handle it differently and it's for each person to express their feelings of loss in the way that feels right for them. That's why this isn't a book on 'how to do grief'. It's not a blueprint for how to grieve. This is simply my personal story of different types of loss with some reflections along the way.

It's also important for me to say that this is not a book about the crash in which my sister and her colleagues lost their lives. The details of the crash and why it happened is not my story to tell. It's also not my place to talk about anyone else's family member, that's their own story to tell. I do briefly outline what happened on the night of the accident, but only to give context to my own experience of loss. It matters to me very much that I tell my own story without telling anyone else's.

In writing my story of loss, I do of course need to mention other people on occasion, but only when necessary and only in minimal terms. I mention my family, for example, but I do not speak for them and neither do I tell their story; I simply reference them in the context of sharing my own experience of loss.

I encountered life-changing loss that knocked me right off my feet and altered me for ever, but I lived to tell the tale and I've learned some powerful lessons along the way about the capacity of us all as human beings. I have discovered first-hand that there *is* life after trauma, grief and hopelessness, that it is possible to feel happiness and joy once again and that there is growth after loss. Life doesn't have to be perfect to be wonderful, there is comfort and hope in that. My experience of loss has influenced my experience of life and I see life so differently now. Nothing matters but being with those I like and love and doing what is meaningful to me. The rest is noise. I know now that the little things in life are actually the big things.

I'd give *anything* to have my sister back, to have my old life back, to be ignorant of the depths and reach of grief. I'd like not to know how the fallout from loss seeps into every corner of your life, like water finding its way into every tiny crevice. It is now three years since my sister died and since my marriage ended, and just a few years since I accepted that I would not become a mother. I still feel immense sorrow and grief, but now I can honestly say that I also feel hopeful. I have an awareness that I can carry the sadness and at the same time live my life.

If I didn't feel that sense of hope and possibility, I wouldn't be writing this book.

Now, I know the truth about loss.

CHAPTER ONE

IT WAS A NORMAL WEEK UNTIL IT WASN'T

spent Monday 13 March 2017 as I would have expected. It was just like any other Monday. I did normal things, such as chat with my husband, go for a walk, have breakfast, feed and walk my dog. I saw clients and scheduled meetings and appointments. Throughout the day I chatted with family and friends over text and by phone. I'm not a worrier by nature, but that day I was probably having the usual thoughts that we all have every day. *Will I have time to get that report done? Should I say yes to that project that arrived in my email inbox because it's in my field of study even though the subject is not really a passion of mine? I must put washing powder on the shopping list and I need to take salmon out of the freezer for dinner. I feel like I'll have lost weight when I go to my slimming group this week. Actually, should I be doing more intense exercise to keep shifting those pounds?* Normal thoughts, normal things taking up space in my head. I went about my business during the day and when I went to bed that night I was ready for sleep. It had been a satisfying day, but a busy one. It was another normal week.

Until it wasn't.

My sister was Captain Dara Fitzpatrick, a pilot with the Dublin-based Irish Coast Guard rescue helicopter, callsign Rescue 116. In the early hours of Tuesday 14 March, Rescue 116 crashed off the coast of Mayo while on a callout. All four crew onboard lost their lives that night: Winch Operator Paul Ormsby, Winchman Ciarán Smith, Captain Mark Duffy, Captain Dara Fitzpatrick. They flew out over the sea to provide assistance to the rescue of someone in trouble and they never came home.

The first I heard about the crash was a phone call from my sister Emer, just before 6.00 am on Tuesday 14 March. My alarm had been set to go off at 6.00 am as I wanted to get an early start to a busy day. But instead of the alarm, it was the sound of my phone ringing that roused me from sleep several minutes before 6.00 am. It's strange the details that stick out in my mind. I remember that I was sleeping on my left side, facing the window. I remember the very first moment that the phone came to life, how even through sleep I noticed right away that it was not the alarm tone sounding but the ring tone.

I grabbed the phone and pressed Accept. Emer spoke five words that would change life for ever: 'The heli has gone down.'

I phoned my mother and without preamble told her that the helicopter was down and that we were coming to get her. I phoned my twin sister, Orla, and she said that she would collect my mother and call our brother, Johnny. Our father had travelled to the UK the day before and his phone was turned off, so initially we couldn't reach him. As I was making those calls, I jumped out of bed, brushed my teeth and threw on some clothes while filling my husband in on what Emer had said. I had a little dog called Buddy, a gorgeous five-year-old Lhasa Apso, and I remember giving him a little rub behind his ear and a kiss on top of his head before I ran out the door. My husband would lock up the house and follow me.

I live four houses away from Emer and Dara, who shared together and with Dara's little son, Fionn, aged two and a half at the time. Sprinting over, it took me only moments to get from my house to theirs and Emer had the front door opened within a nano-second of me standing outside it. I can remember the look on her face when the door opened. She mirrored exactly how I felt – a bit dazed, confused, disoriented. I think we were both still brushing off the remnants of sleep and wondering how on earth we got to be standing on her doorstep at 6.00 am. She explained that Dara had received a callout the night before and had gone to work, leaving Emer and Fionn in the house, and that shortly before she rang me two work colleagues of Dara's had knocked on the door to deliver the news that there had been no contact with the crew of Rescue 116 for a number of hours. Fionn was sleeping upstairs, so Emer took me straight into the kitchen, where I saw the two men standing beside the table.

I recognised one; he was Captain Mark Donnelly, a work colleague and also a friend of Dara's. I had met him and his family on several occasions. I didn't know the other man, but he was introduced as Aircraft Maintenance Engineer Eoin Murphy, who also worked with Dara at the Dublin Search and Rescue base. We had to be quiet so as not to wake Fionn, so we talked in whispers.

I asked Mark and Eoin what had happened and they told me that Rescue 116 had been on a callout during the night and that there had been no contact since shortly after 12.30 am. They knew no more at that point, but it seemed that the helicopter had gone down. I remember seeing fear in their eyes and it struck me even then as being fear with a capital F. I was 48 years old at the time and I honestly don't think that in all my life I had ever seen fear in its pure, raw form like that. I was wondering if they knew more about what was going on but were trying to protect us. So, quite urgently and perhaps quite strongly, I asked them if they had any more information, trying to let them know that if there was bad news, I would rather know it. We're all different in situations like this, but for me not knowing is not protection. Whatever it was, knowing was better than not knowing. But it was clear that they had no other information beyond what they had just told us, so we waited for the rest of the family to arrive, the four of us just standing together in the kitchen, disbelieving. It was like having some sort of out-of-body experience.

Over the next few hours it would emerge that Rescue 116 had been tasked with providing what's known as top cover to a sister helicopter. The Irish Coast Guard has four helicopter bases in Ireland – one each in Dublin, Waterford, Shannon and Sligo. The Sligo-based helicopter, Rescue 118, was heading out to sea to perform the medical evacuation of an injured fisherman from a vessel situated approximately 140 nautical miles/259 km off the Mayo coast on the west of Ireland. Carrying out this long-range evacuation required a second aircraft be present to provide support, mainly in the way of radio communication but also assistance, if required, to Rescue 118. During such operations, top cover means having their backs in case of emergency.

The callout came late on the night of 13 March and Dara got out of her bed and made her way to the Search and Rescue base at Dublin Airport. Rescue 116 set off from Dublin to make its way to the west coast, a flight time of about 60 minutes. Upon reaching the western seaboard they would land at the helipad at Blacksod Lighthouse, which sits at one of the westernmost points of Ireland, right on the edge of the country, next stop America. They would refuel at the lighthouse before heading out over the black-dark sea to support their colleagues. However, en route to Blacksod Lighthouse, at 12.46 am Rescue 116 crashed into Black Rock Island, a rock approximately 9 miles/16.6 km off the coast of Blacksod Bay, plunging into the sea on impact.

Vincent Sweeney is the lighthouse-keeper at Blacksod and from radio communications with the Irish Coast Guard helicopters involved in the rescue mission over the course of the evening, he knew that Rescue 116 from Dublin was due to land on his helipad to refuel. When the Dublin-based crew had not arrived by the time he expected, beautiful man that he is, alert and in tune with what should happen timing-wise and sensing no reason for even a small delay, he wasted no time in raising the alarm.

After the alert went out and it was established that contact with Rescue 116 had ceased, the search began for the aircraft and the four crew. Search and Rescue helicopters and lifeboats began to comb the area of Blacksod Bay. It was after 1.00 am on a dark March night, a fog had descended on the area and the seas were rough and changing all the time, with a swell of about 4 metres, occasionally more than that, meaning incredibly difficult search conditions for all involved. Nonetheless, they soon found debris scattered in the sea around Black Rock Island and it became apparent to those searching that Rescue 116 had indeed crashed.

Dara's body was discovered in the water not long after the search began, located by Rescue 118, the helicopter for which she and the crew had been providing top cover. Weather and sea conditions were so bad that although they located her, spotting her red hair floating out around her in the water under the search lights of the helicopter, several attempts by the crew to recover Dara from the water were unsuccessful. It was too rough and the swell too big to enable the winchman to reach Dara; even with the immense skill of the pilots and winch crew working as a team to manoeuvre the winchline down towards the surface of the sea, positioned on the end of that line the winchman could get to within an arm's length of her, but no nearer. Rescue 118 contacted the RNLI's Achill Island lifeboat, one of the boats in the area searching for signs of life through debris scattered in the water. Under extremely challenging conditions, the lifeboat crew managed to retrieve Dara from the sea and take her onboard the lifeboat, where they carried out resuscitation attempts before pronouncing her dead. Dara was later airlifted from the lifeboat and flown by her colleagues in the Shannon-based Rescue 115 helicopter to the mortuary at Mayo University hospital in Castlebar.

All this took place while we were asleep in our beds, unaware that the girl we love was living her last moments of life.

It was much later when I would find out that these two men, Mark and Eoin, had volunteered to come and deliver the news to Dara's family. During the night, Captain Mark Donnelly was woken and told that contact had been lost with the helicopter. He had been on the shift before Dara, so he had met the crew at the end of his shift when they took over from him and his crew. They had spent some time together on the base and chatted before he headed home. So the moment he received communication to say that contact had been lost, he would have known right away who was in that aircraft and that whatever had happened, his friend Dara was in a very bad situation. As Dara's pal and colleague, he volunteered to come to her house and tell her family. That is the essence of courage in my book, and of friendship. That's what showing up for your friend looks like.

Mark contacted Eoin, his colleague at the Dublin base, and together they came to tell Emer the news. How awful it must have been for them as they stood outside the door of Dara's house, knowing that they would be changing our lives for ever once they rang that bell, bringing the news that as a family member of someone who works in the emergency services you dread, heralding the day that we all pray will never come. In the early days when Dara started in Search and Rescue I worried about her, we all did, but as the years went by and I got to know more about her job and indeed saw her doing her job, the worry mostly faded into the background. I have heard the words 'We're going flying' or 'We're just back from flying' so many times from Dara over the years that flying was the norm. It was what Dara did.

I am sure that my parents, particularly my mother, worried every single time Dara was on shift or got a callout, especially night calls or those in bad weather. For a mother to know that her child was out there in those conditions, instead of being safely tucked up in bed or safely on solid ground, even though she is an adult child who is highly trained, hugely experienced and working with a crew of the same calibre, must have been savagely difficult. It has to go against every maternal instinct, I would imagine, and I expect that over the twenty-three years that

Dara was in Search and Rescue, my mother only truly breathed when she knew that Dara was back on the ground. Mark and Eoin didn't have to break that news to us, but knowing from their own families the worry that loved ones of search and rescue personnel face, they knew that it was the right thing to do, to not have strangers turn up at Emer's door and wake her from sleep, to have at least one familiar face there to tell us what had happened.

Soon the family were gathered in Emer's kitchen, my mother, my two sisters and my brother, Johnny, everyone there except for my father, who making his way back from the UK following our phone call to him that morning. When Fionn began to stir, although his Mama wasn't there he woke to familiar arms waiting to mind him and he was soon dressed and fed. Extended family had arrived and people pitched in and took him to play, finding his favourite toys and ensuring that he had as normal a start to the day as possible. I don't know what a two-and-a-half-year-old thinks of a house full of people so early in the morning, but it didn't faze him and he wasn't at all distressed. He was just happily chatting away to everyone, the way toddlers do. We didn't tell him anything at that stage, of course. He thought that Mama was at work and as he had his aunties and uncle and his grandmother there with him, there was no cause for concern on his part.

For six hours after that early-morning knock at the door on 14 March, all we knew was that the helicopter was missing. Dara's body had by that time been recovered, but she had not yet been formally identified at the hospital. As a result, all we were told was that the helicopter had gone down and there had been no contact from them. None of us waiting in the house knew any more than that; this was all the information that Mark and Eoin had been given. We could do nothing but wait. It was excruciating.

During those hours I remember the feeling of being helpless. I wasn't able to sit still, indeed everyone was just standing or walking the floor. I had a knot in my stomach, a lump in my throat and a weird, almost fuzzy feeling, as if I was outside of myself watching this nightmare unfold. No one would likely have known that from the outside as there was no screaming, no crying, no big show of emotion from anyone during those hours that we waited. Everybody stayed calm. Thinking back on it, that may sound strange, but it's obvious now that we were all in shock. Even in that situation I think that something kicks in and you go into a deal-with-it mode. There was no Fight or Flight or even Freeze mode at that time, we all just went straight into practical mode and tried to figure out what we could do to find out more about what had happened to the helicopter and the crew. But the fear was there, beneath the surface. There was a sense of foreboding in the room, a low-level terror; you could see it in people's eyes.

For me, that fear felt like a cold hand around my heart, icy fingers squeezing, pulsating. The terror was physical, it was palpable. We knew that things were bad. Even from the little information we had been given, it seemed almost impossible that this could end well. But we had no idea what exactly we were dealing with. Catastrophic injury? Death? We didn't know what was facing Dara or what was facing us. Deep down, I think that we knew somewhere in the furthest corners of our mind that we had lost her, but we clung on to scraps of hope, pleading silently for a miracle. Because that's what you do.

We knew that soon the news of the missing helicopter would be broadcast on radio and television and we began to contact our wider family, friends and neighbours, to let them know that Dara was on board Rescue 116. These were people who knew and loved Dara and we wanted them to hear it from us rather than from any other source. To me now, it seems almost cruel that we contacted them by text, but we needed to reach everyone quickly and didn't have the luxury of time to call each in turn. How horrifying for people who love Dara to be woken by such a text message, the shock that they must have felt. We told people that we would let them know as soon as we heard anything, and we asked them to pray. That's all we could do. I think that I knew then the true meaning of the word helpless: we knew that Dara was in trouble, but we could do nothing whatsoever to help her. We just waited, Mark and Eoin by our sides, never leaving us, though they were probably as frightened as we were. It was a living nightmare.

People began to arrive at the house, neighbours, friends, family. Even then I was amazed by the courage of these people, how brave it was to come to the home of a family who had just received news like this. The easy thing to do would have been to tell themselves that it would be an intrusion to call around, or that they would be in the way. But they didn't do that. They called to the house and they wordlessly hugged us. Some cried. We were numb, I don't think that many of us had shed tears yet, but the people who came cried for us. Then they made us tea. They tried to get us to eat. That failed, but the kind thought was there. Some stayed, some came to offer support and said that they would not overwhelm us but would be back later. Several people stayed outside the house, greeting new people as they arrived and directing them towards one of us as they came in. We were minded from the start, surrounded by an army of kind, supportive people who wanted only to find some way to help us get through this horrific situation we found ourselves in. It was the first of many times during this tragedy that I saw the power of community, when a group of people work together to support, to help, to surround you with enough comfort and strength to hold you up as you do your best to find a foothold in the darkest and saddest of times.

On that morning, people offered both emotional support and practical support. For example, one of my friends, Ciara, offered to fly to the UK to drive my father's car back if he wanted to jump on a plane to get back to Ireland faster than the ferry would bring him. I had sent a text to another friend, Liz, shortly before 6.30 am to tell her what had happened, and without asking she arrived over within twenty minutes to take care of my beloved dog, Buddy. She came to Dara and Emer's house, I met her outside and we hugged, then I gave someone the keys to my house and they brought Liz over and she took Buddy home with her to mind him. The assistance offered that day was both practical and kind, people covered every need that we might have and they did it without fuss, drama or pressure. No one there that morning was trained for or prepared to deal with a catastrophe of this magnitude, yet somehow everyone around us did everything that needed to be done and there was no added stress on us as a family.

It filtered through to us that some of the morning news reports mentioned that a body had been found, though no details were given of gender or name. I actually don't think I can properly describe how horrifying that felt, to hear details of a death, to know that a body had been found and to wonder if that body was your sister, but not being able to find out.

Somewhere in that waiting period, my mother quietly said that this date was the anniversary of baby Anna, their daughter who had been stillborn 39 years previously. I think that when my mother heard about the helicopter going missing, knowing that it was Anna's anniversary, on some level she probably felt deep down that she was about to lose a second daughter.

A bit later in the morning I needed to cancel my work schedule for the week, so I went upstairs to sit on Dara's bed and get this job done, and also to take a few moments to try to somehow take in what was happening. It just felt so surreal, as though we were in a parallel universe. The bed was as Dara had left it when she'd got the callout the night before, with the bedcovers pulled back and the pillow still with the indent where her head had been as she slept. That sight was so poignant, a lump formed in my throat. Here I was, standing in Dara's room, a room where as sisters we four had all sat and chatted many times, laughing and making plans, yet the room was quiet now, and downstairs there were all these people coming and going, quietly, respectfully, moving in and out of the house, with Dara's belongings and possessions surrounding us, including photos of her living her life, among them many photos of her with the helicopter, every one of us frightened to death about what had happened to Dara and the crew.

It felt wholly unbelievable. When I had gone to bed the night before, I had four siblings and I woke to find that one was missing. I couldn't take it in. This was Dara we were talking about, our Dara. The girl with the dimple and the beautiful smile who was a sweet and lovable imp as a child. The girl who, when she was small, was so frightened of the car wash that she used to sit on our mother's lap so that she could bury herself under her coat while the machine washed our car. The girl who loved animals so much that she made us all attend solemn funerals for every budgie or goldfish that died during our childhood. That Dara couldn't be missing, she couldn't be in trouble, she couldn't die. I had seen her less than 48 hours earlier and we'd chatted as normal, so this simply couldn't be real.

I pulled back the covers to make the bed and I found Dara's night clothes, which I folded and put back under her pillow. The straightening of the covers revealed her book, which was one from a pile that I had given her. We are avid readers in my family and we share books, passing on anything that we have enjoyed. Dara often read books on her iPad and her well-worn sage green Ted Baker iPad case went everywhere with her. On this night, however, she was reading a paperback and when I saw which one it was, it stopped me in my tracks. It was *No Time for Goodbye* by Linwood Barclay, a book that I had given her after I'd read it myself. That was the first time the tears came. It was as though the book's title made my brain register that this could be real and that we might be about to say goodbye to Dara.

When I was composed again, I went back downstairs and joined everyone to wait for information. I was thinking about how the world was going about its business, preparing for the day, as we waited to find out if Dara and her colleagues were injured or dead. In the houses either side of us and in homes all over the country, people were sitting in their kitchens, eating porridge and drinking tea, listening to the radio report about Rescue 116. Then they were heading out into morning traffic, making their way to work and school, living a normal day. We didn't fully know it at the time, but my family had already lived our last normal day.

Sometime near noon, Mark and Eoin told us that representatives of Dara's employer were on their way to speak to us. Soon after, two men from Dara's company came to the house to tell us the news we hoped we would never hear. Having received word that they were due to arrive shortly, we were mostly all outside, standing in the driveway, waiting for them. I'm not sure why we waited outside, perhaps subconsciously we thought that we'd know what the news was once we saw their faces. Perhaps we needed so badly to know at that stage that we literally went to out to meet the news. Some friends and relatives had taken Fionn around to the green area of the estate to play as he didn't need to be near when we heard what we suspected we were going to hear. As the two men walked towards the house, dressed in dark suits and ties, we stood and watched them. Quietly. No one saying a word. My mother brought them into the house and we all stood in the kitchen where we had spent many happy times with Dara and we listened to what they had come to say about her.

The body recovered from the water had been formally identified. It was Dara.

I don't remember the exact words uttered that day in Dara's kitchen, but I knew instantly what they meant. Dara was not coming back. Ever. She would never walk into a room and flash that beautiful smile at us. She would never hold her young son or hug her beloved mother. She would never spend one more minute with her siblings, family, friends or colleagues. Ever. My mind had registered that fact even before the last words of the sentence had been uttered. Dara was gone.

There was a sharp intake of breath from everyone in the room, then stifled screams, tears and complete disbelief. I can still hear those screams even now, the anguished sounds of sorrow. Dara's mother, siblings, cousins, in-laws and friends all hearing that she was gone. It was as though the world had stopped. Literally stopped. In those first few seconds and minutes as my brain realised that Dara was gone, actually gone, and never ever coming back, I felt as though the world was crashing down around me. Because life as we knew it ended in that moment. Grief made its presence felt instantaneously and the first impact was physical. I could hear the blood rushing through my ears, mingling with the sounds of muffled screams from some others in the room. My breath seemed to catch in my lungs and it was as though an elephant was sitting on my chest, my heart crushed by the weight of the news I was hearing. My stomach dropped like a stone and I felt a wave of nausea wash over me. My heart was the place that I felt it the most, it was instantly heavy, leaden, this heart that had been beating so hard and so fast when the two men came up the path now felt almost like it was going to stop beating. I would say that my heart felt like stone in those moments but that would imply that there was no feeling, whereas this heaviness was the most painful thing I have ever known. If it didn't sound so twee, I would say that it was the pain of my heart breaking into pieces.

Grief hits with a savage punch and the intensity of these feelings was immense. I had never experienced anything like this before in my life. It was visceral, almost violent, such was the force and power of what I felt. I struggle even now to fully capture linguistically what those first few moments were like, but I do remember that I felt grief in my body even before I was aware of any emotional response.

Within a few minutes I started to feel numb, both physically and emotionally, a state of shock that apart from the occasional shift would last for several weeks, and on some level for several months. It felt as though I was on the other side of a glass wall and I could see everything as it happened, all the goings-on, but because of the glass wall I could hear no sounds, so it removed me somewhat from the experience and I couldn't fully feel. It was almost as if a kindly anaesthetist was standing at my shoulder and giving me a few minutes to feel the impact before injecting me with a sedative to numb me physically and emotionally. I think that the numbness is needed because it's all too much to take in and so grief can come with this shot of sedation that wears off over time, revealing the true impact of loss in small pieces rather than all at once. It was almost other-worldly, that feeling of being numb, knowing full well what had happened yet still being able to function, to think and plan and do the practical things that needed to be done. That's part of what the numbness is – a clever mechanism designed to ease us into a state in which we can continue to function. Falling to pieces wasn't an option because there was so much we had to do in the aftermath and I think the numbness was the tool that enabled us to carry on and get everything done.

The first thing that needed to be done was to tell my father, who was still making his way to us from the UK. We knew that news of Dara's death would soon reach the radio bulletins and that he couldn't hear about the death of his daughter on a news report, so we had to act quickly. I stepped outside the house to find a quiet space and I dialled his number. On the one hand, I wanted the call to connect right away; on the other hand, I hoped that he would never answer his phone. You don't expect to have to tell your parent that their child has died, it's just not something that I would ever have considered having to do. In fact, I've had to do some really difficult things over the past three years, but delivering this news to my father was probably the hardest. Just like Mark and Eoin before me, I knew that when I spoke, I would be saying words that would change his life for ever, that there would be no going back from that moment, that it would bring with it a new life, one without Dara. But there was no other option. When he answered my call, I told him gently that Dara's body had been recovered from the sea. Again, I get a physical reaction even now as I think about that call and remember what it felt like. I hope that I never have to do anything like that again as long as I live.

My father arrived at the house at about 5.00 pm and despite whatever they were feeling, both my parents led from the front that day. They felt whatever they were feeling but they held it together and I think that in many ways they set the tone for our family in how we would cope with this from that point onwards. My parents were dignified and courageous, yet at the same time they were completely real in their response to the news about their third-born child. They felt the pain, they just didn't let it break them, either then or since. The rest of the family followed their lead and my three siblings showed considerable fortitude in how they each stepped up and did whatever had to be done from that day onwards. It's not about being 'strong' or about denying the facts or ignoring emotions, sometimes it's just about doing what the situation asks of us. I think that having our parents model an ability to manage their own pain and not add to that of those around them encouraged the rest of us to follow suit. This meant that we didn't add to an already traumatic situation by layering further distress on top. I have great respect for and gratitude to my parents for that lead.

There were many practical things that needed to be done quickly, including making arrangements to travel to Castlebar to bring Dara home from Mayo University Hospital, as well as starting to plan her funeral. Without any big discussion my family stepped into their natural roles and we all undertook jobs that were right for each of us. The Gardaí arrived to the house once we had received the news of Dara's death to introduce us to our Family Liaison Officer (FLO), Garda Paul Flood. At that point I didn't fully understand what a Garda FLO actually did, but in the hours, days, weeks and months that followed Paul Flood provided information, support and guidance that I hadn't even realised we needed. During that first meeting, I was given the role as the point of contact for our family with Paul, so that he could get information to or from the family by going through one person rather than several. The numbness helped me to get these and other tasks done. I knew that the lack of tears didn't reflect my feelings for Dara, that it was a function of the need to carry on, that there would be time for tears later.

I remember a few days later trying to describe to my friend Giles what the whole experience of that morning was like, trying to get across how it felt, perhaps needing to express how it felt. In explaining it to him, I think I was trying to make sense of it for myself, using words to translate and understand my emotions. From the time of that knock on the door before 6.00 am, I described it as feeling as though we were trapped in a car that was stuck on a railway track and I was looking out of the car window and seeing a train coming down the tracks towards us. But I couldn't move the car off the tracks. Nor could I stop the train. I could see that it was going to hit us and that it would hurt, in a way that nothing had ever hurt before. The first threads of terror building quietly inside as the anticipation of the impact grew throughout the morning. Then, that moment standing in the kitchen, Dara's family and friends huddled close together, bracing for the impact that we subconsciously knew was coming. Then, hearing the words that Dara had died, knowing that this was not a nightmare, that it was real, and that we would never again see our lovely girl walk into this kitchen with a smile or a hug. That was the moment when the train hit, crashing with a ferocious speed into the car as we sat trapped inside, the impact catapulting the car high into the air, leaving it to fall back to earth in a million pieces. The fact was that with Dara's death, life as we all knew it was gone – smashed, scattered, left strewn along the tracks, some pieces missing, some broken, some intact and others mangled beyond recognition. This was the new reality for all who love Dara.

That was my introduction to grief.

I used strong, emotive words in my description to Giles because that's how it felt. It was vicious. We were people who, without warning, had been woken from sleep and propelled from our beds with horrifying news. We had spent over six hours waiting for information about Dara and the crew. That whole time we knew that Dara was in trouble, but we could do nothing to help her. And then, when that news came in that Dara was dead, the feelings were what I would expect to feel if I were in some sort of collision or near some sort of bomb that had exploded in our world. It was carnage. Yes, the numbness came quickly, but even with that, both physically and emotionally it felt like violent carnage to me.

I felt Dara's loss in every cell in my body. It was going to hit hard, of course, and there was never going to be any way around feeling that impact, but hearing the loss of Dara confirmed was the single most painful thing I have ever known in my entire life. All the pain of the previous forty-eight years mixed together and multiplied by a hundred didn't come near to what this pain felt like. And that's the truth.

The truth is also, however, that as humans we have a physiological system that serves to protect us and when faced with trauma, shock and loss, that system kicks in to numb us. Those first moments of registering Dara's loss were horrific but they were, I can say now, survivable.

It's interesting that even as I type those words, *they were survivable*, a feeling of guilt seeps in. Is it okay to say that learning about Dara's death was survivable? Does that somehow mean that I didn't love her enough, or that her death doesn't matter? Of course not, neither is true, but this feeling gives an indication of the many complexities of grief. It feels somehow disloyal to say that the loss of someone you love so much is survivable, but therein lies one of the biggest challenges when faced with the grief brought about by death: how to balance carrying the loss with learning how to live with the loss. It is the painful reality of becoming, in time, okay with the fact that you survived the death of one of the most important people in your world. That forms part of the grief, too, and we have to work on accepting it.

CHAPTER TWO

EMPTY ARMS

had experienced loss in my life prior to Dara's death, but it was only when grieving for Dara that I recognised that what I'd felt a few years earlier was in fact grief for that loss. Indeed, it was also only then that I realised the magnitude of that loss. I'm referring to the loss around infertility, that journey of medical testing, investigation and treatment threaded through with optimism and hope and repeated devastation. In my case, I eventually had to come to terms with the fact that I was never going to be a mother. As the waves of grief washed over me after Dara died, I realised that while her death was my formal introduction to grief, I recognised some of the feelings from that journey through infertility a few years earlier. I just hadn't named those feelings as grief at the time.

Just as when discussing my personal truth about bereavement, I want to be respectful and sensitive and not tell anyone else's story here. The loss surrounding infertility is important to discuss in this context, but I will look at it purely from my own perspective. I am mindful that I didn't go through this journey alone, but I will only talk about my personal experience. Therefore, I will reflect on the truth about this loss from the perspective of letting go of the dream of motherhood.

Reflecting on them side by side, the emotions experienced around the loss of my sister felt more intense, more overwhelming, louder and more obvious than those I'd felt around the loss of my hope of becoming a mother. It's not that one loss is greater than the other; I have felt each loss deeply, both powerfully painful, different from one another yet also similar, each having a significant lasting impact on my life. But I found it interesting that it took experiencing the overwhelming and overpowering emotions at the loss of my sister for me to recognise the loss of motherhood as just that – a loss. It was only then I realised that grief is not just about the death of a person, it can be about the death of hope.

Go into any primary school and ask young children what they want to do when they grow up and you'll get a raft of answers, from firefighters to teachers to singers on *The X Factor* or influencers on YouTube. You will also hear from many children that they want to be parents. There is an instinctive drive to create our own family that is present from even a very early age. When we have enjoyed a warm and loving environment in our own family of origin, we sometimes want that for ourselves, to become the parents and pass on life's lessons to our own children, teaching and guiding them so that they grow to be emotionally healthy adults who can go out into the world and contribute. Some may not have had happy times in their own childhood and may want to have their own children and do things differently, giving love where perhaps they received none. But whatever the driver, many of us see being a parent as something that's going to happen in our future. I was no different. Sadly, after a few years of marriage it became evident that having a family and becoming a parent was not going to be as simple as that, and so began the long and arduous journey of assisted fertility.

I think that when the subject of fertility testing is raised in the GP's surgery, grief becomes present on some level, however subtle or hidden. Once those words are spoken, the truth enters the room: you cannot do what others appear able to do so easily, which is to reproduce. The moment you admit this, there's a sense of loss. As a woman, being able to conceive, carry and deliver a baby is an incredible privilege, but it's also one that many of us assume we will experience. I mean, everyone has babies, right? My parents had babies, my grandparents had babies, my aunts and uncles had babies, my cousins had babies, so why should there be any reason to think I won't have a baby? I certainly didn't think there would be any problem. That thought doesn't even enter your head until there's a question mark over whether you're going to be able to have a baby. It certainly never crossed my mind, not until I was faced with the suggestion of fertility tests. Then came a voice that shouted very loudly in my head: *What is wrong with me?* I think that voice echoes the sense of loss, a sense that something that should have been present is missing, that we aren't whole in some way.

When a couple find themselves on the road of fertility testing, it brings others into something that should be private, something that should be reserved just for them. Medical questionnaires. Long lists of detailed questions that poke into every bit of your lives. Blood tests. Physical examinations. Internal examinations. Exploratory surgery. Months of trialling the first level of medications to assist conception. A path worn to various medical waiting rooms until we eventually found ourselves in a fertility clinic. Sitting in a small room, waiting to be called, other couples sitting across from us, no one talking except to each other and in whispers, but even without words each knowing something of the other's story because we were all there for the same reason, because we couldn't conceive by ourselves.

After that, enduring several rounds of IVF, which involved intense daily schedules of scans and blood tests, injections to shut down my hormonal system before other injections to ramp it up again, moving on to an operation for egg retrieval before eventual embryo implantation. Assisted fertility is do-able, but it's not for the faint-hearted. It requires you to give fully of yourself, investing emotionally, physically, practically and financially in the process. I found that physically and emotionally I navigated through it quite well and that by far the hardest part was that it didn't work and I failed to conceive.

What makes it more difficult is that the entire time you're going through all of this, everything you're doing is hidden from those around you. It's a private sorrow that is constantly triggered by the sight of pregnant women and babies. It's as though everyone in the world has a bump or a buggy. Of course, it's not the case that there's a sudden exponential increase in the numbers of pregnancies or births as soon as you start IVF, it's simply that your focus of attention is such that you are hyper-aware of anything to do with pregnancy or babies. I found it particularly difficult to have to walk past the maternity hospital several times a week, on the way to the fertility clinic a few doors away, seeing heavily pregnant women going into the hospital or watching parents emerging with newborns in car seats to go home and start their new life together. It brought a pang of regret that it wasn't us every time we had to make that journey past these scenes of happiness and continue on to our very different reality. During the first round of IVF, I looked at the pregnant women or the new families and felt a sense of hope, a feeling that this could soon be us, that it was a good omen. Then, when that attempt failed and we moved on to the next cycle of IVF, those scenes brought a feeling of anticipated grief, a gnawing sense that it might never be us. I never dwelt on that and I always kept a hopeful frame of mind, but now, years later, I can say with hindsight that it was horribly difficult and that although unnamed, there was most definitely a sense of grief throughout that time.

The grief around infertility is often a secret grief because we don't tend to tell the world what's going on, we keep it to ourselves and go about our usual business of living and working while juggling this schedule of appointments, injections and operations. It's a secret loss, a lonely loss. I remember having to leave a party to go home and inject myself because certain medications needed specific timing in order to fit with the schedule. I made some daft excuse so that I could get away, with no one there having a clue what we were going through because we hadn't told them. As a result, you end up dealing with the physicality of the treatment, the emotional aspect of the treatment and also the practical aspect of the treatment between the two of you. If things don't work out, you also deal with the deep-seated feelings of failure, disappointment, anger and sorrow just between the two of you. And even in that sharing there is loneliness because by its very nature you each experience assisted fertility in different ways, so you're on a lonely path on what is already a lonely journey.

After we had experienced initial failures, we talked and agreed that it was okay to tell some of our immediate family about our IVF journey. I told my sisters, and all three of them were warm, kind and supportive, both emotionally and practically. They were there for me when I needed them and it helped enormously that I didn't have to pretend around them. I hadn't realised how exhausting that part had been. When I was with my sisters, I could cry or rant or just talk about what was going on with the treatment and the three girls listened, individually or collectively, and helped in whatever way was useful at the time. I was very grateful for that.

It's important to remember that there are people among us who have secret losses that no one knows about, losses that they carry alone, silently, heavily, not a soul knowing the pain they endure. We encounter hundreds of people in our everyday life, but we have no idea what they may be dealing with behind what we see. It could be the person sitting opposite us on the bus or the train, our boss at work, the coach of the local football team, the person in the coffee shop who knows what we mean when we smile and say 'The usual' every morning. There are myriad hidden stories of miscarriage, infertility, serious illness diagnosis. Stories of unrequited love or failure to find someone to love. Stories of broken dreams, of shattered hopes for victory or achievement. There are also those who bear the secret loss of a childhood stolen by an alcoholic father or a narcissistic mother who was never emotionally present through those early years of youth. There are people carrying inside the unspoken loss of innocence at the hands of an abuser. Or the loss of safety at the hands of an attacker. All bring grief to our door and, unlike the grief of a bereavement, which is a very public grief, this kind of private grief can go unsupported, adding to the difficulty of carrying that loss. It means having to go on with life with no one knowing what you're dealing with. Someone who has experienced a miscarriage but has to turn up for that meeting, or someone whose adoption hopes were dashed but who has to be there for their godchild's christening, no one having a clue of their private sorrow. It's the particular loneliness of the secret grief. It's why I try to be kind to everyone I encounter because you simply don't know what is going on behind the smile – or, indeed, the angry frown.

On reflection, my feeling is that, depending on the nature of the loss, we may in fact have people in our lives who would be willing and able to support us through the losses that we tend to keep secret, but at the time it can be difficult to see that. It's just complicated. How do we talk to family or friends who have children about our inability to have them? Would they understand? How *could* they understand? It seems impossible, so we tend to say nothing. Even if there are people in our life who we feel might understand, there's the worry about how they will react once we tell them. Will they hold our secret with kindness and respect? Will they keep our secret? Will they tell others? Will they treat us differently once they know? Or give endless supplies of well-meaning but unhelpful advice about how their sister's friend's cousin got pregnant at 44 when she stopped fertility treatment and 'just relaxed'? Or how Sandra at work had three miscarriages but went on to have four children? There's a lot to consider, so when it comes to things like infertility or miscarriage or forbidden love, so many of us stay quiet and absorb the loss ourselves without support, feeling lonely as well as full of sorrow.

Adding to the loneliness around this sense of loss in trying to have a family is the fact that at the time of doing fertility treatments, you're usually at the age when many of your friends and family are having children. It's just the stage of life you and your peers are at. This means that while you are navigating the rigours of fertility treatments, fervently hoping that this time it will work, you find yourself in the middle of pregnancy announcements, birth announcements, christenings and toddlers' birthday parties. You have no choice but to dry your tears, put on your lipstick and a big smile to go with it and help your friends and family celebrate these momentous occasions in their lives. That's just how it works, that's what life asks of us. I did that for a while, but when hope began to fade that things would work out for us, I had to step away from some of those occasions for a while. When invitations arrived, I made excuses. I pressed pause on expecting myself to attend every single one because it was just too difficult. I know to some that may seem selfish, but to me it was self-preservation, an instinctive need to protect myself from constantly looking at the future I was starting to realise wouldn't ever be ours.

The problem is that questions run around in your head during these child-centred occasions that act as a Petri dish for that grief to grow and develop. How could we not manage to do what so many people can do without difficulty, what many manage to do without even wanting to? What if this next time worked? What will we be in life if we are not parents? Will we fit in any more with those around us who are parents? That whole world of parenting, children and family was a world that we weren't part of, no matter how much we wanted to be. It felt like being outside a building with a big window, peering in at life inside the building, looking through the glass at a lovely warm scene that we couldn't get to join. It was tough.

During the time when we were doing one of the IVF cycles, the singer Michael Bublé had a song out called 'Haven't Met You Yet' and as I travelled to and from those medical appointments it was played over and over on the radio. Perhaps to some people it will sound daft, and even to me now it sounds a bit silly, but while going through treatment the words of that song resonated with me and each time I heard the chorus it was as if I was saying those words to the child I hoped we would meet – 'I just haven't met you yet'. I know that's not what the song is about, but that's the meaning that felt like a fit for me so that's how I related to the song. When it became apparent that success was unlikely and the end of fertility treatments closed the door on that dream of meeting our own child, while it wasn't the death of a person, it was the death of hope and of a life I had banked on living. I can see now, only now, that I began to grieve after that point. I was never going to have my own child and that was a huge loss.

I retreated into myself for a while after that. My mood was stable in that I wasn't depressed, but I just didn't feel like I wanted to be around people. I probably didn't even notice that I was retreating at the time, but with the benefit of hindsight I can see that I stepped out of life for a bit. I had all these feelings of loss and I didn't know what to do with them because I hadn't even named them as loss or grief and I think that, unconsciously, I was making space for myself to feel those feelings. In some situations in life we can be unaware of what we're feeling and if we don't identify those emotions, it is pretty much impossible to process them and move forward. When this happens we can get stuck in how we feel, perhaps engaging in some behaviours that don't help us, feeling that we are existing rather than living yet continuing on the same path regardless. Looking back, I can see that this was me then, but I genuinely couldn't see it at the time.

I had gone to see a counsellor towards the end of fertility treatment, when we were asked to think about further options for different types of treatment, and that psychological work was very useful in helping me to figure out what my own limits were and what felt right for me in that regard. But it never entered my head to go back to the counsellor after the fertility door had closed fully. I think that had I done that, I would have known that what I was feeling was grief and that understanding would have enabled me to process those feelings of loss properly and would have prevented me making that retreat into myself. Instead, after the IVF ended I experienced a range of symptoms that I didn't know how to interpret: for a long time I had trouble sleeping, I was exhausted all the time, I just didn't feel like myself, I wasn't engaging with life and I stepped away from connecting with people in the way that I usually would. When I look at all of that now, it just screams grief to me. At the time, though, no one had died, so the concept of grief wasn't on my radar. I completely missed the fact that I was in the throes of it.

In a way that is either really kind or really cruel, life went on and in time things settled down and I eventually felt like myself again. We then began the process of an adoption application, knowing that we could give a child a warm and loving home. Assisted fertility had honed our form-filling skills, which turned out to be useful for the adoption process, which involved plenty of form-filling along with course completion, homework assignments, interviews and assessments. It was a necessarily rigorous assessment of our suitability to be adoptive parents. It was an arduous process in a different way from the fertility journey, and I found it an enjoyable process, strange as that may sound. There are many variables in the adoption process besides suitability to be parents and for different reasons many people do not become adoptive parents, even having gone through the full application process. Sadly, that was to be our story. The day our adoption journey came to an end marked another unsuccessful outcome on our path to have our own family. I can see now that I grieved after our adoption journey ended, too. I once again retreated and stepped away from people for a bit. It wasn't depression but it was grieving. I needed time to process that loss, the end of that great dream of becoming a mother. But yet again, I didn't identify what I felt as grief. This seems almost inexplicable to me now, especially given my profession. I've even counselled elite athletes about the loss and grief of retirement, but it was never apparent to me that it was going on in my own life. I wasn't able to see it for what it was. I shake my head even now as I write these words – how could I have missed it?

As I got older and I passed the age at which it would have been possible for me to have been a mother, I accepted that I wasn't ever going to hear a child call me Mum. I was never going to be that guide to a child, someone who would teach them about life, shape them, help them to find their feet in this world. It took a long time and a lot of work, but eventually I made peace with this.

What I mean by work is that I allowed myself to feel what I felt. I gave myself permission to feel angry, sad, resentful, jealous and all the less than pleasant, unpalatable emotions that come with living in a world that values family when you cannot have a family of your own. I think that even though I hadn't consciously registered the presence of loss and grief in my life, I had recognised that it was significant to have gone through those years of all we had gone through and yet not to be parents at the end of it. I knew that it was normal to feel wrung out by the experience, worn out physically and emotionally. Most of all, I instinctively knew that it was important to be compassionate towards myself and to let myself heal in my own time. I see emotions as being like the warning lights on the dashboard of a car; they indicate that something needs our attention. I knew that how I was feeling meant that I needed to work on myself, which meant to give myself some time, to show myself some kindness and understanding, to drop any expectations to be 'normal' or to feel like myself, to take a step back from situations that made me sad until I felt okay to step back in again.

I also think that reaching my late forties helped me to achieve acceptance of this loss. At that point I realised that I felt too old to be the mother of a young child, even through adoption. The window of opportunity had passed and arriving at that realisation helped me to move towards a peaceful acceptance of my life as it was and would be.

I knew that I had worked my way through the loss when one day, talking to someone about having a family, I heard some wise words and they resonated with me. This person said that although she was a mother herself and had friends with children and friends without, when it came to being a parent she saw it as a case of 'blessings with and blessings without'. In other words, whatever place we arrive at in the parenting situation, there are blessings. As she pointed out, having children brings joy but it also brings responsibility and endless worry. On the other hand, not having children can bring loneliness and grief, but it also brings freedom and exciting new chapters in life. I was ready to hear this at that time, and I realised that of course life could be good even if we weren't parents. I appreciated that we had great family and friends and that life was indeed already good. I also realised that there are many ways to contribute to this world and that if raising a child was not an option, I could still be a valuable member of society and know fulfilment. For sure, lots of life is geared towards families and children, but not exclusively so. I could make my mark in the world in other ways. *Blessings with and blessings without.*

There is a poem by Ralph Waldo Emerson that I like for this reason:

> To laugh often and much;
> to win the respect of intelligent people
> and the affection of children,
> to leave the world a better place,
> to know even one life has breathed easier because you
>   have lived,
> that is to have succeeded.

I figured out eventually that there's no right or wrong way to do this thing we call life. There's no foolproof definition when it comes to what constitutes a happy life or a life worth living. Being in a relationship, being married, having children, they are all options, but they're not standards that we have to live up to, with unhappiness being the only alternative. I don't feel defined by either being a mother or not being a mother. Humans are so much more complex than one aspect of our lives and we can have a full and rich life on a variety of paths. It was quite a relief to figure that out. In time, I began to feel happier emotionally, after enduring a significant period of what I now recognise as grief before I arrived at this understanding.

When Dara died, according to her wishes, alongside my two sisters I became a guardian to Fionn. I wasn't going to be his mother or even his primary care-giver, but it was an odd moment to realise that my years of yearning for motherhood and my subsequent years of working to accept that I wouldn't ever have that nurturing role in someone's life took a sudden turn after Dara's death. This unexpected new journey of becoming a key person in my nephew's life brought challenges for me that were additional to grieving for Dara. My sister Emer already lived with Fionn and Dara and in an incredible act of love for her sister, Emer moved into the primary care role in raising Fionn on Dara's behalf. My twin sister Orla stepped up and began to co-parent with her, and I share the load with them both.

In the early days, weeks and months after Dara died I found myself staying over in Emer's house a couple of nights a week, putting Fionn to bed, getting up in the middle of the night to soothe him back to sleep when he needed it, taking care of this little toddler whose mother had disappeared from his life overnight. And while I was delighted to be able to help in any and every way I could, I have to be honest and say that having made peace with not being a mother only a year or two earlier, I really struggled when I found myself in that space: that nurturing and caring space, taking care of a small child in a way that was more than babysitting or being an auntie. It really messed with my head. It was a complex situation and I found myself wanting to help and at the same time struggling with giving that help. It was a wound that had healed over being opened up again, I suppose, and during that time I had a few meltdowns. Looking back now, I can see that in those moments I was as far away from myself as I have ever been and I put that down to the additional layer of the struggle with that nurturing/parenting space coming in on top of grief for Dara. It was just too much. Perhaps in there, too, was the fact that not only had I lost the opportunity to be a mother but now, just when she had become a mother, Dara had lost that opportunity as well. I felt such a depth of sadness around that.

When my two sisters saw how much I was struggling they kindly agreed to move me into a less full-on supporting role for a while, so I got to step back a little until I got myself together. It was around this time that I began to see a psychologist and started working through the onslaught of emotions with him. This helped me to find a sense of balance again and in time I found my comfortable space in that role as guardian. Since then Emer carries out the parenting role, with me coming in alongside Orla and the rest of my family to provide support and cover each week as needed, there as back-up and stand-in when called upon. It works very well for everyone and in the middle we have a healthy, happy and well-adjusted child, which is the most important thing.

The IVF journey and the ultimate loss of my dream to have a family showed me that grief isn't only about death, it's also about change and the end of hope. We grieve for how our life has changed, either from how it was or from how we wanted it to be. It's okay to grieve even if no one has died; indeed, it's not only okay, it's necessary. You have to give yourself permission to feel whatever you are feeling, whatever the loss that caused it, because your emotions are valid. Whatever the source of your grief, it's important to lean into the feelings rather than try to avoid them; they won't go away just because you don't acknowledge them. The truth is that facing the pain, naming it, recognising that it is grief and sitting with that grief enables us to begin to process the loss we have experienced, and that can be the start of healing.

CHAPTER THREE

WHEN 'I DO' BECOMES 'I DON'T'

Before Dara died my marriage had been in trouble and around the time she died it was near to breaking down. I want to respect my ex-husband and our marriage, so there's no need for details other than to say that there was no victim or villain in this piece, just two people who had many happy times together but who were unable to find their way back from significant sadness in the preceding years. Together, we made the decision to end the marriage.

I think that the years of trying to become parents had taken their toll and I guess that we both knew that after twenty-one years together we had come to the end of the road. Life is not linear, we meet obstacles and challenges along the way as we zig-zag through our choices and their consequences, and in any long-term relationship there will be many times when we are tested. Many couples come through those times but, sadly, while we had come through quite a lot, as a couple we just couldn't find our way through the challenges of the recent years. My ex-husband was one of Dara's oldest friends, it was she who had introduced us, and after she died, with me grieving for my sister and him grieving for his friend, it was just too much sadness to bear given that we were already buckling under the pressure of those other losses. There is an element of marriage breakdown that is worse than death in that Dara never meant to leave us, whereas we chose to leave one another. That's a heavy burden to bear.

I remember arriving at my parents' home two days after Dara's death and there was no one at the house except my parents and a friend of my mother's, who was there with her husband. I came into the sitting room where the latter three were seated and as soon as I saw my mother and heard her voice, I burst into tears and my legs went out from under me. I heard a wailing sound and it took a moment to realise that it was coming from me. I cried and cried, and they just hugged me and let me howl. And it was indeed a howl, an anguished sound. The realisation had dawned overnight that I had lost Dara and that I was about to lose my marriage as well, and that layering of grief on top of grief was too much for me in that moment. Emotionally, the cumulative impact of grief for Dara and grief for my marriage was like being in the ring and being felled by a punch, knocked out, then being hit again when I was back up on my knees but not yet on my feet. The fact that the relationship was ending just as Dara died brought an added poignancy to things because she had introduced us. It had all started with her and, coincidentally, it was coming to an end just as her life was ended, and there was something so awful about that. I took off my wedding ring on the night of Dara's funeral. We would go on to work on things for a while, but deep down we both knew then that it was over. It felt as though I said goodbye to my sister and to my marriage on the same day.

The months between that point and the official end of the marriage felt like the long goodbye as we worked through the process of deconstructing our lives together. It was a process of taking apart the life we shared and creating separate lives for ourselves. Emotionally. Physically. Practically. Financially. Socially. After all we had been through together over the twenty-one years since we'd met it was hard to believe that we had reached this point, yet that was the reality. I often found my mind wandering back to when we first met, to the many happy years together, and then on to the latter years when we faced a lot of sadness.

We remained amicable throughout the process but I still found it excruciating, as no doubt did he. What had happened to the two people who had been so happy together for so long? How did we come to this? As we had known such happiness together, it was a huge loss. The fact that you both have some responsibility for it coming to this adds another dimension to the grief because there's such sorrow alongside a sense of regret that you weren't able to make it work.

There's no funeral or sympathy cards, no eulogy or public expression of sorrow when a marriage ends, but pain and grief are present nonetheless. There is the loss of love, perhaps a loss of mutual respect and understanding, as well as the loss of a shared future. It's a private grief, but it features all the feelings that accompany the death of a loved one: sadness, anger, disbelief, hopelessness, fear. This is wholly normal and understandable when coming to terms with the end of your married life together and the start of a new life on your own, but it's still very tough.

The grief I felt at the ending of my marriage was therefore similar to how I grieved at the loss of Dara. I cried, raged and felt numb, unable to believe that we had got ourselves to this point. On some levels I ground to a halt because the combined effect of both losses hit very hard and I struggled badly for an awfully long time. My husband and I had been together for twenty-one years and married for fifteen and he's a good man, a kind man, and some of the happiest days of my life so far have been spent with him. There were many years of adventure, laughter, support, encouragement and love between us. It was such a lovely relationship for so much of our time together and I mourned that loss.

The ending of a marriage feels like you're swapping one sadness for another: you feel sadness at the loss of the marriage, but at the same time you are letting go of the sadness felt during a marriage that's not working. That's a particular kind of loss and a particular kind of sadness. Being in a relationship with someone yet being so far apart that you almost don't recognise one another any more is brutal. It's so painful. No matter how nice you may be towards one another, being in a relationship that's not working is one of the loneliest places to be. Both of you may be feeling that loneliness and it's horrible. I don't hate anyone, nor do I have any enemies, but if I did, I wouldn't wish that pain on any of them.

Over the following eighteen months, we went through the legal, financial and practical steps to end our marriage. You don't end a marriage without anger and upset on both sides, so of course we had elements of each, but we managed to keep things amicable between us. The time period between the emotional end and the actual end of the marriage was still awful, though. As we stayed on friendly terms, we were able to remain living in the same house until all the legal and financial elements were completed. This was a good thing for various reasons but sharing that functional space when we no longer shared the emotional space was another one of those toughest things that I have ever done. It's the relationship equivalent of having to turn up to work each day after you've parted company with your employer and sit in an office with people you used to work with, meeting them at coffee break and over lunch and having to chat, even though you no longer have much to chat about because you're all on different paths now. It doesn't matter if you're friendly, what matters is that you're no longer all working towards the one goal, so by definition that leaves you alone. It's heartbreaking and dreadful. Sometimes I just had to get out of the house. I would drive somewhere like the seafront and sit and look out, trying to find some sense of peace because it felt like I was living in such turmoil. I was always aware that this was the experience of an amicable marriage breakdown; I can only imagine that the distress accompanying a turbulent separation must be almost unbearable.

The question of what to do with our house was made more difficult and pressing because of my need to stay living there. The house was four doors away from Dara, Emer and Fionn's house and I was very happy living there and needed to continue to be close to Emer and Fionn. It would have felt so wrong if I'd had to go and live somewhere else and leave them. I would have felt as though I was abandoning them both.

Also high on the list of reasons to remain in my home was the fact that so many of my recent memories of Dara were tied up in that house. My house is perpendicular to theirs and ever since Dara and Emer moved into the estate, each morning while blow-drying my hair upstairs in the boxroom I'd see them through the window as they left in the morning. I wasn't stalking them or anything, but any movement over in the direction of their house would catch my attention and I'd glance over to see who was doing what. Emer heading to work with her wet hair tied up in a ponytail if she was running late, Dara heading out for a morning cycle or a hike before starting an afternoon shift at work. Some days if I was in the boxroom later in the day, folding clothes or ironing, I'd see Dara leaving the house and heading to work for one o'clock. In typical Dara fashion, she managed to make even her flying uniform look good. It was a black boiler-suit type uniform, a style that would look like a sack on many people, but Dara somehow made the look her own. In the summer I'd often see her with the top part down, tied around her waist, a crisp white T-shirt on underneath, boots on, rucksack in hand and her jaunty ponytail of red hair finishing the image that I saw so many times through that boxroom window over the years.

In time to come, when Fionn came along, I'd see her coming out of the house with him, first pushing him as a baby in his buggy, then later holding his hand as he toddled about. When he was small, Fionn loved to look through the grate into the drain at the end of the driveway to see if he could find any worms. I don't think there ever were any worms in there, but someone had put the idea into his head and it was a favourite thing for him to do. In the winter before she died, I often saw Dara out there with him, helping him look for the worms, her warm North Face jacket zipped up to the neck and her woollen beanie hat pulled down to keep her warm. Fionn would be dressed the same, with the addition of little woollen mittens. He would be down on his hunkers, the way young children seem to naturally sit, and she would get down on his level while she chatted with him, a steadying hand on his back, matching his enthusiasm and hope of finding some elusive worms. Some days I would holler out the window at them – like the classy person I am! Then I'd grab my keys and run down the stairs and out the door to join them for a minute and say hello before we headed our separate ways for the day.

From that house I have wonderful memories of such simple things that I may not have given a second thought to at the time, but they mean an awful lot to me now. For some people the grave is where they go when they want to remember their loved one, but I remember Dara every time I look out my window or drive past her house and on up to my own. So when my marriage ended, I just could not countenance leaving this house. I knew I had to at least try to remain, because of my happy memories and because there's something about grief that makes you want to be in a place where the person who died has been – at least that has been my experience. I couldn't contemplate living somewhere that Dara had never been without having made robust attempts to stay put. In addition, as one of Fionn's guardians, if I had to sell our home to strangers and move somewhere else, then each time I went to Dara and Emer's house to mind him I would have to look four doors over towards my own house and see other people living there. I am a fairly hardy person and I can withstand a lot, but the very thought of that was just too much.

Therefore, for a variety of legitimate reasons, after the marriage ended I needed to remain living in my home rather than having to move away. I always say that if you want to marry someone who is hot, go ahead and do that, but if you can marry someone who is kind, that's much better. My ex-husband gave a powerful demonstration of kindness. I only had to ask him once if he would agree to me buying him out of our home and he agreed immediately. This was an act of compassion on his part, one he wasn't obliged to engage in. There's many a spouse who would have insisted on selling the home, so that both people would have to move away. I will always be grateful that in that time of sadness heaped upon sadness, he didn't put me through that. He just knew in his heart that it was right that I stayed in the house, near my sister, so that I could continue to be a support to her in raising Dara's son.

All I had to do then was to apply for a mortgage so that I could buy him out, which was my next step. I gathered together all the necessary documents over several months, submitted them to the bank and then I waited, a wait that felt interminable. It was one thing to have secured my ex-husband's agreement to buy him out, but quite another to secure a mortgage from the bank to allow me to do that. When your marriage ends, everything is up in the air for both of you because you don't know what life will look like now that you're no longer a couple. Everything changes and there is immense upheaval and distress on several levels. In the back of your mind you know that the turmoil will be temporary and that you'll get through the loss of your old life as part of a couple and that, at some point, you'll begin to get a sense of what your new, single life will look like. You have an awareness that in this regard there will be light at the end of the tunnel. But in the midst of all the change, one of the greatest concerns is the worry around your home; certainly that was the case for me. For those of us who are fortunate to have a home, it is our safe place, where we go to retreat from the world, where we can relax and recharge and process what's going on in our lives, the safe port in the storm. Therefore, not knowing where your home will be can be extremely unsettling. It feels like you're floating out to sea on a boat with no motor, no oars and no anchor – you have no idea where you're going to end up.

Not knowing where my home would be and if I would have to leave the place that meant so much to me was the aspect of marriage breakdown that brought me the greatest distress after the actual loss of my relationship. It was torturous. The idea of the possible loss of my safe space on top of the loss of my relationship, the safe space that also housed so many of my memories of life with Dara, that possibility pushed me to the very edge of my limits of coping. But still, I had to wait. The wheels of finance and the law move slowly, so month after month I lived with that crippling uncertainty, knowing that I had already lost so much and wondering if more loss was on the way. It was a feeling I hope I never have to experience again. I felt so vulnerable during that waiting time, in that limbo state where I could do nothing to decide matters.

In the most incredible of coincidences, on 14 March 2018, the first anniversary of Dara's death, I arrived back to my hotel in Mayo after attending the ceremonies held to mark the anniversary of the crash to find an email from the bank. It notified me that my mortgage approval had been granted. I stared at the screen, reading and re-reading the words to make sure that I hadn't imagined it, or that I wasn't somehow making a mistake. But there it was, in black and white: I could remain in my home, my safe place, my memories intact, able to continue to support Emer and Fionn. The relief was indescribable. I cannot find adequate words to express what that felt like once it sank in. Gratitude of epic proportions comes nearest, I think. It was an additional loss averted. After months of waiting, hoping and wondering, of all the days for that approval to be granted, that it came through on that particular day, a day that was already heavily laced with emotion, was just astounding. If that wasn't Dara Fitz looking out for me, then I don't know what it was.

Over the next few months we went on to complete the sale of the house over to me and at the end of summer 2018 the day came that my now ex-husband was moving out of what had been our home and into his new home. I remember so clearly that moving-out day because it felt like the day of a funeral, which I suppose it was in many ways, given that we were saying goodbye to our marriage and setting out to live apart for the first time in two decades. There is anticipatory grief when someone is terminally ill, whereby we begin to feel grief before they die because we are anticipating their loss. Similarly, I had known this day was coming and had been experiencing a sense of anticipatory grief in the months leading up to it. I didn't recognise or label it as grief at the time, I just felt that I was emotionally unsettled in the lead-up to the final parting of the ways. I can see now that it was like waiting for an axe to fall, a different version of waiting for the train to hit on the day that Dara died.

On the day that he moved out, going through our belongings and deciding who got to take what from the items we owned jointly was painful. We did it with kindness and consideration, but it was still awful. When it came to dividing up photos of us together, I really struggled. I nearly want to put my head in my hands even thinking about it now. When we fall in love we start off as individuals, but little by little we move towards one another, linking our lives together until eventually people tend to say one name with the other not long after it. Joint mortgage, shared goals in life, Christmas cards sent to the two of you, spending occasions with each other's families, helping each other through life's ups and downs. Even though we all have friends and family outside of marriage, as a committed couple you become each other's number one person. When something happens, your spouse is often the first person you want to tell. They're the one you discuss life's big decisions with as well as the small decisions, and it's often them who sees you at your best and worst and everything in between. Being entwined in this way for so long, it's understandable that taking apart that life piece by piece will be difficult and painful, to say the least.

Around that time I was having renovations done in the house because I wanted to make it my own and to make it different from how it looked when we lived there together. On the day my ex-husband was moving out, I had painters, electricians and gardeners working in and around the house. I needed to have a chat with each one, to go through the work they were doing that day, but I had tears rolling down my face most of the time because I just could not stop crying. They were those endless streaming tears, the ones that cannot be held in, the ones that no amount of tissues can mop up, they just keep coming and you just have to cry it out. Even knowing that I needed to get it together to have those conversations with the workmen was not sufficient to stem the flow. I ended up just telling the guys that it was a sad day and asking them to ignore my tears but to hear my guidelines about the jobs to be done. They were lovely and kind and they did ignore the fact that I was wiping my red eyes each time we spoke. Everything got done, including my ex-husband moving out of our home and settling into his new home, but it was a horrible and exhausting day.

Later that evening I had to go out on an errand. When I returned that night, it was into what was now my own house for the first time. I turned the key in the lock and walked in through the front door and down the hallway. It felt very strange. Standing in my now quiet kitchen, with just the sounds of the house to keep me company, the ticking of the clock and the hum of the fridge, I didn't know whether to breathe or weep. In the end I did both. I had received many kind offers from family and friends to come and stay with me that night so that I wouldn't be on my own, but I didn't fear that. At any rate, I knew that I needed to be by myself, to feel the feelings of that first night alone. I knew that avoiding emotions doesn't work. I cracked open a cold bottle of Bulmers, focused on the gratitude I felt at being able to remain in my home and drank a toast to the new chapter in my life as I became single again at the age of fifty.

I think that a marriage or relationship ending is tough at any age, that the sense of loss is felt full force no matter what decade you're in when it happens, but there are probably some extra layers to the loss when it happens at a later point in life. When we experience the end of a marriage later in life, we know that the hourglass has turned over for us and the sands of time are slipping through on the second pass. I'm fifty-one now and while I don't feel in the least bit old, either in body or in mind, I know that it's unlikely that I will live to be 102, so I'm well aware that I'm in the latter part of my life and there is less time for a do-over. I had a long-term relationship or two in my twenties and when they ended, while I was devastated at the time, I knew that there was both time and opportunity if I wanted to find that relationship that might be the lifetime one for me. It felt different when my marriage ended, however, because there was a sense of loss not only for the ending of the marriage but also perhaps for that side of my life. Would I ever meet someone and fall in love again? Would anyone even find me attractive? Would I ever find anyone attractive again? All those things go through your mind and add another seam to the loss. It makes it feel even bigger because there's a fear there that it has obliterated the future as well as the past.

Fortunately, the flip side of that coin is that being older, we tend to have developed a good perspective on life. While those questions did flit across my mind initially after my marriage ended, I soon came to remember that there are no rules and that age isn't a barrier to love or happiness. I'm not looking for a relationship, but if one day I meet someone I like and who likes me back, then who knows? I'm open to finding like or love again, but I don't feel that I need either to be happy. I already have all I need in my life to feel happy. The response I have received since Dara's death from family and from both existing friends and new friends tells me that I matter to people, that there are people on this planet that I care about who care about me back, because I have never felt so utterly broken yet at the same time so utterly loved as I have done over the past three years. That to me is true contentment and whatever else might happen or not happen in my life relationship-wise, I already have what matters; a combination of the perspective that comes with age and surviving loss tells me that.

Now, fifteen months after we began to live apart as single people, when I think of my marriage and of my ex-husband I focus on the happy times we had together because I see that as the most useful thing for me to do. I could focus on the ways in which we were different and incompatible. I could see our time together as a waste because it didn't work out. I could go over and over things that I wish I had handled differently. Or I have the option to guide my mind towards accepting that we gave our marriage the best we each had at the time, but that the 'death do us part' bit didn't work. That leaves me free to focus on any of the many happy times we shared over the years. Nothing will change the outcome, but it makes for a significantly nicer place in my head when I have thoughts and images of happy times together, so I choose this option. To be fair, that choice is an easy one for me to make because I married a lovely man and while we couldn't make our marriage work, there was never any of the toxicity between us that some people endure. We aren't in contact all the time, which is important as it allows each of us to heal, but we have godchildren in common and so we come across one another at events and it helps both us and those around us that we can be friendly with one another. With a bit of distance from the end of the marriage we can now sit and have a coffee and a chat whenever we meet. I think that we both see it as honouring the good times that we had. We may not have been able to make our marriage work, but we seem to be able to make our separation work, and I think there is healing in that.

CHAPTER FOUR

EVERYTHING HAS CHANGED, YET LIFE GOES ON

The death of a loved one is a public grief and because of that it comes with a network of supports that kick in immediately. The wake, the removal, the funeral, the house visits, the month's mind – these are all designed around the bereaved and allow the family and community to come together in sorrow and to help one another. It is like a warm, consoling embrace when faced with a sudden and inexplicable loss. It's very different from the private grief I had experienced prior to this. We were facing into a nightmarish period of time, dealing with the immediate aftermath of Dara's death, but we felt that support, that embrace, and we leaned into it.

Dara died in the early hours of Tuesday morning and as a family we travelled across Ireland that same day to bring her home from Mayo University Hospital in Castlebar. It made good sense to let others drive and soon we found ourselves divided between three chauffeured cars, with a Garda escort clearing the way for us through the rush-hour traffic on the motorway, bringing us safely to the toll bridge, where we picked up the route to the west of Ireland.

I remember sitting in the front passenger seat, looking out the window at the countryside going by as we drove, my phone silently alerting me to message after message of support from people wanting to send their condolences, unable to wait until they could post a sympathy card, needing to reach out that very day. With nothing else to do on the journey I read the messages and began to respond, but it seemed that I was hardly making a dent in the numbers that were coming into my phone. I remember the over-riding sense of shock and disbelief in the texts – people were stunned. To me, it still felt unbelievable. Otherworldly. I knew cognitively that this was happening and that it was real, but I couldn't yet feel it. My head seemed to understand, but after the initial physical response to the news my heart had gone dead and silent and I still couldn't actually feel anything. What I was experiencing was the blanket of numbness that drapes over you after a shocking loss.

Earlier in the day I had been contacted by another of Dara's colleagues, her friend Captain Cathal Oakes, a pilot with the Shannon-based Rescue 115. Cathal told me that Dara had been recovered from the water by the RNLI Lifeboat from Achill Island, airlifted from the lifeboat by Rescue 115 and taken to the hospital in Castlebar. He told me that the crew of Rescue 115 had carried Dara, their friend and colleague, from the helicopter into the hospital, waving aside offers from hospital staff to bring Dara in; it was the last thing that they could do for their friend. That must have been a very difficult thing for them all to do, and

I know that in that crew were two people who had known Dara for over twenty years, from back in her early days of search and rescue, Winch Operator Eamonn Ó Broin and Captain Carmel Kirby. Carmel and Dara were the only female pilots in the company for a long time and they were great pals, real friends who supported one another through all that life threw at them, professionally and personally. My God, what must that walk have been like for Eamonn and Carmel, those steps from the helicopter to the mortuary as they carried the body of their friend? I just cannot fathom how difficult that must have been for them and it makes that last gift to Dara even more special.

Cathal and Captain Ciarán Ferguson, another long-time friend and colleague of Dara's, drove up to Castlebar when they heard that Dara was there and Cathal said that between them and the crew of Rescue 115, someone would stay with Dara at all times until we got there that night. As we drove west and darkness began to fall, knowing that Cathal and Ciarán were sitting with Dara gave us huge comfort. Dara always said that when she died, she didn't want to be left on her own. I have no idea if they knew this or if they instinctively sensed that someone needed to be with her, but we were very grateful for this kindness.

After a long journey from Dublin to Mayo, seeing Dara for the first time was going to be surreal. We were met at the hospital by some local Garda members. They told us that as well as having Garda Paul Flood as our Dublin-based Family Liaison Officer, we would also have a FLO based in Belmullet, County Mayo, as this was the Garda station attached to where the crash had taken place and from which investigation information would come as it arose. I was chosen to be the point of contact for our family with this second FLO as well. Just as with Paul Flood,

Garda FLO Sinéad Barrett would become a vital lifeline for our family over the next few years.

I walked into the hospital's mortuary with my family that Tuesday evening sometime between 9.00 pm and 10.00 pm. I had seen Dara only two days earlier, fifty-three hours earlier to be precise, when we had been walking along, chatting and laughing, no idea that they were our last moments together. The whole thing felt as though it was happening to someone else, nothing about it felt real. But I knew that once I saw Dara, it would all become very real and that my mind would begin to grasp on a deeper level that this nightmare was our new reality.

I think that at that point, if I could have stopped time and paused it for a bit to let my mind and emotions catch up, I would have done so in a heartbeat. It was all happening so fast and I had no time to wrap my head around what was going on. Less than twenty-four hours earlier our lives were normal, I would have been getting ready for bed, mentally winding down from the day and preparing for the next day, but here I was in a mortuary, about to see my sister laid out in a coffin. I knew that we were very lucky that she was found and that we were blessed to get her body back, so being able to walk into a mortuary and see her was awful, but it was also a privilege denied to others. Nonetheless, it was a lot to take in, but there wasn't the luxury of taking time to process it all. I just took a deep breath and went in to see Dara.

When we got to see her, it was different from how I imagined. On the journey across the country, I had played over in my mind what it would be like to walk into that mortuary and see Dara with my own eyes. Because I was feeling so numb all day, I imagined that I would see her and perhaps feel somewhat removed, my feelings still deadened by the shock. I also thought that the day had already brought the worst, that the piercing stab my heart experienced when I heard that Dara was dead was the saddest moment. I was wrong. I found that standing over the coffin and looking at my sister's face, a face I knew as well as my own, was the saddest moment. I wasn't in any way numb. As soon as I saw her face, I felt that crushing sensation in my chest from earlier, that punch, that body blow, the visceral expression of grief barging in. I was looking at her face, but Dara wasn't there. She was gone. Dara was dead at forty-five years of age, killed doing the job she loved. It was unbelievable. And I felt the full impact of her loss again in that moment. Although even in the midst of that sense of disbelief and the pain of loss, I did take comfort from the fact that she looked at peace, there was some small solace in that.

We stayed with Dara overnight and, as is usual when it comes to Irish traditions around death, we traversed between sharing memories of funny and happy times spent with her and feeling the sadness as we drifted back into the present moment and the cold hard reality of where we were. It was a strange night, sitting in that mortuary with Dara, with blankets over our knees, cold hands around mugs of hot tea brought to us by mortuary staff who were eager to do anything to help, as we told stories and remembered good times we had had with Dara. It was strange, but I'm so glad we did it, because it's one of those things that brings comfort now, the privilege of experiencing that sense of solidarity, us all being there together with Dara in that moment in time. I couldn't be there for her when she needed help the night before, but I could be there with her and with my family that night. That brings solace now.

By the early hours of Wednesday morning I had been up for almost 24 hours straight. I was exhausted, numb and still very much stumbling around in that feeling of this being wholly surreal. I went back to my hotel room to shower and change and discovered that the room was too hot, so I turned off the radiator, pulled back the curtains and opened the windows. I heard the sounds of birdsong and something in me just exploded. I went from exhausted to furious in a matter of seconds. I was livid. When the tears fell, they were hot, angry tears. How on earth could the birds sing and the dawn break when Dara was dead, leaving a child without his mother, parents without their daughter, siblings without their sister, loved ones without their friend, colleagues without their crew member? How could the world still go about its business when our world had ended? That didn't compute.

I realised, in a lightbulb moment of understanding, that in the world nothing had changed. Yet in our world everything had changed. As we were preparing to bring Dara back to Dublin to say our final goodbyes, people were rushing to get out of the house to commute to work or school, worrying about being late or forgetting their homework; radio stations were playing songs and chatting about the latest showbiz gossip; people were celebrating birthdays or wedding days; at a time when we were the saddest we had ever been, others were the happiest they had ever been. To me, the world was now a different place because it was empty of Dara, and yet the reality was that the world itself wasn't any different; life was quite simply going to carry on as normal. The injustice of that angered me in that moment. I felt a disconnect between what was going on emotionally in my own heart and what was going on physically in the world. The two just did not match up.

As before and throughout, there was no real time to process these feelings or make any sense of them. When the eye of the storm had passed and my anger had died down somewhat, my professional training kicked in and I remembered that even in these difficult moments in life, we have a choice. I could either give rage permission to take over, which would take up all my headspace, or I could take a breath and compose myself. I chose the latter and turned my attention to the mundane tasks of getting showered and dressed in clean clothes. Numbness took over again and I focused on what we had to do that day, because there were so many jobs that required our attention. I might have wanted to sit and think and feel and process, but it was a busy and demanding time and I just had to keep moving. I had to keep up with all that was happening around me.

We brought Dara back to Dublin and to my parents' home, the house in which we'd spent our childhood. It was always a warm and welcoming family home, surrounded by the fields where we played chasing and the river we splashed about in as children. In the tradition of the Irish wake Dara would remain at home for a few days until her funeral, and mourners could come to pay their respects to her. Kindly, so as to let us get some sleep, some of our cousins and uncles stayed up with Dara each night, ensuring that she was never alone in the days before she was laid to rest.

The undertakers at Collier's funeral home dressed Dara in her Irish Coast Guard dress uniform, a smart tailored black skirt and jacket with gold buttons down the front and stripes on her sleeves, her flying wings on the left breast pocket, worn over a crisp white shirt with a black tie. I had seen her wearing this uniform on several occasions over the years when she attended ceremonies with her Coast Guard colleagues. Dara was Chief Pilot with the Waterford-based Rescue 117 for several years and during her time there I remember she wore her dress uniform to a civic reception held by the Mayor of Waterford in honour of the crew of Rescue 117. She also wore it when she attended the People of the Year Awards with her colleagues to collect an award for a successful rescue mission. Seeing Dara dressed in her uniform on those occasions, standing beside her colleagues, all looking polished and distinguished, I could never have imagined that one day I would see her wearing this uniform as she lay in her coffin. Considering that over her career she was involved in an estimated 800 rescues and there are people alive today because of Dara and her colleagues, it was fitting that this was her final attire.

Dara was laid out in my parents' house from the Wednesday evening until her funeral on the Saturday morning and hundreds of people came to the house over those days to pay their respects to Dara and to offer their condolences to us. There was a steady stream of people from morning until night, every room was filled with people and it was a sea of faces and a constant hum of conversation.

I had been to wakes before, of course, and had sat and chatted with families who had lost a loved one, people telling stories and sharing memories, but I'd never lost someone that close myself before. Prior to Dara's death, I might have imagined that when it was me who had lost a member of my immediate family, I would be crying constantly, unable to stop the tears of sadness. I might have imagined that having all those people come to sympathise would be difficult and might get in the way of me feeling whatever I needed to feel. I suppose I had always wondered if some of the traditions around death are a help or a hindrance to the bereaved. But the reality, as I found it, was that those rituals of the wake and the funeral were beneficial on many levels and while they may hurt, they also help.

As it turned out, during those days before Dara's funeral I still felt numb, sort of empty and a bit hollow and, except for the odd time when the tears spilled over, I remained composed throughout that week. I don't see that as either a good or a bad thing, it's just how it was. I think it was down to the fact that we had so much to do that my system kept me numbed, keeping me at a remove so that I could function and do my part. After all, we had a funeral to plan and visitors to look after, so I needed to be present and, in all honesty, I also needed to be useful. Nature seemed to take care of that for me and that sense of being anaesthetised stayed with me for the duration.

I remember that week feeling a sense of admiration for those who came to see us. I thought it was a courageous thing to do, given the circumstances. The horror at the loss of four lives in such tragic circumstances had impacted on the whole country. About two days after the crash I went into a local shop to pick up some milk and when I spoke to the person at the till I got the same reaction I still get today if someone realises that I am Dara's sister: their eyes widen and their face almost freezes for a second as they register the depth of the loss. It is a difficult thing to encounter, so I think it was very brave of our visitors to come into a home where they knew that they would face loss of that magnitude head-on. But people are kind, they just wanted to see us, hug us, be with us. Most said the same thing to us: 'I have no words.' I would hear that phrase over and over again during those days, and it sticks out in my mind because it was so apt.

What do you say at a time like this? How do you put into words what you feel in this situation? Shock. Disbelief. Anger. Sorrow. Sympathy. I think that people found that they didn't know how to encapsulate their emotions and so they just said it as it was ... they had no words.

Sometimes I hear people say that they don't know what to say to someone who is distressed or bereaved. My feeling is that if you come when I am distressed, then you say all you need by standing in front of me. You don't need words because your presence says it all. It's the same with attending a funeral, you don't need profound or original words when you shake my hand as I stand beside my sister's coffin. The fact that you stand in front of me and take my hand or hug me gently says all I need to hear. Or if you send a card or letter, don't worry if your words seem inadequate to you. I just see that you went to the trouble of selecting a card or finding some writing paper, that you took time out of your day to think of my family and that you found the best words to write. I see that you left your house and posted this envelope filled with care and love. I see support. The simple words such as 'I'm so sorry for your loss' or 'I'm thinking of you and your family' send a strong message of support. It's also very important when you're grieving to know that your loved one will not be forgotten, so those people who said things like, 'Dara was a lovely girl, she was so kind whenever I met her' also brought me comfort, as I knew that on some level they would remember her.

One of Dara's great friends from Rescue 117, Winch Operator John Manning, arrived to the house one night to lend his support to us and he brought a gift. Several years earlier he and Dara and the Waterford crew had landed the helicopter at a local school to teach the children about water safety. As part of these educational talks they showed the helicopter to the children and on this occasion John, a keen photographer, captured a photo of Dara as she walked towards the heli with a line of children trailing after her. In the photo she is turned to face the camera, looking at her friend John, smiling and waving over at him with a look of pure joy on her face as the children follow her in a line. She looks so happy. She's right where she wants to be, proud to be about to show off the helicopter she loved so much, to tell these young children all about her job in search and rescue. It's a beautiful photo. John printed the image, framed it and gave it to us that night. As it was passed around, it made everyone smile. It was far more eloquent than any words he could have said. It was a perfect and thoughtful gift.

Amidst talking to mourners, receiving and relaying information between the two Garda FLOs and my family and vice versa, I was also involved with my parents and siblings in planning Dara's funeral. We did all the usual things, such as picking out readings and music, preparing the mass booklet, composing prayers. They all sound easy when I see them written down here, but they take time and we wanted to get it right. This funeral had to be a celebration of Dara's life, a fairly incredible life by any standards. Her loved ones were of utmost importance to Dara and we wanted to include as many of her family, friends and colleagues as we could and have them participate in different areas of the funeral mass.

Over the few days that week, we worked together as a family and got all the planning done, ready for the funeral on Saturday morning. By late on Friday night the only job I had left to do was to write my speech for Dara's eulogy. Captain

Cathal Oakes was giving a eulogy on behalf of her work family, I was giving a eulogy on behalf of her home family. However, after the preceding four days I was exhausted, completely spent, there was nothing left in the tank and I had no eulogy prepared. I desperately needed sleep, so I decided to set my alarm for 5.30 am on the day of Dara's funeral and get up to write it then. This was a risky plan, I knew. It would be one of the most important speeches I would ever make, I had one shot at it and it needed to do Dara justice. At the same time, I knew that I had to be fresh in order to get it right and I felt that rising early was the best strategy, so I trusted myself and went with that plan, heading home to my house to sleep.

That night felt like the opposite of Christmas Eve. You know that feeling of anticipation the night before Christmas – the sense of waiting, excited by the knowledge that tomorrow would be a big day, different from other days? It was just like that. Only this time, it wasn't going to be different in a good way. We would be waking up to say our formal and final goodbyes to Dara. I'm never short of words, but I actually don't think I have words to adequately describe what that felt like going to bed that night. It felt so odd, like I was living someone else's life. To add to the sense of things being surreal, that night on Twitter I was tagged in a tweet from someone asking me if I was aware that the official number given to the road on which the church in Glencullen where Dara's funeral would be held was R116. This was one of those examples of truth being stranger than fiction; it would be deemed far-fetched if this coincidence was written in a novel or shown on screen. I don't really understand why, but I did find this somehow comforting. The bereaved clutch on to anything that may offer solace of some sort, a connection, a meaning. I'm okay with that. I'm glad that I was told about this link, and I liked knowing that the place that would provide Dara's final resting place had the same name as her helicopter. It seemed fitting.

At 5.30 am on the day of the funeral my alarm woke me and I sat up in bed with a pen and paper, letting my thoughts and emotions flow out onto the page as I wrote Dara's eulogy. I found that once I began to write, I didn't actually worry too much because I knew that everything I wrote would come from the heart, which meant I would get it right and say what needed to be said. It took perhaps 30 minutes to put my thoughts together and I then typed them into a document on my laptop before transferring them to a memory stick to bring to my parents' house for printing before the funeral. Despite, or perhaps because of, the early hour in terms of time of day and the lateness of the hour in terms of proximity to Dara's funeral, when I read over my notes I was happy that I had covered the essence of what we were feeling and that my family would feel that I had represented them well and had done Dara justice.

I arrived at my parents' house early. I went to see Dara and then the undertakers arrived and gently told us that they would be closing the coffin shortly, in readiness to move it to the church. I took out my memory stick and went upstairs to print out a copy of the eulogy. I discovered that the printer was out of ink and try as I might, I couldn't find any new cartridges. I could feel tension building inside me as I searched frantically and I got so stressed about it that I was on the edge of a meltdown. It was mostly immediate and extended family in the house that morning, and I shouted downstairs to ask someone to help with the printer. I could feel my voice getting higher and my breathing getting shallower as the panic began to rise, until I was almost yelling at the top of my lungs for help. I am probably a hot-head by nature, a bit fiery in character, but my psychology skills have trained me to be composed, so while I might have yelled as a child it's not something I would often do as an adult. It was completely out of character for me to do so that morning, but that's one of the facets of grief – it can make you a stranger to yourself. Of course, beneath the panic was fear, and beneath the fear was my own voice telling me that this wasn't about the ink, it was about the finality of closing the coffin. The emotions roller-coastering about inside me were making it hard to think, hard to stay calm and so I blew up at the slightest thing. It was never about anything but grief and emotional pain and yet another moment of facing the truth of Dara's death.

A kind and, let's be honest, brave person came upstairs to help and we got the eulogy printed. Afterwards I felt awful for behaving so badly, until I remembered the words of the psychiatrist Viktor Frankl, words I have often quoted to clients. In his book *Man's Search for Meaning*, Frankl notes that 'an abnormal reaction to an abnormal situation is normal behaviour'. In that moment, this thought was comforting and allowed me to both forgive myself and interpret my shouting and panicking with compassion. There was absolutely nothing normal about this situation. My sister was lying in a coffin and I was about to see her for the last time. Unknown to my family, I was also holding in the secret of my marriage breakdown. On top of all this I was mentally, physically and emotionally exhausted after the events of the previous few days. It was fair to say that a meltdown was allowed. It was normal, so there was no need to feel ashamed or angry with myself or disappointed in myself. I simply accepted that it was an emotional reaction, forgave myself and left it behind.

I rejoined my family and spent some time with Dara. Then I said my goodbyes before the coffin lid was closed. That was a truly horrible moment, seeing her beautiful face for the very last time, it brings a lump to my throat even now as I remember it. But at the same time, I'm very glad I did take the time to be with Dara and say goodbye to her in that moment, because I can appreciate now, with hindsight, that it helped me to face the reality and accept what had happened.

Flanked by motorbike outriders from the Garda Traffic Corps, the hearse and funeral cars escorted Dara from her childhood home one last time. The tricolour was draped over her coffin, her Irish Coast Guard hat lay beside it and as the hearse drove the few kilometres up into the Dublin mountains to the church people lined the route to pay their respects as she passed by. Silently they stood, making the sign of the cross or bowing their heads as the hearse drove by slowly. If it wasn't so sad, it would have been beautiful.

I think there's an added layer of sadness when someone dies in the fact that they never hear or see the outpouring of love, warmth and respect when people express how they feel about them. For example, Dara never saw the staff at Mayo University Hospital lining the driveway to pay their respects as the cortège passed by when we left the mortuary; she never saw the huge group of her neighbours from the houses in our estate standing outside her house, shivering in the cold, when we brought her back to her own home one last time; she never heard all the stories and memories shared by the hundreds of people who visited my parents' house that week, colleagues telling us how much they enjoyed working with Dara and how much they respected her, or friends sharing how they loved having her in their life. I would say that Dara knew that she was loved by her family and close friends, but she would have had no idea whatsoever that she was so well regarded on a wider scale, either personally or professionally. That would have been such a surprise to her, and probably an embarrassment because Dara was kind of shy. There's a learning in this for us all: don't wait. If you feel it, say it; if you like, love, value or respect someone, tell them. Those words can mean so much to someone and it's important that they hear them when they are alive.

I hadn't given any thought to what it would be like when we got to the church, so I was astounded by the sight that greeted us. Crowds of people everywhere, Gardaí and stewards on site to direct the flow of people, each piece of ground both outside and inside the church gates filled with people, mourners standing several deep as they waited for the coffin to arrive, the click of cameras flashing from the bank of journalists positioned opposite the church. Stepping out of the car I could hear the tolling of the church bell, but aside from the bell all I noticed was the quiet. There was not a sound from what we later learned to be more than two thousand people, many standing since early morning in the drizzling March rain, wrapped up in winter coats and holding umbrellas, waiting for Dara.

The job of the Coast Guard is to bring people home and it felt right that the men and women who flew with Dara would be the ones to bring her to her final resting place. In their dress uniforms, just like Dara, they slowly and gently carried her coffin round the winding gravel path from the church gate to the entrance door, accompanied by the strains of a piper playing

Dvořák's 'Going Home' as we walked behind. All I could hear was the piper and the crunch of gravel underfoot, it was perfectly silent otherwise. The church grounds were filled with people as far as the eye could see and standing in front of those crowds, at the edge of the winding path, were more uniforms than I had ever seen in one place. Emergency services colleagues had come in huge numbers to pay their respects to Dara, from the RNLI, Fire Service, Ambulance Service, Mountain Rescue, the Coast Guard, as well as representatives from the Defence Forces, Naval Service, Civil Defence, Air Corps, Gardaí and many from the aviation world. They stood shoulder to shoulder, in their uniforms, providing a guard of honour for Dara as she was brought to her final home.

Inside the church we took our seats in the front rows. It was important to us that the funeral mass balanced the sadness with the joy of Dara's life and I think we achieved that. We had asked the choir to 'sing Dara home', and they performed a mix of rousing and poignant songs. Family, friends and colleagues participated in readings and prayers as well as bringing up the gifts, which represented the different aspects of Dara's life.

Towards the end of the mass Cathal delivered his eulogy, a touching tribute full of respect and admiration for Dara and the work she did over her twenty-three years as a search and rescue pilot. Then it was my turn to speak about Dara. I had been so in the moment throughout the funeral, trying to take in every piece of this beautiful tribute to Dara, that I hadn't thought about that part when I would need to stand up and walk across the church to the pulpit to deliver my eulogy. When the time actually arrived, I felt quite emotional. For a fleeting moment I wondered if I could get through the whole speech without losing control of my emotions. But Cathal had previously told me that he would remain standing behind me for the duration and as I spoke I felt his hand on my back, gently reminding me that I had support from everyone, and although it was one of the most difficult speeches I have ever given, I was able to keep my composure and to get my words and sentiments across.

We expect to survive our parents but no one expects to outlive a sibling, we don't ever give consideration to that possibility. For those of us fortunate to have good relationships with our siblings, they are the people in our lives who are always there. They have been there for all or most of our life and it is such a special connection. Sibling relationships can survive the arguments of childhood and the disagreements of adulthood and still remain intact. These are the people who share the highs and the lows of our life, from youth through to being fully fledged grown-ups, and whatever other relationships come and go, siblings feel like the constant in our world, and perhaps there is an unconscious sense that they always will be. Hence it was understandable that I had that brief second of mental hesitation before I left my seat to speak, because you do not, and maybe cannot, really picture speaking at your sibling's funeral until you are actually doing it.

As I neared the end of my words, I wanted to suggest a way for people to remember Dara and bring some of her values with them throughout life. When someone dies, the idea that they might be forgotten is too awful to consider. I wanted to help everyone gathered there to remember Dara and think of her often. So I introduced the expression 'Do a Dara' and I explained what it meant. It wasn't easy for Dara to start from a zero base and become a pilot, to gain entry to and then smash glass ceilings and succeed in the largely male-dominated environment of search and rescue. But every obstacle that Dara Fitz encountered along the way to doing her dream job she found a way over, around, under or through. She did not let anything stop her, not in a bulldozing way, but simply that in her own unassuming and understated way she found a path through every single challenge and difficulty. Dara was persistent, hard-working, dedicated and resilient. I suggested to the congregation that a lovely way to remember Dara and to bring her with us in life would be to stop and think about what she would do whenever we each encountered obstacles in our lives. Dara would find a way.

Since that day, that phrase 'Do a Dara' has been quoted back to me on many occasions and each time I hear the expression I know that someone is remembering this warm, funny, kind, loving girl who also had a backbone of steel. There's comfort in knowing that she is not forgotten.

I finished my eulogy with a concept that I felt was helpful for those who love Dara to consider. *Death ends a life, not a relationship* (Morrie Schwartz, from *Tuesdays with Morrie* by Mitch Albom). Dara had been ripped out of our lives without warning, and the idea that the connection we had with her was gone was unbearable. When I'd read those words on a card earlier in the week, they'd resonated with me because I had realised even then that one of the truths about grief is that it is, in time, about finding new ways to relate to the person who has died. Because the love you feel for them doesn't die with them, they just aren't here to experience it any more. So what do you do with the love, respect, admiration and other feelings you have for someone who is no longer here? You can't sit across from them and chat any more and show them that you care by listening to their worries. You can't laugh together at life's funny little moments or share the big times of joy or celebration in their life. There's just nothing. Only emptiness. A big gaping space where the person you love once was. That's the truth.

However, time, learning and healing have taught me another truth, which is that a lifetime of feelings and memories are held intact in my heart and no matter what life holds now in this new reality without Dara, that old reality will always be there in my heart. I can't engage and connect with Dara in the physical world, but I can do so in my cognitive world and I find comfort in those memories. Those little moments gifted randomly when something in my current life sparks a connection to that old life and out of the blue, I see Dara in my mind. Those memories and feelings from our life together can be a gateway to maintaining that relationship, enabling us to keep the memory of the person alive and relevant even when they are no longer there. Grief is about finding a way to be okay with that, getting to a place where we can welcome those memories rather than being resentful that they are all we have left, accepting that if this is the way we will now relate, through memories and stories and a love re-lived, then we'll take the joy that brings. I needed to end my words about Dara's life and about her death by giving some hope to those left behind about the place that Dara would have now in our lives, and the sentiment behind Morrie Schwartz's words helped me to achieve that.

Just as it was fitting that Dara's Irish Coast Guard colleagues and friends had carried her into the church for her funeral Mass, so it was fitting that her family carried her coffin out to the waiting hearse to take her to the crematorium. As the crowds milled around us, wrapping us in love and support, we heard the familiar sound of the Irish Coast Guard Sikorsky helicopter as it arrived to do a fly-past. The crowd went silent. People stood looking up to the sky at the approach of Dara's colleagues from the Waterford-based Rescue 117, who had flown to Dublin to pay their respects to their former Chief Pilot. Two winch crew stood tall in the open doorway of the helicopter as it circled slowly overhead before coming to a hover in front of the hearse. It remained in the hover for a few moments, watching solemnly over the crowd, a respectful silence disturbed only by the sounds of the aircraft. The pilots dipped the nose of the helicopter down towards the coffin in a bow of respect to their fallen colleague, saluting Dara, saying farewell to their friend. It was sincere and poignant, a beautiful end to her funeral mass.

The funeral cortège set off from the church and headed for Mount Jerome Cemetery and Crematorium in Harold's Cross. There, Dara's colleagues once again bore her coffin, carrying her into the Victorian chapel, a beautiful old building with high ceilings, wooden beams and arches and large stone pillars. Going into the chapel I was behind my sister Emer, who was carrying Dara's little son, Fionn. He was too young to really understand what was going on and as we walked up the aisle, we were all chatting quietly to him, keeping him settled. As we walked, Fionn reached over, tapped my shoulder and said, 'You're beautiful, Niamh.' It was so lovely and unexpected. He was used to only ever seeing me in jeans; this was the first time he had ever seen me in a dress and, observant little fella that he is, he let me know that he had noticed the difference. It was a lovely moment, one that I like to think would have made Dara smile.

The sight of Dara's colleagues lining the walls of the chapel, resplendent in their Coast Guard uniforms as they and our family, friends and colleagues surrounded us with a swell of support, was a huge comfort. And I really needed that comfort because I knew that alongside seeing Dara for the last time before the coffin was closed earlier that morning, this was going to be the hardest part of the funeral day. Once the prayers were said, Dara's coffin would slowly move away from us and she would be gone. I knew, of course, that she was already gone, but the idea of that moment when I would see her coffin for the last time terrified me.

It's an indication of the complexities of grief that only an hour before, I had stood at the pulpit in the church and spoken about how death is the end of a life, not of a relationship. I had brought into the conversation that sense of finding a new way to relate to a loved one who has died. I believed those words when I shared them with the crowd at the funeral. Intellectually, I knew that there could be comfort one day in the bank of memories housed in our heads and hearts and that, in time, through those very memories we could continue to have Dara in our lives. Yet as I took my place in the chapel for the cremation service and I faced into the moment when Dara's earthly body would be no more, emotionally that concept was of no use to me. It wasn't enough to console. Where would she be? Where would I find her if not in her physical body? What shape and space would she have in my mind if the shape and space that she had occupied for forty-five years was no more? How could she just be *gone*? The days of having Dara at home before the funeral had been so precious, but after cremation she would no longer have a physical presence on this Earth. She would quite literally no longer exist except in our hearts and minds, a dawning realisation that trailed terror it its wake. The idea that a loved one will be eradicated from our life, leaving only a space where they once were, is a most painful and frightening part of the reality of loss. The emptiness. The nothingness. In the chapel that day, emotionally I buckled under the weight of that. On some level I struggle with that fact even now, to be honest. Dara as I have known her all my life doesn't exist any more. It's very hard to get your head around that. I don't dwell on it because it would drive me into a state of angst, but somewhere in the recesses of my mind there is still a silent scream at that truth.

As the coffin moved out of view, our chosen song for this moment played around the chapel. It was 'Run' by Snow Patrol, a band and song that Dara had really loved. Either I had never properly listened to the lyrics before or hearing them in that particular context brought new meaning, but as soon as the song began to play I could feel myself starting to lose control of my emotions. There's nothing wrong with that, crying is healthy and healing, but I tried to keep it in because if I let go, I wasn't sure what would happen and I was conscious of not upsetting others. Everyone was distraught and me wailing wasn't going to help the situation. But had I been on my own in that chapel during the few minutes of that song, I honestly would have probably dropped to my knees and howled in pain. I could feel it in my chest, pure pain, a heavy, crushing sensation as though my heart was being compressed. The resonance of the words Gary Lightbody was singing intensified that moment and all the emotion of the previous few days came flooding over me.

To think I might not see those eyes
It makes it so hard not to cry
And as we say our long goodbyes
I nearly do ...

Towards the end of the song, as the melody builds and circles, I did lose control and I broke down. I couldn't hold myself together any more and I cried and cried and cried. It would have been obvious to those present that I was very upset, but I did manage to let my own feelings out without intensifying the distress that everyone else was feeling in that moment, and that mattered to me.

At the end of the cremation service, we walked down the aisle of the chapel and out into the afternoon light, but really, we were walking nearer towards the reality of daily life without Dara. In the week of a death and a funeral there is a suspension of real life and nothing feels normal. Surrounded by people who are not normally there and busied by tasks that don't normally need doing, we move from one day into the next in a bit of a daze. But after the funeral, when the cups are washed, the sandwiches have gone stale and everyone returns to their own lives, we must face what comes next: returning to real life without the buffer of distraction. With the focus in the days leading up to a funeral on planning the details of the funeral itself, there is little or no time to consider the details of life *after* the funeral. Going home that evening, I found that both my mind and my heart were focused on a sense of emptiness as I sat feeling lost in a world without Dara in it. She no longer even had a physical body. Dara didn't exist any more. There was nothing where she had once been. Incomprehensible was how it felt, wholly and completely unbelievable. No matter that I had heard the news of her death with my own ears, had seen her body with my own eyes, and had been present for her funeral, I still found myself asking over and over again in my head if this was real.

The funeral day had been harrowing, yet also brought a sense of comfort in seeing the love and respect that people had for Dara and in feeling the blanket of support that they wrapped around us as her family. That day and the rituals of death brought, in addition, a heightened sense of her loss and of the finality of that, deepened by the physical end to her existence on Earth with her cremation. Dara didn't exist any more. The rituals of the wake and funeral were over and she was gone. It was a Saturday night and only a week earlier, my sisters and our mother would have been chatting among ourselves about *Dancing with the Stars*, discussing which dancer we were rooting for. But now … Dara didn't exist any more. I know I keep saying that, but this overwhelming sense of the finality of her loss was at the core of the sadness I felt that night. As I went to bed it was in the knowledge that I would wake the next day and it would be time to come face to face with the cold, hard reality of what the previous few days had been leading to, and for the second night in a row I fell asleep with a sense of dread for a day that I knew would be particularly difficult. In truth, there was nothing that could help me that night. In order to begin to process Dara's loss, I needed to first know the acute pain of her loss. In time I would be able to feel her presence in my life, but first I had to feel the full force of the fact of her total absence.

Even if you cannot hear my voice,
I'll be right beside you dear.

CHAPTER FIVE

FEEL THE FEELINGS

When you experience a loss, especially a sudden and traumatic loss, the onset of shock and the numbing of your feelings is a natural reaction that allows you time before the full impact of the loss hits you head-on. The sense of surreal disbelief provides a buffer zone between the old normal and the new normal, while you struggle to process the new normal. As the initial sense of numbness begins to dissipate over time to reveal different emotional states, such as anger, fear or sorrow, of key importance is that you feel those feelings. They can range from the unpleasant to the unpalatable or the intolerable, but being present with them all and experiencing the truth of your loss is a vital part of that journey towards learning to carry the loss.

One of the unexpected things about loss is the amount of admin surrounding it. At a time when you are depleted, both emotionally and physically, you are suddenly required to perform a huge list of pressing tasks. Your attention is constantly dragged away from the source of your grief to the practicalities of the loss, at a time when it's important to avoid hiding from your feelings. It can be a real challenge to not let the practical details around loss swallow you up, failing to pay attention to the emotional details in the process. It's a strange situation, but it is the case, as I described before, that the numb state in those early days of loss can help you get through the jobs to be done. I think of it as the admin of grief, and I had to manage it in the wake of all three losses in my life. The challenge is to make sure that we neither use the admin of grief as a way to avoid feeling the feelings of grief nor let it become a distraction from feeling what we ultimately must feel.

I am an organised person and tend to be methodical in how I approach things, so I'm not fazed by having a lengthy to-do list. Indeed, I usually quite enjoy the satisfaction of getting through the admin of life. We might assume that those who are so inclined in normal life would, in grief life, easily handle the conveyor belt of tasks and decisions that require completion after loss. However, my experience is that after the initial numbness had worn off, when I was feeling the full force of loss, the admin of grief became the straw that broke the camel's back and those jobs and decisions often became too much, pushing me over the edge, triggering a heightened sense of emotion, exhaustion and bone-deep weariness.

In the case of a death, there is personal admin and then the job of preparing the public managing and expression of grief. In terms of personal tasks, each person has to cancel work, reschedule, talk to their boss and explain the situation, make

apologies for an absence that might have unwelcome consequences for colleagues and clients. It's difficult to focus on these
things that now seem utterly pointless because your world has
fallen apart, but I found that taking the time out to focus on
them and tick them off one by one provided a quiet, controllable
space in the middle of all the noise and the horrible feeling of
my life being utterly outside my control. There was something
balm-like about the mundane ordinariness of making phone calls
and sending emails. It can be a means of slowing things down
and allowing you to take a breather, if you can see it that way.

In the days after Dara died, we had to prepare for hundreds
of visitors, organise for Dara to be in the company of people at
all times of the day and night and think through the funeral we
felt she would have wanted and that we wanted to give her. It's
a busy, busy period and it can be overwhelming at times. In our
particular case, there was a distressing extra layer of admin in
the fact that the circumstances of Dara's death meant we had to
liaise with the Gardaí and the Coast Guard. This required one
person to be the point of contact for each agency, available and
able to answer questions and make decisions about all sorts of
things. Initially these were decisions around the post-mortem,
finalising arrangements around my father's return from the UK,
where he was for the week, making plans to get the family up to
Mayo to bring Dara home, getting a photograph of Dara for her
company to release to the media and so on and so forth. There
was an awful lot to be done.

When the Gardaí came to Dara and Emer's house on that
Tuesday and told us that we would need to choose someone to
be that point of contact, my family all physically turned towards
me, simultaneously unified in the instinct that this job had my

name on it. I'm comfortable dealing with people, I'm good with gathering and disseminating information, my communication skills are effective and I'm reliably reachable at the end of a phone, so it made sense that I would be a match for the role and I was okay with that, it made sense to me too. I felt a deep need to do something, anything, to contribute in some way to navigating through the living nightmare we found ourselves in and stepping into the point of contact role was one way I could be of use. Once I was confirmed as point of contact with the Gardaí, it made sense that I would take the same role with the Coast Guard. From that day I began to work with Garda Paul Flood and Captain Mark Donnelly, relaying information to and from my family and responding to requests for information or decisions.

In normal life we tend to have roles within a family unit, spaces in which we find ourselves within the dynamic of the group. Some are personality-based roles: the funny one, the sensible one. Others are task-based roles: the fixer, the peace-maker. In grief life, we also fall into roles within the family and, as in normal life, these roles are often based on a natural fit given a particular skill or area of competence. After a parent dies, for example, if one of the adult children is an accountant, they might take the lead on tasks around the financial admin of death. There are situations too, of course, that require people to fill roles not because of particular knowledge or expertise but simply because they may be the person best placed in terms of availability or geographical proximity, and it can be challenging on many levels when that happens. A family grieving is made up of individuals dealing with the loss in their own way, not always in sync or sympathy with one another's perspective, and on top of this some will incur the added layer of responsibility around dealing with solicitors or packing up and selling a house. It's very tough.

Where possible, when selecting tasks from the admin of grief, it's useful to have even a brief conversation to check in around what feels comfortable for each person. This is about having a calm, open, honest chat about what needs to be done and who feels able to do it. It's about suspending judgement and remembering that behind the form-filling or meetings there are people hurting from the pain of loss; people whose lives have been changed for ever with the death of a loved one. It's about appreciating differences and acknowledging that we won't all deal with death in the same way, but that's not what matters. What matters is that there are jobs around the practical, legal and financial end to a loved one's life that must be completed and those tasks won't wait. There are timelines and deadlines to be met, schedules that don't care about the feelings of grief. So when a family can work to their strengths and work together, these tasks can be shared and completed, in a mark of respect to the person for whom we ache, and that in itself can be connecting and perhaps even bonding for a grieving family.

The grief admin means that very quickly after cognitively registering the loss of a loved one, you are required to move into a functional space rather than a feeling space. It felt overwhelming, the volume of jobs to be done, but there simply wasn't the time to dwell on that. The tasks had to be addressed as they arose, so I had to park my emotions and engage my brain and get things done; we all did as everyone pitched in. As the investigation into the crash got under way, I became my family's point of contact for all the different agencies involved, including the Air Accident Investigation Unit, the Gardaí in Mayo and the

Coroner for North Mayo, Dr Eleanor Fitzgerald. All communication to and from these agencies and my family came, and still comes, through me and it's a significant volume of correspondence. I felt welded to my phone in those early days, unable to be far away from it because of a need to be ready for the next request, report or piece of information that came in. There was an onslaught of new information and vocabulary, as through those requests and reports we had to learn the meaning of a host of terms previously alien to us, aviation terms, search and rescue terms and even medical terms.

An additional challenge features with a death that necessitates an investigation or an inquest because, like a rock thrown into a pond disturbing the surface of the water, admin of that nature tends to bring back to the top those waves of emotion that may have somewhat settled into a more manageable state at that point. Although these particular pieces of admin are both welcome and necessary parts of the process in a situation such as ours, every time I have to read sections of an investigation report or hear clinical details at the Coroner's Court inquest it brings on that tsunami of grief, a rush of waves and a wall of water knocking me off my feet, reminiscent of those first few moments after I knew of Dara's death. All over again it becomes hard to speak because of the flow of tears or the size of the lump in my throat. I feel that tightening in my chest as my heart contracts with the pain and circumstance of her loss. My body feels winded from the sucker punch to the gut yet again. It feels as though a wound is opened anytime these really difficult pieces of admin arise and when I've closed my eyes on the nights after I've read certain things, there are images in my head that I can't get out. Then I have to go out the next day and smile and put my best foot forward when I had been reading such horrifying details only hours before.

When I struggle with the trauma of Dara's death, triggered by reports or articles that go into detail that as a sister is hard to read, I lean into the grief and let myself feel it fully. Sorrow. Anger. Hot tears of rage at the utter waste of life. Then I ground myself in the present moment, tuning into what I can see, hear or feel in the room around me. And when I am in the present, I bring that to the horrific details of what I've just read and I remind myself that Dara is no longer suffering, that however horrific her last moments were, she is at peace now. That's how I get through those most awful times when I have to face details of her death that I don't want to face.

But although my heart is breaking all over again as my brain takes in the information, there are still administrative requirements around that report or inquest that need my attention and I have often had to put aside my emotions and deal with those first. Over the three years, this point of contact role has been what I would describe as a heavy piece of grief admin, full-on emotionally, practically and in terms of volume, and although I was glad to do it and wouldn't have had it any other way, it has undoubtedly been tough.

It must be said that there have been times when the admin around Dara's death has allowed for moments of comfort, such as when my family was invited by Dr Eleanor Fitzgerald to submit some words about Dara to the Coroner's Court before the inquest. I wrote a piece about her life and once it had the approval of my family, we gave it to the Coroner's office. Then, in the courtroom in Belmullet, at the end of the inquest proceedings I sat in the witness box and read out our words about Dara. We took the chance to speak about Dara when it was offered to us because we wanted to balance out the cold, clinical facts about her death with some warm, personable facts and observations about her life, so that the last words about Dara that day were about her life, not her death. I cannot say that this piece of admin was enjoyable, but it brought comfort at a difficult time on that inquest day.

I suspect that any family who finds themselves dealing with an investigation or inquest surrounding the death of their loved one would say that it adds a layer of complexity to the grieving process and that they feel relief when that side of things comes to a close.

In addition to all the above, I also found myself having to spend time and effort contacting members of the media who had published articles quoting me in ways that were quite simply inaccurate and untrue. They each responded quickly and kindly, to be fair to them, and the articles were removed, but neither the distress on first reading them nor the time taken to resolve the situation were welcome. I also have to contend with the ghouls and conspiracy theorists who send emails with information they purport to have about the crash, under the guise that they are sharing it to 'help' me. I ignore these, save for reporting them to the relevant authorities, but again, it is an added stress on top of what is an already distressing situation.

There were unusual and particular circumstances to be handled with regard to Dara's death, but every bereaved family is pitched straight into funeral and grave arrangements and announcements, dealing with the undertakers, writing death notices and answering texts, calls and letters of condolence. It also requires working with solicitors, figuring out wills and probate and possibly even involving the Revenue Commissioners. This is all brand-new territory to most of us, so it's very difficult to find the head space to understand what's required and how to go about it. Then, as the weeks go on, you also have to address the question of the clothes and belongings of your loved one, cancelling things like phone contracts, changing names on utility bills, selling cars, reorganising the deceased person's online world and ensuring their files of documents, both hard and soft copy, are all dealt with safely and appropriately. As time goes on, it becomes about things like designing memorial cards and putting In Memoriam notices in the paper to mark a year since their death. It's hard to read a list like this, but these are only a few of the myriad of admin tasks facing someone who is bereaved. Given that when we're grieving we feel overwhelmed and exhausted, and we feel challenged in terms of our cognitive capacity, it's easy to see why the admin around grief can be too much for many of us.

It is also understandable how ordinary everyday life admin can pile up when we are grieving, those little jobs that we put off because they don't shout as loud as either the pain of loss or the meeting with the estate agent to sell the house. The energy it takes to deal with both the emotion and admin of loss is all-consuming and depletes our tank right down to empty, leaving little or nothing to deal with other demands. We sift through the calls for action in our email inbox or on our to-do list, picking out the urgent and the important, and then scramble to complete the tasks in these categories. But jobs that could be seen as a nice-to-do rather than need-to-do can stack up as they never make it to the top of the list. Birthday and Christmas cards aren't bought, never mind sent. Searching for new curtains for a spare bedroom becomes an aspiration rather than an action. Even routine checks-ups with things such as a car service can wind up pushed out further than normal. And those beneficial-but-non-urgent tasks, such as shopping around for better car insurance rates or switching energy supplier, don't even get a look in. I even discovered that my car tax was several months out of date because, mired in grief, when the notification came in I had filed it away under 'must do that soon' and it had slipped through the net because the admin of grief made its presence felt more strongly than the admin of life.

It is important to carry out these grief admin tasks, and although they can provide a welcome distraction for some people, it's also important to realise that you can ask for help, you can ask for extra time, you can delegate. Extended family and friends are often delighted to be given a concrete task to do because it can allow them to feel useful. In the twilight world of surreal grief, the sense of being helpless is one that affects everyone and people tend to feel very uncomfortable in that space. Giving someone a job to do can be a help to them, so don't worry that you're burdening others if you ask for assistance with particular jobs.

A death is particularly admin-heavy, but there will be requirements to be fulfilled around all types of loss. I found the admin around infertility difficult for several reasons. First, it was linked to such a huge emotional consequence; this was form-filling and appointment-scheduling in order to bring life into the world, which adds an intense dimension to the tasks. Second, it is work that has to be done on top of normal life, which continues on as normal, with the usual demands asked of you while you are going through fertility treatment, so it was a big extra load to carry and took up a huge amount of time (and indeed money). Third, the admin around fertility was all tackled privately, without that ability to call in help from others; there was a lot to be done in terms of form-filling, answering probing questions about things that you don't normally discuss with anyone, let alone your family and friends. There was also a steady list of appointments to be scheduled, including trips to another country for medical investigation, all of which had to be managed without inconveniencing or even alerting colleagues or family. We just got on with it quietly and got it done, but looking back now I wonder how we managed it all. What's most striking to me now is the fact that all that was happening, but for a long time no one knew. It was a private world we entered and had to navigate on our own. That brings a layer of loneliness.

There was a similar administrative load with the adoption process. More copious form-filling, attending meetings and courses, doing homework that was lengthy and detailed, it was like preparing for the Leaving Cert again, when your whole self is consumed by thoughts of what is done and what remains to be done. Funnily enough, within the admin around the loss of parenthood, the adoption process was the one that felt enjoyable and most manageable to me. I struggled in different ways with the admin of the other aspects of loss, but while it was a significant workload, I enjoyed the adoption process as a process in itself. I think there were a few influencing factors in this, a significant one being that the adoption course is done as part of a group, so you attend for a period of weeks with other couples or individuals who are in a similar situation to yourselves. This was very different from the quiet waiting rooms of the fertility clinics, where things understandably felt more private and couples didn't tend to interact. However, from the first coffee break on the first day of the adoption course I found myself chatting to others, everyone sharing their stories and talking openly about their journey to become parents. There is healing in togetherness, in this kind of personal connection, and for me there was something healing about meeting that lovely group of people. It normalised where I found myself, but in a way that felt more palatable than being around other people in the fertility clinic who were unable to conceive.

Infertility is not shameful, not in the least, but the truth is that adoption felt easier to talk about than fertility treatment. Is it because adoption is about a positive process in which you are about to actively participate, whereas infertility is focused on your biological capabilities? Whatever the reason, while others weren't aware that we were undergoing fertility treatment, many family and friends knew at the time that we were going through the adoption process. That also helped me to enjoy the process because it was something normal rather than something secret. It didn't have to be hidden and privately juggled. A final factor was that I found the adoption process educational. I learned so much from the course and through completing the homework. It felt like I was expanding my knowledge base but in a way that was interesting rather than distressing.

By comparison, the grief admin that I found most difficult and stressful was that around the end of my marriage. The sheer volume of tasks to be completed in order to officially end a marriage feels intensely demanding and utterly endless. There's consultation with solicitors, agreeing the means and terms of the separation, forms, forms and more forms, spreading out your financial and personal lives for strangers to pore over in detail, which feels invasive and can make you feel vulnerable and resentful in equal measure. Then the house, selling it, buying or renting a new place, audited accounts for the bank, so many documents to track down and sort so that you can be assessed from top to toe. And now, you're doing it on your own as a single person, which takes some getting used to as well. It's terrifically difficult and prolonged. The admin around Dara's death has been the most distressing but it was definitely the separation admin that I found most stressful – and that was even in a situation where all parties were amicable and cooperative.

As I reflect now about the admin of grief around these three losses in my life, I notice that my feelings are still very strong and raw as I write about anything concerning Dara's death, but they are more settled when I think about the admin around the end of my marriage, and actually I feel neutral when I write about those tasks around infertility and the loss of the hope of motherhood. Is this because that loss is so far in my past? It is seven years since our adoption journey ended without success and I wonder if that distance plays a part in how I feel when I recount the challenge of that admin? It was incredibly challenging and distressing at the time, but it is no longer so. Or do I feel differently when I write about those tasks because I have now fully made peace with not being a mother? Would I find my mind going over aspects of the inconvenience and intrusion of those jobs if I were not in a place of acceptance in that regard? I suspect that I might.

Timing meant that the admin of grief around the loss of my sister and of my marriage rolled into one another, so I was simultaneously dealing with matters in the aftermath of Dara's death as I was gathering documents for the end of my marriage. As I've mentioned, the suddenness and the circumstances of

Dara's death meant that the admin around this loss has been incredibly distressing. To have the cumulative layer of the marriage separation admin on top of that has brought me to my knees at times. It was savagely difficult dealing with two significant losses at the one time and having to handle the emotions of grief, the admin of grief and the life that carries on around grief.

There is something about having to deal with the admin of grief when a loved one dies that heightens awareness of the admin around your own death and this taught me an important lesson. I saw how organised Dara was, how much time and attention she had given to every last detail of getting her affairs in order in the event of her death. She showed great sense when she took the time to put plans in place to ensure that her own wishes were met. She also showed great kindness towards us because everything is so difficult when someone dies without the added complications that arise if they have not left a last will and testament. I have now done this piece of admin for myself so that when I die, my family will be similarly met with a well-thought-out, clear set of instructions around my estate and some guidance around my wishes for funeral and cremation. I think that any way that we can lift the weight of burden from the shoulders of our loved ones when we die should be grabbed with both hands and taken eagerly, for it is appreciated beyond measure after the fact.

It's good to be aware of the demands that are placed on us with regard to loss, but it's also necessary to be aware of ourselves in the midst of these tasks and how they are affecting us and our grief. As I said, it's really important to ask for help when it's needed, to allow us to cope with the many demands on our time and attention. But also to ensure that the grief admin does not get in the way of facing our feelings in the aftermath of loss. These jobs are necessary, but they can be a distraction, an annoyance or a source of distress or avoidance and can take us away from emotionally processing our loss. We can end up being too busy to feel at a time when we need, above all else, to feel our feelings. So being aware of the admin around grief means being aware of the equal necessity to make space for feeling, for thinking and processing, for not hiding behind a to-do list.

For the most part, as we go through life we move towards pleasure and away from pain. It's not that simple, of course, and there are exceptions to every rule, but generally speaking we seek to avoid discomfort and gravitate towards comfort. For example, if you're someone who finds relationships to be a place of love, warmth and acceptance, you will seek out friendship and love, welcoming that feeling of being connected to others. If your experience has been that relationships are about criticism, judgement, coldness and rejection, then you may be more likely to keep your distance and refrain from getting into connected relationships, because when it goes wrong it can feel too painful for you, an old injury triggered again. These are survival mechanisms that we use to try to control what happens to us and to protect ourselves from difficult situations and emotions.

When it comes to loss, however, it's a case of having no control. I couldn't prevent Dara's death. I couldn't make the IVF work. I couldn't bridge the gap that grew between myself and my ex-husband. I would have done anything to be able to do those things, but I couldn't. That's where the grief comes in, as a result of what's happened and our inability to prevent it happening. As children, we are taught about the concept of fairness and we also hear that if we work hard, we can achieve anything. So later on, as an adult, it can be difficult to accept that life is sometimes random and uncontrollable. The grief we experience from loss is pain on steroids. Bereavement grief is immense pain because it arrives when we lose someone we love, they are gone from this life for ever and we can do nothing about it. What else are we going to feel except sorrow, anger, loneliness, confusion and a range of other emotional states? When we know that we'll never hug that person again, or spend the day with them, or listen to their worries or share their joy, we'll never see their face or hear their voice, that has a massive impact as we scrabble to adjust to life without them.

It's the same for the other losses in life. The grief they bring might not always be quite as sharp-edged as that from the death of a loved one, but it still smashes down the door and barges into our world, bringing sadness, rage or loneliness as we realise that the life we wanted is not the life that we will have. The grief brings us directly into a painful space, one that we cannot move away from. It is one of the most difficult experiences that we will go through in our lifetime. From my own perspective, grief is *the* most difficult experience I've ever encountered.

Whilst it may seem counterintuitive, one of the important responses when faced with grief is to feel that pain and not to give in to what might feel instinctive, which is to try to avoid it. It is a pain that we need to lean into rather than run away from. This is because it is only by acknowledging the pain and feeling it that we can begin to process the loss. This isn't always easy because right from the very first moments of loss I found those feelings of grief truly awful, arriving with no mercy, like an ambush, hijacking my body and my emotions.

I recognised at the time that I felt numb and even then I had a sense of that being a useful state. That numbness or sense of distance in the days following Dara's death allowed me to function without falling down and I think I knew that this was what was going on and that it was a help to me. It's very strange to find yourself with dry eyes in those first few days, comforting others who are weeping, but on some level I knew that the numbness was there to help me, so it didn't cause me to question myself or my feelings for Dara. In the many conversations about death and grief that I've had with people over the past two years, lots of people have mentioned that they were unable to cry when their loved one died. They describe feeling empty and hollow and it worried them, because they wondered if it meant they didn't care enough about the person or didn't really love them. Anytime I have been asked my own experience, I have explained that in my case I saw the numbness of those early days and weeks as a positive thing, a natural response to the shock of Dara's sudden loss, and it was my psychological and physiological systems protecting me, ensuring that the full horror of the situation would not hit all at once because that would have been too much. The realisation that feeling numb and not being able to cry doesn't mean a lack of care or love makes sense to people and can bring great comfort.

If we think of grief as a journey, it is one we embark on as soon as we understand the loss has occurred, and there is no way back to port. Like it or not, the journey has begun and we are on it and we cannot jump ship. We might hate it, resent it, scream at it, but we are on that path and there is nothing for it but to follow it. It is our path, there is no other. That is very hard to accept, but if we try to avoid it, that only prolongs the journey.

It means we are stalled, with the engine turning over, waiting to move off. It uses up resources but gets us nowhere. The thing is, the path stays stubbornly right there, waiting to be travelled. We are simply avoiding a process that is unavoidable. That's why I mentioned how grief admin can be used as a delaying tactic. It can be helpful in getting us through the initial days, but it's important not to let it take over completely in order to prevent reflection and feeling. We have to make the space and time we need to face up to what's happened and embark on that journey of processing and accepting it. That's essential for our personal health and well-being.

In my own situation, the numbness shifted in time and other feelings began to put in an appearance in the weeks and months after Dara died. They were intense feelings of sadness, rage, fear, loneliness. They all arrived at some point and I knew that the same rule applied – I had to feel them, to sit with them and experience them, no matter how unpleasant. Dara's loss from our lives was immense and I was going to feel those feelings whether I acknowledged them or not, so they could either come out in a healthy way once I'd named them and given myself space to express them, or they would seep out in the weakest spot, leading to angry outbursts, like yelling over printer ink. It was going to happen one way or the other.

The week that Dara died I received many messages from people wanting to offer support and help. One such person was Dr Eddie Murphy, Clinical Psychologist with RTÉ's *Operation Transformation*, a television programme that guides participants through a healthy and sustainable weight-loss programme. I've carried extra weight all through my forties and my first thought when I saw Eddie's name come up on my phone was, 'Don't tell me that this fella is recruiting people for *Operation Transformation*.' It's amazing how a sense of humour can emerge, even at times of great sadness. Eddie wasn't looking for volunteers for the programme, of course, he was offering to help handle my client caseload and we began to chat. One of the first things he said to me was that I needed to remember that at this time I was not a psychologist, I was a sister. This was so sensitive and helpful as it allowed me to let myself feel whatever I was feeling without pressure to 'cope' or to 'handle it'. It gave me permission to take myself out of the therapist's mindset and just be Dara's sister. I took his advice, but it wasn't until much later that I realised just how valuable and prescient that advice had been.

Chatting with Eddie got me thinking about what I would expect of myself over the coming days and weeks. I decided that the best thing I could do was simply aim to put one foot in front of the other and get through this time, that was all I would ask of myself. That simple plan served me well. I really felt the value of having this as my only goal, not thinking too much, not expecting to feel okay, just dealing with each task as it arose until, inch by inch, I got through each day. I was lucky to have had that advice from Eddie so early on in the process because it helped me to ease myself onto a useful path right from the start.

The truth is that we can help ourselves when we find ourselves thrashing around in those deep waters when the ship has wrecked. Loss leaves us floundering and gasping for breath, desperately trying to survive the waves, but we can do things to help ourselves stay afloat until support arrives. For me, deciding to focus only on the micro goal of putting one foot in front of the other on repeat was an example of that. I took responsibility for my own grief by asking for and listening to the advice of someone who was qualified and experienced enough to know what mattered at that time. By doing so I helped myself onto a path that was emotionally healthy, as opposed to one paved with unrealistic expectations around grief – that's what I think of as being an active participant in our own grieving. While it may not be easy, I would suggest that it is not only possible but indeed both necessary and, crucially, beneficial, to help ourselves when grief comes to stay. For as I lay my head down to sleep each night, those small wins, knowing that I had put one foot in front of the other and dealt with the day task by task, hour by hour, or sometimes even moment by moment when I was really struggling, gave me a sense of having found myself a life-raft to cling to. I was surviving. I was helping myself. That counted for something.

As we continue to help ourselves in the eye of the storm after loss, I feel as though there's a selfishness about grieving, by necessity really, a focus that is purely on ourselves as we learn to carry the weight of loss. I once messaged a friend and asked whether she and her family were well. Then I added that I was truly sorry to not have been around enough in order to know the answer to that question myself. I didn't know what was going on in her world, and I usually would have done. But surviving the waves and feeling the feelings of grief around the loss of my sister and the loss of my marriage took up all I had. I was depleted and I just wasn't in a place where I could widen out the lens and focus on others. When faced with loss, I think it's important to forgive ourselves for such apparent selfishness, to know that it is not a reflection of us as a person but of the situation we find ourselves in and of the need to survive. It's important also to know that this self-focus is temporary and that when we feel more able to bear the weight of loss, we will return to showing consideration for others once more.

When Eddie learned that my marriage was also in trouble and he realised the extent of loss that I was dealing with, he suggested that I talk to a professional who specialises in trauma. The person he recommended was Clinical Psychologist Mark Smyth. I set up some appointments with Mark and was very glad I did so. During our sessions Mark provided a safe space for me to express even the most unpleasant feelings I was experiencing. What does that actually look like? It's about seeing what comes up naturally in the conversation, noticing what topics I gravitated towards, paying attention to what triggered different emotions in me, letting myself follow the thread and exploring those emotions further, with Mark gently probing, encouraging reflection and offering guidance and perspective so that I could come to understand what I was feeling and, in time, accept those feelings. He never judged me. Whether I was crying and unable to speak or raging and swearing, he was very much present with me while I felt all those feelings and from his position of objectivity he helped me to identify what I was feeling. He accepted all those feelings as normal and he met my emotions with compassion and understanding, which allowed and encouraged me to do the same. That was a powerful tool in helping me to grieve in a way that was healthy rather than hindered.

Those sessions with Mark were about naming and expressing feelings, permitting even the most unpalatable to exist, and in doing so facilitating authenticity in my grief. I could be whole rather than partial in how I met my experience of trauma, loss and grief. In the wake of Dara's death and the end of my marriage, that therapy space gave me a place where I did not have to censor what I thought or felt; there is immense healing in that experience. The truth is that in life and in loss, by and large we show the world a sanitised and edited version of our cognitive and emotional experiences, but we all have feelings that we are ashamed of and we have a sense that they aren't the 'right' feelings in the situation. But they are real feelings and we do feel them, thus they deserve a right of expression. So you might be furious at the person who has died, raging in pain and cursing them for leaving you. You might harbour huge resentment towards them for leaving you alone to deal with the practicalities of children and of life. All of this can feel at odds with your sorrow, which somehow feels more palatable. We can go farther than this and say that these real feelings not only deserve expression, they *require* expression in order to allow us to process the loss and move towards acceptance and acknowledgement of the new life that we now have. Unpleasant, unpalatable, unspeakable feelings exist; we need to let them exist before we can let them go.

Thinking about how I felt around the loss of motherhood, those feelings were different from how I felt when Dara died. It was a much quieter, more subtle set of feelings, and there were no big overwhelming waves of high emotion or blocks of numbness. It was a sharp but quiet sorrow. I notice now that I keep feeling the need to use that word – quiet – because whereas the feelings of grief for Dara seemed to shout loudly, my sadness at realising that I would not be a mother seemed to whisper. It felt like a private loss, a personal grief that needed to be borne alone, by myself, rather than shared with others. Did I feel that I had permission to share my grief for Dara, but had no sense of that permission when it came to grief for the loss of motherhood? Perhaps. Whatever the reason, those feelings of sadness, anger, resentment and isolation that I experienced at the end of IVF were quiet, but they were also oh so strong. There was sadness that I would not continue our bloodline and give my parents a chance to see their lineage in the face of my child. There was anger that I would not be giving love, support and guidance to a child who was looking for a warm and loving home. There was resentment towards people who have children and mistreat them, and resentment towards people who have children and treat them well. There was isolation from society because I wouldn't know both the joy and the worry of being in that parenting club, a club that includes many of my family and most of my friends. These aren't nice feelings to have, there is an ugliness to many of them and reflecting now, I think that perhaps I might have perceived those feelings of loss as being less palatable than my grief for Dara. But at that time, I didn't understand that they were real nonetheless and required expression; that realisation only came later.

I didn't go and talk to a professional once that door on motherhood had completely closed with the end of both assisted fertility and the adoption process. Most likely, as I mentioned earlier, because no one had died I didn't identify it either as a loss or as grief, at least not valid grief that was worthy of time and space and attention in the therapy room. I just saw it as a case of things not working out as hoped and that it was up to me to process that in private and carry on with my life. So besides talking to my sisters and one or two good friends every now and then, I essentially endured those feelings of loss alone. In fact, I probably didn't really even share all of what I was feeling with my husband, because it was too painful and because he was already carrying his own pain for this loss. I think that in that place of infertility there can be a feeling of blaming yourself, of feeling not good enough, of feeling somehow as though you have let your partner down because you can't give them a child. I would be pretty good at walking the walk when it comes to dealing with my emotional life, so I never engaged in any significant apportioning of blame, but I do think that wondering if my age or my faulty reproductive system was to blame blocked me from having more conversations with him about how I was feeling in the face of that loss. I had no idea about any of this at the time, but it's interesting to realise now how ideas of what grief was or what I was allowed to grieve for led me to be blind to the reality of the grief I was feeling around the loss of my life as a mother, a life I was so hopeful would be mine.

My feelings around the loss of my marriage were different again. They were similar in some ways to the grief I feel about Dara's loss and for not being able to be a mother, but also different from both. When I realised that the marriage was truly in trouble, my first emotion was fear. Sadness would come much later, along with anger, frustration and loneliness, but I recall clearly that fear took centre-stage when understanding crept into my mind that we were possibly approaching the end of the road in the relationship. The end of a marriage is an enormous loss. I had been with this man since I was in my twenties and I was near the end of my forties when I realised we were most likely going to end, and the terror was overpowering, it was those cold fingers of fear wrapped around my heart. Because you know that when your marriage ends, your life as you know it will end, too. It's not only about the loss of that person from your life, though that is immense. For at one point in time, the two of you stood in front of your family and friends and promised to love one another to the end of your days, choosing each other over all others. That is not done lightly. So at another point in time, to be saying publicly that neither of you can uphold that promise, it's a huge loss and immense sadness. But it's also fear, because a marriage ending is also about the loss of that life you know as well as the back of your hand. It is a terrifying uncertainty. You look to your future and see only a big scary blank because you've suddenly no idea how it will look or how you'll go about filling it.

When I recognised that we were floundering, I went to a relationship therapist to explore my feelings and to help me emotionally process what was going on. After Dara died and it was clear that the marriage was over I went back to the relationship therapist for a session or two, which was very helpful, but working with Mark Smyth around the traumatic loss of Dara gave me space to address my feelings around the loss of my marriage as well. I used that space to deal with my feelings of grief for the end of my relationship. Those feelings were ones of fear for what was going to become of both of us, sadness that we had somehow gotten ourselves to this point of no return, anger at the unfairness of it all, that we had not been able to become parents and that we had then lost Dara and now our marriage was ending. It just seemed incredibly unfair, to be honest. I noticed that my emotions remained high throughout the long-drawn-out legal and financial processes we had to go through. It was not until we were legally separated and living apart that I began to see a reduction in the intensity of those feelings. That made the grief for the end of my marriage feel unending, but there was relief from it once everything was sorted and certain. Then, I was able to begin the process of moving forward into my life as it now was.

In the grief journey that stemmed from all of the losses I experienced, one of the big lessons I learned first-hand was that in the heart of the chaos and the uncontrollable, I could make a choice. I could choose how I was going to view what had happened and how I was going to live with the grief, and in doing so I was able to give myself a sense of taking control, which was important for me to feel. My world had been kicked out of all recognisable shape, it felt alien to me, and that was frightening, but I could still choose how to reshape it. It was back in the late 1980s, while at university studying psychology, that I was introduced to *Man's Search for Meaning*. It is a short but powerful book, written by Viktor Frankl, a psychiatrist who had been a prisoner in the Nazi death camps. He experienced and witnessed the worst and the best of humankind and had some powerful observations about survival. I found his words both a comfort and a strength as I struggled to choose the best path for myself:

> We who lived in concentration camps can remember the men who walked through the huts comforting others, giving away their last piece of bread. They may have been few in number, but they offer sufficient proof that everything can be taken from a man but one thing: the last of the human freedoms – to choose one's attitude in any given set of circumstances, to choose one's own way.

In *The Choice*, psychologist Edith Eger, who as a young girl was a prisoner at Auschwitz, echoes Frankl's words when she talks about 'your choice to dismantle the prison in your mind, brick by brick. You can't change what happened, you can't change what you did or what was done to you. But you can choose how you live now.'

For me, these are two of the most powerful examples of the fundamental choices that we have as human beings: the ability to choose what we pay attention to and focus on; and the ability to choose what we value in life. Of course, there will be people who experience trauma so horrific that they are not in a position to make many, or indeed any, choices, such is the degree to which they have been traumatised. This is not an infallible approach and I do not raise it to simplify trauma, this is simply what resonated with me in my own situation. I understand the potential for choice and I find it a deeply comforting and helpful concept. I first got a sense of it that day in the hotel room in Mayo as dawn began to break on the day we would take Dara home to Dublin in her coffin. As the anger swamped me, when I heard the birds singing and realised that life was carrying on as normal, a reminder gently tapped on the edge of my consciousness, telling me that from here on in, I had a choice. Yes, being angry was wholly understandable and there was nothing wrong with anger per se, there would be a need to express and process that anger, but I knew that if I let it fill my head and run riot, there would be no room in my mind for the happy memories of Dara. These would be wasted, left to rust like scrap metal in a junkyard. The reminder that I had a choice came with the sudden clarity that I needed to exercise that choice wisely.

I have only so much space in my head and I decided there and then in that hotel room to only ever fill that space with a focus that would be useful to me, to give my attention to things that would help me rather than hinder me in whatever lay on the path ahead. My gratitude for that moment is huge, as that simple advice of making *useful* choices is one of the key things that has helped me to navigate so many challenges in the time since Dara died.

Death is normal. Grief is normal. But knowing that the person you love is not coming back and that life goes on regardless is an abnormal situation when it happens to you. In the face of that traumatic realisation, I chose to give myself a break and to be okay with feeling whatever I was feeling because the emotions were completely understandable. I chose to lean into the feelings and I believe that was an important moment in my grief journey. But, crucially, I also made a choice very early on not to dwell on anger and let it rule me. Life *must* go on, it's just how it works. Once we understand this, it can make the journey more bearable.

Given this truth, I think that the time after a loss of any kind, but particularly after a death, is about being kind to ourselves, being good to ourselves, going easy on ourselves. I think that if we colour outside the lines a bit in terms of our emotions, especially in those early days of grief, that's perfectly okay, because those hours, days, weeks and even years after a loss are not normal times in our lives. It's about remembering that we have experienced significant loss and that life feels different now because it *is* different. Self-compassion is important: we have to show the same understanding to ourselves that we would show to a friend who had lost a loved one. No judgement, no impatience, just understanding and kindness. The starting point is to accept that life is different now and that it will take time to come to terms with that.

There's no right or wrong way to respond to loss and it's vital not to fight whatever we feel, but instead to let ourselves feel those emotions, even if those around us are responding differently. A healthy approach to grief means taking what feels like the more difficult route, which is to let the feelings come. Sometimes people use alcohol, drugs, food, denial or distraction in order to prevent themselves from feeling grief, but this is not going to work, it will merely delay the inevitable. Indeed, sometimes the emotions around grief can be intensified and made more complex by that delay. When you encounter a loss, particularly the death of a loved one, you might scream or run out of the room. It could be that anger descends and you begin to roar and yell. Or maybe you just stand there in disbelief, motionless and without expression either internally or externally. You may cry for weeks or you might spend your days in a rage. Others around you may have different responses. It's all okay and it's all normal. There is no correct response, there's just *your* response. Your only job is to give yourself permission to feel it, whatever it is. Acknowledge the feelings. Step into them. Experience them however you want. Don't let the admin of grief or anything else distract you from feeling them or enable you to avoid them. Let them out and express how you feel in whatever way feels right for you. But above all, *feel the feelings*. For me, certainly, this has been one of the most important truths about loss.

CHAPTER SIX

A NEW LIFE AFTER LOSS

The common thread through loss is that we don't want to accept the truth of it because we don't want the new normal it's giving us, but we do have to make our way towards acceptance so that we can continue to live our lives. When a loved one dies, we may not want to die but sometimes we don't really want to live either. But life does go on and we must go on with it. The grief journey leads us towards acceptance, even if we want to resist that change. This is why it's so difficult when the numbness starts to wear off and we have to feel the reality of life without a longed-for family, or a loving partner or a person we thought we'd grow old with. Alongside this personal struggle, we also have to contend with the reactions of other people to our new status and how they behave around us and either help or hinder us in moving towards acceptance.

There were many tough times before I got to the point of acceptance of not being a mother. Standing in a local shop in September, for example, and hearing the shop owner say, 'I'll bet you're delighted to have the kids back to school now after being under your feet all summer!' I felt bowled over by a wave of grief, silently and privately bowled over in that moment, feeling knocked off my feet by the strength of emotion. Obviously I looked like a woman of an age where she would have children who had gone back to school, that's what society expected of me, and in fact that's what many of my friends were – mothers of school-going children. So there was no harm intended by this remark, it was normal chit-chat that he had probably repeated with countless other people who came in and out of his shop that time of year, but in me it triggered that awful sense of loss. Equally tough was sitting around a table at a Christmas party and being the only person who wasn't a parent, listening to conversations about what Santa was bringing and taking time off to attend a nativity play, and so on and so forth. I just felt that I hadn't really got anything to contribute, so I probably didn't contribute much, which of course only served to help me feel left out of things. It was a case of my emotions influencing my behaviour and my behaviour further influencing my emotions. I also remember walking down the aisle at a christening and someone saying to my parents-in-law, 'I'll bet you've given up on this pair to produce a grandchild for you!' Again, no harm intended, just a harmless remark meant to fill space in the conversation, but like other similar remarks it was like an emotional neon sign, pointing to the pain of loss and bringing it all back into the present on that day. Of course, you feel you have to be 'adult' about it and smile and not show any signs of what you're really feeling, because sometimes in life we need to remember to not take things personally, although the truth is that's really tough, too.

Thinking about how others reacted to news that our marriage had ended and we were now separated, I might have expected those around us to be awkward or uncomfortable, but actually it has been smooth and amicable in that respect. Although things have obviously changed for each of us in that we no longer really spend time in the company of one another's family or friends, we do have some friends in common and when we do meet them or each other's family or friends, it is within an atmosphere of warmth and respect. I think that we were such an important part of each other's lives for so long that those around us have the same attitude that we have ourselves, no one wants to have acrimony where there was affection. I also think that possibly because almost everyone we both knew was still reeling from the shock of Dara's death, our family and friends have a perspective on life that might have been different had they not been acquainted with traumatic loss. The end of the marriage brought sadness to those we love, but people recognised that each of us still had our life and there was gratitude for that fact and context within it.

I haven't found that anything has changed in terms of not being invited to dinner parties or events because I am now single. I have continued to be involved in plans by others. In fact, reflecting on that now, I would nearly say that it has been the opposite, in that I possibly receive more invites now than I did when I was married. Do people assume that if you're in a couple you are in some way 'sorted', perhaps? I'm not sure. But I can say that finding myself single in my fifties, I feel loved and cared for and included rather than out on a limb socially. I have not experienced anyone viewing me differently because I'm separated. I have been met with kindness, compassion and unlimited space to find my way through the pain of separation. Similar to the link I feel with those who are bereaved and with those who have wished to be a parent but have been unable to make it happen, I do also notice a particular connection with others who have experienced a marriage breakdown, which is understandable.

The grief that comes with sudden and traumatic loss has a different texture, naturally. When I woke the morning after Dara's funeral, I felt more of an edge to my emotions than I had all week. Once the funeral and other rituals around death were completed, I found that something felt different straight away. The numbness from the shock was still there, but now I felt a sharpness running through it, a bit of reality was starting to push through the anaesthetic, I think. It was like watching a movie, then realising that you're in it. Although the shock would take perhaps a year or so to fully dissipate, that morning, for me, was the start of having to let go of the numbness and step forward into the new reality, which was my life without Dara in it.

The day after the funeral was a Sunday and when I woke up, I found words repeating in my head on a loop: 'Dara's gone … Dara's gone …' Exactly one week earlier she was still alive. Incredible. In fact, one week previous was the last day I saw her alive and this kept coming into my mind, reinforcing the stark reality that she was now gone. As with all my family Dara and I always saw each other regularly, but over the four days before her death we happened to meet every day except for the Monday, the day before she died. On the Friday evening I was driving down the road on the way to give a talk in a local school and I spotted Dara in her front garden with Fionn. I stopped and rolled down the window and we had a chat. I remember the chat because the first thing Dara said to me was that I looked nice and she asked where I was going. She said it with a big smile and she meant it, that was typical Dara. At the time I was doing my usual thing of trying the next diet and exercise plan to burn off the extra weight I was carrying. Although she kept herself slim and fit, Dara would often kindly tell me that I looked well, reminding me that I didn't need to be at my goal weight in order to be lovely. My family would gently and affectionately tease me for my perennial 'shift the weight' New Year's resolution – which sounded a bit like Del Boy's, 'This time next year, Rodney, we'll be millionaires.' But I kept trying and, like the others, Dara was always ready with a compliment to encourage me, as she did that Friday evening.

The next day we bumped into one another in almost the same place and we had the normal chit-chat that sisters have before we each went on about our business for the day. On Sunday morning I went with my twin sister Orla to meet our cousin Rosemary for a walk along Sandymount beach and then for lunch. When Orla and I got to my house that afternoon, we noticed that Dara was back from work as her car was there, but she wasn't home. We figured she was out with Fionn on his little tricycle somewhere nearby. I have no idea what possessed me, as I have never done it before or since, but I suggested that I look up Dara on the Find My Friends app on my phone. We saw from the map that she was indeed over in the green area nearby. Orla and I followed the map and in less than ten minutes we found Dara and Fionn, playing on the grass. My husband arrived too as he was walking our dog home from a ramble, so the five of us ended up there chatting. Soon enough, with his usual sense of fun, Fionn seized the opportunity to have us adults and the dog run up and down a small incline with him, 'racing' to see who was the fastest.

It was a chilly enough March afternoon and I remember Dara with her beanie hat on, her hands buried deep in her pockets, trying to keep warm as she stood laughing at how Fionn had the rest of us eating out of his hand, doing whatever he wanted. We had great fun for a while and then we all set off for home, walking together, chatting and laughing. Even now I can still see us on that walk home, and it feels so strange thinking that we had no idea those were our final moments together. When we got back into our estate and went to our own houses it was an ordinary goodbye that I said to Dara, the same goodbye that I said to the others. I don't even think I hugged her that day. I just said something like, 'See you later', the usual way that many of us sign off when we depart. Only this time, there was no later.

I have not had the experience with my immediate family, but there have been others in my life who were terminally ill and I was aware that they were dying. In those instances I found there to be a heightened sense of awareness around conversations in the months and weeks before their death. Each time I visited them, I always had that feeling that this could be our last time to talk, that we might be seeing each other for the last time. I don't recall ever replaying any of those meetings or conversations over in my head after their death, but I have found myself reliving that last meeting with Dara. I suspect that this is because there was no warning that this could possibly be the last time we would see each other, the last time we would talk. My experience is that a death under those circumstances brings a need to go over that final conversation again and again, behind which is a desire to be sure that, although ordinary, the interaction would somehow have shown Dara that I care, that I love her, that she matters to me. With advance warning of death we can have that luxury, so when the person dies we tell ourselves that we may not have been able to do anything about their death, but we did what we could to ensure that they knew how we felt about them. But when there's no notice, we have no opportunity to make sure of this, to take care of that business of putting our emotional affairs in order. I know without question that Dara knew that she was loved by her family and that she felt that love and yet, regardless, there is a need to replay our last conversation and search for proof of that within. I have wondered about Dara's last moments on Earth and while I know that they were by all accounts focused on survival, I wonder if any fleeting thoughts visited her at that time, if she knew that she was going to die and if she thought of her family. There may have been no time for this, but if there was, then I needed to know that in those moments Dara *knew* our love. That, I think, is why after forty-five years as sisters our last ever conversation takes on a greater significance and I have felt the need to replay it in my mind.

I've wondered since what it would have been like to have known that it was the last time I would see Dara alive. If she had been terminally ill and lying in a hospital bed and we knew that her death was imminent, I would have told her that she is loved more than she probably ever realised. Is loved, not was loved. Whether Dara is alive or dead, I love her. I would have let her know that she was a great sister and friend to me all my life. I would have told her that she made a difference in this world and that the world is a better place for her having been in it. And I would have told her that we would love and mind her little boy and raise him as she wanted, guiding him to be the person she knew he could be. Then I would have hugged her so tightly, trying to breathe in the feel of her, attempting to imprint the sound of her voice into my mind, knowing that whatever I got from this final meeting would have to last me for ever.

There's a gift in being able to say those things, in having the time to let loved ones know what they mean to us. But what those thoughts have shown me is that we can do that anyway, of course we can. It doesn't require the threat of death to make us speak truthfully and lovingly. I do know from how we all lived our lives that Dara knew she was loved. That is a comfort to me. But I do wish I'd had a chance to speak to her honestly. I have that chance with the people I love who are still with me, and it's important to me that I take that chance when I can. It's a good lesson to take from Dara's sudden death. Live *now*. Live life to the full. If you like someone, take a chance and tell them. If you respect someone as a person or in their work, tell them. If you love someone, tell them. If you are not comfortable or confident in expressing your feelings verbally, then show them through your actions so that they unequivocally know how you feel about them.

In terms of trying to accept our new reality, one thing that helped me in the week of the wake and the funeral was getting more pieces of information about what had happened on the night of the crash. Crew members of the rescue helicopter that located Dara in the water visited my parents' home to pay their respects and I asked them about the crash. I didn't barge in with direct questions, I sussed things out first, to see how they themselves were coping. Once I felt they were open to talking about the crash, I looked to find out whatever I could about the events of that night, trying to fill in the gaps in the picture. They were very kind in answering my questions, even ones that appeared to me to be stupid. I think they understood that I needed to hear some details, to understand as much as I could bear. I'm the type of person for whom information is vital. I like to know facts, to build a complete picture in my mind. Even if something is awful, I would rather know what I'm dealing with than wonder or speculate, so I found those conversations hugely helpful. Each time I received another piece of information about what had happened to Dara, it helped me to process her death another bit more. We're all different, so this won't be the case for everyone, but for me information has been a key factor in the grieving process and in helping me to accept what happened. It wasn't nice to hear, but it was necessary for me emotionally.

The heightened sense of the new reality that I experienced the day after the funeral meant starting to think about the next items on the list of jobs that needed to be done, one of which was to get Dara's phone and iPad from her workplace because there was information on both around Fionn's care that we needed to access. I decided to do this quickly. I think on some level I already knew that I had to try to move towards acceptance, and that was my way of making inroads towards that.

The day after the funeral, two of Dara's work colleagues drove me and my cousin Stephen to the base. They had suggested I bring someone with me because they knew it wouldn't be an easy task to go through Dara's locker. These men were good friends of Dara's for many years, they are pilots themselves and they respected her as a pilot and cared about her as a person and after she died they extended that care to her family. I was grateful for their thoughtful suggestion and for having Stephen at my side.

It was nearing dusk when we drove up to the base near Dublin Airport. There were bunches of flowers placed at the gates, with notes of condolence written on them, handwritten words of sorrow for the tragic loss of life. Dara's car would normally have been parked in the small car park to the left of the gate when she was on shift. I looked for it, but was told that they had moved it inside the hangar.

We went into the base and I met some of the crew I had seen the day before, at Dara's funeral. We stood in the corridor and talked for a long while, I can't even remember what about, just general disbelief about what we were all going through. They had suffered such an immense loss in the organisation. My family had lost one person, but the crews of the Irish Coast Guard had lost four people. Four colleagues. Four friends. A crew of six had been on shift that night of the callout, two winch crew, two pilots and two engineers. Four of those six departed the base in the helicopter to provide top cover off the coast of Mayo. No one came home. That is such a huge loss, it's unthinkable. I can't properly fathom the magnitude of that loss. My heart went out to them all.

After we chatted for a while, I asked if I could see Dara's car. They hesitated and said that it was a very hard thing to do, that most people had found it extremely difficult when they walked into the hangar. But they said that if I was sure I really wanted to do it, they would bring me to the car. I wasn't even sure why I needed to see it, but I just did, and the men, including Stephen, understood that. We walked into the hangar and I have to say that they were right, the sight of Dara's car sitting where the helicopter should be hit like a punch in the gut and a lump formed in my throat as we walked over to it. They gave me the keys and I got inside the car to get that sense of Dara, the way we do when we sit in someone's car with their belongings around us. Her hand cream and hair bobbins in the console, along with loose change, water and healthy snacks for Fionn in the side pocket of the door, his car seat in the back with his little mirror with the teddy-bear cover so that he could see himself on car journeys, a very faint trace of her perfume. The others left me on my own for a few moments and as I sat there in the driver's seat, I closed my eyes, trying to process it all. This was real. I was sitting in Dara's car and she would never sit in it herself again.

Why did I need to do that, to sit in Dara's car among her things? It's not like she was there herself, only her belongings were there, random objects that she had collected and stored in her car, and even then they were just functional, everyday objects that held no value. So why was I drawn to sit in her seat and pick up her hand cream, to hold her hair bobbin in my hand? I think it's because those physical belongings were what was left of Dara and the life that she had lived with us. That hand cream was the hand cream I could smell when she threw her arms around me in a hug. That hair bobbin was one that I had seen tied around her wrist so many times. These weren't, in fact, just random objects, they were evidence that Dara had lived, they were memories, they were laughter and togetherness and all sorts of ordinary and I needed to feel them so much because Dara was gone.

I think that we feel the presence of those we love from their belongings because we know that they chose them or wore them or used them. And when we hold those objects, we see them alive again, just for a moment, memories of the life we had with them feeling like a soothing rub of balm when we need it most. Comforting. Consoling. Connecting. Death breaks that connection and rips the person we love from our lives, but we need it and so we'll seek to find it wherever we can. I think that's why personal belongings mean so much to those of us left behind.

Some people might imagine that being among the possessions of a loved one who has died would be upsetting, that it would serve only to remind us of the love that has been lost. And for some who have been bereaved that is the case, they don't like to have to walk past the chair that their loved one used to sit in, or to smell the scent that they used to wear. And that's okay, because the item itself is not the issue, it's the association that the person has with the object that will influence whether it is helpful or hurtful to be around. Does it bring with it a sense of comfort and connection, or a sense of loss and pain? For me, even from that day in the hangar at the base, Dara's belongings most definitely bring a sense of connection and comfort. I love to see my sisters wearing one of her scarves or tops because seeing it on them reminds me that Dara was alive and that we did have that life together and that this void in our lives was not always there. Just for a moment, that's a lovely feeling to have.

After a while I locked Dara's car again and walked back over to the three men, who were standing in the office. There I met another crew member, one of the engineers who had been on shift with the crew that night. As we chatted, he told me how

Dara was in great form that day and there was lots of laughter and chat on the base. It was comforting to hear little things like that, to be able to picture her in my mind going about what would be her last day, happy in herself and her work.

Dara's colleagues then took Stephen and me to Dara's locker. On the way I saw a kit room and inside was a big unit divided into square cubby-holes, with crew names under each one. It was where they left their helmets when they weren't wearing them. There was a cubby-hole with Dara's name in black print on a white ticker tape underneath it. Empty. I stood looking at it, imagining her taking her helmet out of that space on the night she died.

We got to Dara's locker and I opened it and found her familiar work rucksack and I swear to God, I had to work so hard not to do what they do in the films and pick up her clothes and smell them. I wanted to do that so badly. Instead, I located her phone and iPad and took them with me. We would come back another day and clear out her locker and take her car from the base, but this was enough for now.

The whole visit to Dara's workplace that night was difficult. It was a tough confrontation with reality, very emotional for all of us there. I found it almost eerie to be in that place and see evidence of Dara's everyday existence, knowing that she was gone. Yet at the same time it was also very helpful because it put me on the path of seeing things that forced me to face the fact that this was now a life without Dara. I was going to have to accept that life as I had known it was over and that what lay ahead was an entirely new life. We aren't the same people after we experience loss, and life isn't the same either. We don't live it the same way and we don't look at it the same way. That's the cold, hard truth. Everyone will face their new reality in their own way and at their own pace, there certainly is no right or wrong way, but sooner or later we must accept our loss. For some people, that first true sense of reality will be going back to the home they shared with the person who died, seeing that empty chair. Or lying in a bed with a space beside them where the other person used to lie. Others might reach for the phone to call their loved one and that's when it begins to dawn on them that this is the new reality, they will never again call that person. For me, it was my experience at the base the day after Dara's funeral. It was like another death, in a way, yet another moment of loss, another prising away of Dara's life from mine. But it was necessary, and I chose to embrace it as such.

This doesn't mean that it's easy to process the grief, of course. I'm talking about acceptance being a goal, but it's a goal without a timeframe because it happens at each person's own pace and you can't plan it out or rush it. It's an ongoing process and it can sometimes be a case of one step forwards and two steps back, but that's okay. Sometimes, we can be thrown back into the raw grief by a comment, a song on the radio, any small thing. Since Dara died, for example, the first few times that I was asked how many siblings I have, I wasn't expecting the question and I scrambled around a bit, unsure how to respond. My heart wanted to tell the truth, but my head didn't want to make the other person feel uncomfortable. I eventually settled on a response that felt right and now I gently reply that I had five siblings but one sister died before birth forty years ago and another sister died in 2017. Emotionally, I still feel like I should have four siblings, so when I look at family photos taken since Dara died, the photos feel wrong, the shape of our family doesn't look right any more. The outline of us as a group, and especially as siblings, looks like someone else's family because one of us is missing. Dara is one of us and she always will be, but she's not with us, so the photo looks wrong to me. I don't even know if that makes any sense, but I expect that to some people it will.

It can be the case that well-meant comments from people can trigger those grief emotions as well. By people I really mean random strangers, because those who know you do not tend to say some of the things I've had said to me by strangers over the past two and a half years. People mean well, of that I'm sure, but the truth is that their words can strike the wrong chord emotionally. Some people say things like, 'It will be a while before you'll get over the death of your sister, I imagine' or 'Do you feel you've moved on yet after the death of your sister?' I would never say anything out loud to someone who is so kind as to have a conversation with someone who is bereaved, because my focus is on the intention behind the interaction. But in all honesty, when anyone uses these expressions, inside there is a part of me that feels like whispering to them that they would be best advised to walk as fast as they can in the other direction. I *hate* these expressions. The reason is that, for me, they completely misunderstand loss and grief and fail to appreciate that grief is not about getting over or moving on from a loved one's death, it's *never* about that. Grief is about learning to live with the fact of their death and with the loss of the life they might have had, as well as their loss from your life. I don't *want* to get over Dara's death or to move on after her death. To me, there is an implication in both expressions of leaving Dara behind and there's no way in hell that I will ever do that, so when I am asked about *getting over* or *moving on*, I feel irritated. I don't show that irritation because I'm grateful for the kindness, but the truth is that when I'm asked if I have gotten over Dara's death yet or if I have moved on yet, inside a part of me is irrationally irked beyond belief. I may be keeping a lid on it, but those feelings are there nonetheless. Professor Lea Waters wrote about life after her sister's death and she said, 'I haven't moved on. But I have gone on.' The moment I read that, it made sense to me. When referring to the loss of Dara it feels okay to go on, just not to move on.

I also get annoyed when people say things like, 'You were close so at least you have lots of good memories' or 'At least you saw her shortly before she died.' It doesn't matter that we had great times and a happy life with Dara, she's not here now and the first doesn't negate the second. There is no 'at least' with death, so don't say that to me, I don't like it. I think there's a sort of urge to 'fix' the grief by pushing the bereaved person on away from it, but it doesn't work like that. We all need to be more okay with sitting with those uncomfortable emotions and allowing people to feel what they need to feel. Dara's great pal Sarah Dunphy sent me a quote that captures this beautifully: 'When you can't look on the bright side, I will sit with you in the dark.' The person experiencing the grief needs to allow themselves to feel it, and those around them also need to give them the space to feel those emotions without trying to minimise, dismiss or push them aside. We won't always feel sad or lonely, but we do need to feel emotions like these until we are ready to feel something else. We need to sit in the dark.

When it comes to sitting with those emotions, never underestimate the power of small: a phone call, a message or a card; bringing flowers in a pot or homemade bread; pulling someone in close for a big strong hug; lending a listening ear; sincerity, kindness, these can all do so much good for the person who is bereaved. You may not be able to fix things, and they don't want or expect you to, but with small gestures you can stand beside someone as they feel their pain and that can help them as they learn to live with that pain. That is the kindest and bravest thing to do.

If you're talking to a bereaved person online and it's someone you don't know in person but you would like to say something, helpful comments include things like, 'I'm so sorry that you have to feel such pain,' or 'I can hear that you miss your Dad very much.' Ask them about the person who died because we don't get to talk about the person we love very much when they die and when someone does present us with that opportunity it feels so welcome. So perhaps you could ask, 'What is your brother's name?' or 'What was he like?' If the person isn't ready to talk in this way, it will be obvious in their manner, but many people who are bereaved will jump at the chance to talk about their loved one. It's often our favourite subject and inviting us to do so is much better than trying to steer us away from our pain, however kindly that is meant. And don't ever think that you'll upset someone by mentioning the name of the person who has died, fearing that you'll 'remind them'. First, what is truly upsetting is when you meet someone who you know is aware that your sister has died and they never mention it. I'm not talking about in a work setting now, but in a personal setting. I do believe that the first time you meet someone after they are bereaved you need to acknowledge the loss. Second, we *never* forget. The loss we experience is indelibly inked onto us and there's not a moment when we aren't aware of it, so you'll never remind us because there is no forgetting. If you talk to someone and mention their loved one and they cry, you haven't upset them, the tears are not something that you have caused, they were there anyway, lurking near the surface, and the conversation was simply that extra drop of water that pushed the salty drops to the top. Crying can be a release and a relief, so don't ever worry about a grieving person crying in front of you. Just be with them as they cry, that's a generous gift to give them.

I also get annoyed when people try to tell me how to grieve by saying things like, 'Don't be sad' or 'Don't focus on the pain, think of the happy times.' One day I even had someone say to me online, 'That's enough. Time to focus your energy forward. Grief is not to be dwelled on.' *Really?* You're actually going to tell me when it's time for me to change my focus? Keep on scrolling, lady! That one astounded me, to be honest. In my opinion we don't have the right to tell anyone how to grieve, we can only share our own experience of grief.

I feel angry when people tell us that the best thing we could do for Dara's son, Fionn, is to not talk about her around him, to 'help him forget about her'. That one is so bad that actually I don't even respond when someone says that to me. I can see that they genuinely do have a good intention behind the suggestion, but it's one that is so awful that it's not even worth getting into a conversation about it.

An expression that is used an awful lot, one that has me clenching my jaw to bite back a sharp response, is when people talk about how Dara 'passed away'. I really dislike this phrase, because I think that we need to be accurate in our own language around death. Dara died. Dara is dead. Psychologically, it's important to use these terms and face the truth. I also dislike this phrase because it sounds peaceful and serene, someone slipping from this life when they are finished living. I don't doubt that some people experience an end to their life that is like this, like a passing, but the last minutes and moments of Dara's life were anything but peaceful and serene. She fought for her life in the cold, dark waters of the Atlantic, so to me she didn't pass away, she died, and I prefer to say it that way, it feels more accurate and it honours her story more. For some people who are bereaved that expression will feel like the right way to describe their loved one's death and that's okay, but it doesn't sit well with me at all and I feel myself tensing each time someone says it to me.

I also dislike when someone tells me to 'Stay strong.' I think what they're trying to say to me is 'Be okay,' or 'You're handling this, keep going,' but 'Stay strong' grates on me because grief isn't about being strong, it's about going on. It's about feeling what you feel and it's about surviving those feelings. It's not strength that helps us do that, it's kindness towards ourselves and compassion and accepting help and indeed asking for help. I don't see strength as being a part of the grieving space. In fact, I'd like to get rid of this idea of being strong in the context of grief. No. We should feel whatever we feel and not be afraid of it. Anyway, because you're bowled over by sadness, anger, loneliness or fear doesn't mean that you're not being strong, those aren't mutually exclusive.

The notion of being strong seems to be something that features in people's thinking when they're watching a tragedy from the outside because people have said to me many times, 'I don't know how you cope. I couldn't cope with what you all have had to cope with.' But the truth is that if you had to cope, you could. I didn't have a choice. Coping was the only option. What else could I do but cope? Am I going to add to the tragedy of losing Dara by crashing out of life and refusing to accept what is fact? By turning into some bitter version of myself who stays stuck in the 'what ifs'? Never. That would be tragedy on top of tragedy. Death has already taken enough, it's not getting any more from us. Instead, I see it that this is what life has asked of us and that even under such difficult circumstances, we have a choice. We can fall apart or we can find ways to stand up in the face of tragedy. I choose to work always to find ways to stand up. I intend to live my best life and to bring Dara Fitz with me in that life, sharing her qualities and her values, doing good in her name whenever I can. That's not down to strength, that's down to survival. It's down to love for my sister and a wish to do right by her.

When I talk about things that annoy me, I might sound as though I'm in a permanent state of irritation but I can promise you that I'm not. I just want to speak honestly about loss and highlight some of the experiences I've had when dealing with people because most of the time interactions are positive, but sometimes even a well-intentioned but misguided assumption can stoke the fire of grief for someone who is bereaved. It's also important to say again that I am hugely grateful for any ways that people express their support and that I respond to all support with genuine gratitude. In being honest and open now, I don't want in any way to appear ungrateful because that's not how I feel at all. I only mention these things here because people don't talk about them much and because I am setting out my personal experience of loss. What bothers me might not even register with someone else, but it's worth pointing out how these things sound from inside the world of grief. And it's really worth hearing that plea for grief to be allowed its place, for emotions to be given space and not 'fixed'.

All of this applies equally to the more private griefs as well. Those losses – like miscarriage, failed IVF, marriage breakdown – also require a period of grieving and the person needs time to move towards acceptance and be okay with how their world looks now. When I had to accept that I wouldn't have a baby, I needed to get used to being asked, 'How many children do you have?' or 'Have you kids?' They are normal questions often asked when people are seeking to find common ground in the early stages of a conversation. But initially they can push the pain button and intensify the feelings of loss each time you have to say that no, you don't have any children. You do in time find ways to say it without inviting discomfort into the room. Now I tend to say in a light voice, 'Sadly that wasn't my path, but I'm okay with it now.' I also had to learn to be okay hearing terms like 'childless', which is factual, without automatically making it emotional. Once again, it took time, but I eventually got there in that regard.

It's interesting that some of the expressions that irritate me when used with regard to Dara feel perfectly apt when talking about the end of my marriage. I think I am 'getting over it' and 'moving on', although those things are impossible in terms of accepting Dara's death. The grief is different, so the acceptance feels different, too. Certainly, in the past couple of months I have found myself thinking that it feels as though I am beginning to get over the fact that our marriage didn't work out and move on. I don't mean moving on with regards to seeing anyone else, I have no interest in that right now and I'm not sure if I will, only time will tell. I mean that my brain and my heart seem to

have accepted the reality of us not working out and have assim-
ilated that loss, leaving me with a clear understanding that this
means a new chapter of life on my own.

I think that, for me, the grief I feel for the loss of my marriage
is somehow cleaner than what I feel for the loss of my sister, by
which I mean that it's somewhat less complicated. I have so many
conflicting and complex emotions around Dara's loss and while
I am working through those, it has been murky waters, because
that grief feels much harder to work through. Is that because I
knew that my marriage was in trouble for some time and I had
begun to prepare subconsciously for the end, so that it was a
sort of anticipated grief? Whereas Dara's death was sudden and
shocking? Is that why the grief feels different? Is it because I
was an active participant in the marriage and I therefore share
in the responsibility for it not working out, but there was never
anything I could have done to save Dara? Or does grief for the end
of my marriage feel less complicated because I understand that
sometimes relationships just don't work out, while I can never
understand why Dara was taken from us after only forty-five
years? Are these factors contributing to me feeling further on in
processing grief for my marriage than for my sister? I have no
idea, but these are questions I wonder about.

What I do know is that the process of grief is a process of
learning to live with the new reality that the loss has created. I
have learned that this process is difficult, mostly exhausting and
that's it's ongoing, a work in progress. For the quieter griefs,
there is a greater sense of moving on and accepting the loss in
full, whereas for bereavement, 'acceptance' means accepting life
without the person you love in it, accepting absence, but never
forgetting what came before. It means living with it every day

but living nonetheless. They are perhaps subtle differences, but they are important. The process will be individual to each and every one of us, but the key truth is that we must engage with it and must do so at our own pace. We have to be kind to our own needs while we navigate this pain. We have to give ourselves permission to grieve, to be 'abnormal' in these horrible circumstances. But we should also keep at the forefront of our minds the fact that we have a choice. We should do that because that is where hope lies, and life.

CHAPTER SEVEN

A FUTURE ROBBED

have a video that Dara sent to me in February 2017, only a few weeks before she died. It's a family video and in the shot you can see her little son, Fionn, holding the lead as he brings my dog, Buddy, for a walk. Dara is talking to him, encouraging him as he walks the dog. Then Fionn lets out a little squeal and drops the lead, whereupon my husband comes into shot and picks up the lead before my beloved dog could make a run for it. I love that video. It brings a smile to my face when I see how proud my nephew was of himself as he brought my dog for a walk, and then the panic of the adults as they scrambled to pick up the lead so that they wouldn't have to come back and tell me that my dog was missing! But in many ways that video encapsulates how life changed for me in 2017. My sister is gone. My marriage is gone. My life as I knew it is gone. Even my dog is gone. I felt unable to take care of him and me in the aftermath of Dara's death, so my friend Michelle kindly adopted him.

Thankfully, my beautiful nephew is still here, but now he and I have a different relationship than when the video was taken. Then it was a straightforward auntie situation but now, along with my two sisters, I am one of his guardians. One day, Fionn will understand how that same video marks a watershed in his life. In it, he is safe and happy with his mother, learning to care for Buddy, his doggy pal. His life, like mine, no longer looks like that. After Dara died, when Fionn was still a toddler, whenever he came over to my house he would go into the kitchen and flick the little metal door-stopper that Buddy used to play with, to hear the spronging noises Buddy loved to make. Then he would say to me, 'I miss Buddy.' And a heartbeat later, 'And I miss my Mama, too.' His level of understanding was obviously that of a small child and he connected these two events in his mind. He knew that his mother and my dog both left us on the same day as we never saw either of them again after that day. So back then, he couldn't think of one without the other. Mama and Buddy were his normal life, the life he loved, and now he was living without them. I'm sure it was bewildering for him, especially in the immediate aftermath.

The grief of bereavement is marked by 'firsts' and 'lasts' – we can't help going over and over the last meeting, the last conversation, the last sighting of the person who has died, and we also feel it deeply the first time we celebrate something without them. The day after Dara's burial brought an immediate 'first' as it was Mother's Day. We all spent the day together as a family, and I was thinking equally of my mother and of Fionn: a mother without her child and a child without his mother. I was also thinking about Dara, of course, another mother without her child. What she would have given to have been there in the middle of everyone, with her son and her mother around her on Mother's Day, doing the ordinary things that families do when they come together for lunch and chats. It just felt so poignant to be there without her on that day of all days.

Not that we needed it, but that day was a stark reminder that in the midst of all that was going on was a child whose mother had been lost from his life overnight. We needed to tend not only to our own grief but to help this little child with his grief for his mama. With this in mind, the day after Dara died I sought advice from Dr Eddie Murphy and from Early Childhood Psychologist Dr Mary O'Kane and both were a great help in the days leading up to Dara's funeral, providing practical advice on how to talk to a child about death.

Thanks to their expert guidance, my family and I soon understood that there are many factors that influence how you might have those difficult conversations about death with a child and what those conversations might look like. Things to consider, for example, include the age of the child, their stage of development and their capacity to understand, their relationship to the person who has died and what they might already know or believe about death. We learned that it was important to tell the truth, to be honest and accurate, but also brief, using plain language within a frame of reference that a child could understand. We knew not to use euphemisms such as 'passed away' or 'gone to sleep' as they can create confusion in a child and might even trigger fears of going to bed at night. We understood that with young children it is important to talk about concrete aspects of death, about how the person's body doesn't work any more and how they no longer need to eat or sleep, how they can no longer walk around or talk. We were advised that it was vital to not overload a child with information but to provide them with the basics and then with space to ask questions, to seek clarification as and when they feel the need. We learned also that as adults we don't have to hide our feelings of grief from a child who is grieving because it is helpful for the child to see us feel our feelings and talk about them, rather than hiding them, leaving the child confused about what is going on with us and, indeed, confused about what to do with their own feelings. As adults, we need to model that healthy response to loss for them.

We knew that a child may not respond to news of a death in the way that adults might expect them to, so they might not cry, for example, or they might be intensely curious about specific (even gory) details. None of this means that they aren't feeling the loss, it just means that they are processing it differently from us. We were warned that children might have to hear about a death more than once, that they might need to come back to the conversation and hear it again, both at the time and as they age and move into a different frame of reference. Their three-year-old self might have understood death, but their four- or five-year-old self might need to hear it again so that they can understand it with their more developed level of processing. We learned that it's good to talk about how the person we love will not be physically here with us but will always be in our hearts and how we can think of them whenever we want and feel the love we have for them whenever we remember them. We heard how it's important for children to be involved in the funeral process, that even if they are very young and it may mean nothing to them at the time, to know later that they were there can be of enormous comfort. It shows that their grief was acknowledged and accounted for, not dismissed because they may have been too young to have full understanding of what was going on.

Vitally, we learned from both Eddie and Mary about the importance of reassuring a child who is bereaved about what will happen to them now. Who will mind them? This is particularly important if the person who has died is their parent. Will they continue to live in their home? Will they still see their friends? Will they continue to attend the same school? Someone central to the child has just left their world and the child understandably needs to know that others won't leave them too, that they won't be left alone. They need plenty of reassurance that they will always be minded and loved, even though their world has changed beyond measure, *especially* when their world has changed beyond measure. It's also about being prepared for follow-up questions such as, 'Will you die, too?' Key here is not lying to the child because we will all die one day, so saying, 'No, I'm not going to die' isn't a good idea. The best approach is to give answers that are factual yet reassuring. A reply such as, 'I take good care of my health and I plan to be here for a long time, to see you run in the sports day and finish school and go off on some adventures, if that's what you want to do' can provide a child with the reassurance they need to help them at that time.

The information from and conversations with both Eddie and Mary gave us a great framework for helping Fionn to understand and to grieve. We had gained an understanding of some of the advised dos and don'ts when it comes to talking about death with a child. It was a huge amount of information to take on board and process, but it was invaluable in those days after Dara died and we had to prepare Fionn for the future.

On the morning of Dara's funeral my sister Emer sat down with Fionn and gently explained what had happened, and what would happen next. That is their private conversation and I'm not going to share specific details of it, but there was no talk of his mother 'going to sleep' or any other euphemisms. It was a gentle but honest conversation. Emer reassured Fionn that we would all be there for them both. I cannot imagine the courage it took for Emer to have that conversation, holding her own grief for her beloved sister and at the same time telling Dara's child that she had died. There are some people who have stood out in this time after Dara's death and Emer Fitz is one of those who stands tallest. Most people get forty weeks to prepare for parenthood; Emer took it on with only six hours' notice. That was the length of time between the initial knock at her door before 6.00 am and the moment when we knew that Dara had died, when Emer stepped in to take over the primary care-giving role of Dara's son. I have witnessed and heard of some powerful examples of courage, but that is right up there with the best of them.

Fionn has three guardians – Emer, my twin sister Orla and me. Orla also stood in beside Emer right away to help with Fionn, and while Emer raises Fionn, Orla has been an incredible co-parent alongside her, both women's lives changed for ever by these roles, in ways that no one knows about. The bond and connection that Fionn has with both of them is beautiful.

My mother also provides great support. She is a constant presence in Fionn's life, wrapping him up in that special kind of love that grannies give – both she and Fionn are besotted!

She is a source of welcome wisdom for us, too, having raised five children of her own, and I often ask her advice and opinion when Fionn is with me. My father is very hands-on as well and he and Fionn have a great relationship, sometimes seeming more like brothers given the joking and trick-acting that goes on between the pair of them. That grandparent relationship is such a special one and observing my parents and Fionn together, the mutual love between them, my feeling is that they are helping one another through the pain. My brother Johnny is the strong silent type and Fionn looks up to him, literally, slightly in awe of this gentle giant of a man who is at the same time wise and great fun, an important presence in his life. Johnny's wife, Olga, is a princess in Fionn's eyes and he will drop any of his three aunties like a hot potato when Olga is around and he has the option of her to read bedtime stories.

My cousins Stephen, Rosemary and Andrew and their respective spouses and children have been regular companions for those wonderful times that grow the bonds of extended family into solid, lifelong connections. Rowdy afternoons of cushion fights or rugby tackles; bracing morning walks on the beach followed by the tastiest chips out of brown paper bags while sitting on the wall afterwards; movie trips; sleepovers; birthday parties; Christmas Day visits and present swapping. I love to see the fun and the love between Fionn and his cousins and their parents. I hope that Dara knows that her child is enveloped and cocooned in this big, noisy family of Fitzes, raised not on his own but as part of a tribe. Fionn's godfather also plays an important part in his life and together they enjoy everything from the educational to the active when it comes to time spent together, another beautiful and consistent relationship.

They say that it takes a village to raise a child. Well, there truly is a village around this lovely child, a warm, loving, cohesive village of people who stepped in the moment they were needed and have been there ever since.

I have the height of love and respect for them all, most especially for my two sisters, and I think that Dara would be eternally grateful to them for how they have put themselves second and minded her baby when she wasn't able to mind him herself. As a family, we are heartbroken for little Fionn and what he has lost, but we are also privileged to have him in our lives and to take responsibility for raising him in Dara's name.

During the afternoon on that first Mother's Day after Dara's death, I received an email from a woman who showed courage and kindness when she shared her story with me, and by doing so sought to comfort us on this day without Dara. She told me that as she stood at her own mother's grave that day, to wish her a happy Mother's Day, she thought of our family. Her mother had died when she was very young, less than five years of age, at a time in Ireland when the dead were not talked about. People would go quiet whenever her mother's name was mentioned and she was put in the corner at school when her class made Mother's Day cards because she had no mother and so she wasn't permitted to make a card. It's shocking to think of this happening to a child, but it's the truth of how many people experienced death and grief at that time, forced to put their emotions into a box and lock them away, not allowed to speak or feel. The way this courageous woman spoke about her experience proves that the 'best to just forget about them' approach that some people tried to push on us for Fionn is completely wrong and that ignoring it only brings more trauma and far-reaching grief. Knowing that my sisters and I were Fionn's guardians, raising him on Dara's behalf, this woman wanted to let me know that she was telephoning the women in her life who had raised her and wishing them a happy Mother's Day. As someone who had lost her mother, she was letting me know that she valued and loved those women who stepped in and raised her and she was also letting me know that she was okay. I knew that when she wrote her email she had been thinking about this little boy who had lost his mother only weeks before and it was such a kind message to send on this particular day; it was reassurance that we could do this job for Dara and, most important, that Fionn would be okay.

I received hundreds upon hundreds of emails after Dara died, too many to respond to them all, but I did write back to this lovely woman. I remember our conversations and her kindness even to this day, her email just stuck out in my head. I also had messages from people who told me that they send Mother's Day cards to their aunties each year, again letting me know that these situations can and do work out for all concerned. We are strangers to these people, yet they felt compelled to get in touch and pass on lovely messages like these, proof that human beings can be so kind.

Only weeks after Dara died we had Fionn's first birthday celebration without her as he turned three. We had people round and there were balloons, cards, presents and a gaggle of children, the adults chatting while the children played games. It was a great day, but as soon as everyone began to sing 'Happy Birthday' the tears just fell, hot tears that I couldn't stop, the pain of Dara's loss so acute and the rage of injustice at the situation. She should have been there, holding her child in her arms and singing, instead she was lying in a grave. I couldn't bear it. Not wanting to spoil the moment I slipped back into the kitchen and cried quietly, joined by one or two others who also couldn't hold back the tears.

On days like this we're not only carrying our own grief for the loss of Dara as a sister or daughter, we are carrying the loss of Dara as a mother, too. There's that sense of their future robbed, the mother and child who had their whole lives ahead of them to do the normal things that many of us did with our mothers. Helping to make dinner or set the table, constant to and fro about tidying bedrooms, the comfort of always being minded when we're sick, pleading to be let go somewhere and trying to get round her so that she says yes, her homemade sandwiches on the beach in summertime, or your favourite cake baked for your birthday, but, most of all, that one person who is in our corner no matter what. She might be the first one to give out to us when we've done something wrong, but for some of us our mother can also be the first person to stand by us when we've done something wrong. That fierce protective instinct is a shield, a cloak, even when we are adults. That has been my experience with my own mother and I feel so sad knowing that Fionn and Dara will never share that beyond the two and a half short years they had together. He does of course have Emer in that space now, and the rest of us, but there is a loss for him and Dara.

I suppose there's another angle to this as well, which is my own sense of being robbed of motherhood, albeit under different circumstances. It is odd to work so hard to accept the unwanted reality of not being a mother, and then for a tragedy to create a situation where you assume a role of guardian. It's not being a mother, but it is a role that has elements of the mothering space. In those early days I found that difficult because it required a whole new way of thinking. It meant more work as I had to confront and think through the old grief, the new grief and my new relationship with Fionn. As I said, I greatly admire my sisters and how they stepped wholeheartedly into this role, which has reconfigured their lives. They were so kind in allowing me a little space and time to come to terms with things, given my own history of IVF and the adoption bid. Now I am into the guardian role, and that nurturing relationship with Fionn is one of the most important relationship in my life.

I think it's important to realise that our feelings about stepping in like this might not be straightforward. This is where the idea of giving ourselves permission to feel, without judgement, comes in because we might not like our thoughts or reactions, we might be annoyed with ourselves for even having certain thoughts, but it is a lot to come to terms with and we have to give ourselves the space for that. It is such a complex and layered grief, to lose a sister or daughter and then witness her child lose their mother. It's necessary, for everyone's sake, to acknowledge the strangeness and the difficulties of this new situation. As the experts told us in the immediate aftermath of Dara's death, we cannot hide our grief and anger from the children involved. That's not a healthy approach because it ignores the impact and reality of what has happened. It is our role, as adults, to model healthy grieving, which means expressing emotions, crying, talking about the person we have lost and how much they mean to us – being real, in other words.

We have watched Fionn progress from his babyhood to now being five years old. He lives with Emer and is surrounded and supported by a loving, reliable family. These things matter hugely because they give a child a sense that they can trust the people who love them to be there for them. After a death it's necessary to reassure them and reinforce the message that lots of people love them, so there will always be someone there. Children are deeply affected by loss and they grieve, too, even if they don't always behave in grief the way that adults do. It's important to let them process the loss at their own pace, which might be much slower than that of an adult. They will have questions at every age, as they develop mentally and start to grasp how the world works. In terms of answering those questions, honesty is most definitely the best policy. Clear, simple answers are what's needed. It is a source of deep sorrow and grief to see a child lose his mother, but we have to be the best role models we can be to show him that we can learn to live with that grief, so he knows that he will too.

CHAPTER EIGHT

SURVIVING THE FIRST WEEKS

Those early weeks after the funeral were strange times, a sort of a hybrid between the totally surreal feeling of the week that Dara died and the weeks much later on when life began to look some way normal again, or at least the new normal that life became after her death. I didn't return to work for about six weeks and those days were a mix of the practical and the emotional. This was a time when the waves of grief were a hundred feet high, coming in rapid succession, with little or no time to catch my breath in between.

There were so many moments when the enormity of what had happened hit like a sledgehammer and I felt overwhelmed by grief. It brought new perspectives to words that I'd used many times in my life but perhaps I never really *knew*. Words such as heartbroken, anguish, anger, pain and, of course, my old friend numb. I knew what those words felt like now. I understood emotionally what they meant, whereas before I had probably only ever really had a concept of what those words described. In my life I had been angry before, but never like this. The anger that came with the grief was a new kind of rage. I had been in pain before, but nothing that came close to this, no pain had ever felt as though it would rip me in two, but that's what the pain of grief is like. I knew what the word anguish meant, of course, but I had never felt truly felt anguish until those weeks when the concept of never seeing Dara again began to solidify into reality.

Physically and emotionally that whole period of time was non-stop, hectic, with very little rest, a life turned upside-down, I suppose. It was tough going. The balance of surviving such a time in your life is that it also showed me the meaning of other words that I had used before but never really knew: love, gratitude, support, kindness, hope. I also felt these words in a way that I never had felt before. I can see now, with the benefit of time and hindsight, that having to face reality head-on and early was a good thing for me personally, but it didn't always feel like that at the time.

In the early weeks after Dara died, when my emotions were all over the place, I found myself agreeing to do something that I would never have done under normal circumstances. I agreed to go to a psychic reading. I'm open-minded and naturally curious, but I just don't get it when it comes to the whole psychic thing, it doesn't make sense to me. I understand that for some people it makes sense, but personally I don't believe in it. In my twenties a psychic was doing readings for a group of friends and I got roped into going along to make up the numbers, but that was seen as a bit of fun. Certainly, the visit did nothing to change my mind and make me believe that a person can actually see the past, present and future by reading cards or by any other method. But in those weeks when I was struggling so hard to make sense of my life without Dara in it, I wasn't thinking like myself, sometimes I wasn't acting like myself. It was a strange feeling, like another person had got under my skin and was sharing it with me, someone very different from me. As a result, I was vulnerable, I suppose, maybe a bit suggestible, so when some friends said they were going to see a psychic, I ended up going along with them. Initially I said no, but the truth is that at that time I was so lost, so lonely for Dara, that I think I would have agreed to anything if it held out the promise of a connection to her.

Three years later, I feel silly for having even entertained the idea, but at that time I felt that I could be missing out on some link to Dara if I didn't go. I think that's a measure of the emotional state we can be in after our loved one dies. We are searching for them, in a way, and willing to go anywhere if there's a chance of finding them. So I went along and while the woman was very nice, within minutes I knew that this was nothing more than a con. Whether she believed herself that she had psychic powers or whether she knew darn well that she didn't and was scamming desperate people like myself I don't know, but I do know that if she had psychic powers she kept them hidden that night because I saw no sign of them in the time I was with her. As a psychologist I work in a profession that values evidence-based data, so I am aware that it doesn't paint me in a great light to be sharing that I went to see a psychic, but I want to tell the truth about what grief is like, and part of that truth is that in those early days I felt lost and scared about never again having contact with Dara. When we are mired in those emotions, we can do things that we wouldn't normally do.

I think that this holds true for whatever loss we experience in life. The loss of a relationship or a job can lead to people behaving in ways that are out of character for them, doing things they wouldn't have previously considered. One reason for this is that the loss has changed our perspective and that can colour how we make decisions. My observation is that how we are in grief tends to be in line with how we are normally as a person. By that I mean, for example, that I'm someone who is used to talking about feelings, both given my character and the profession I'm in, so I have been similar in how I have approached grief. I've spoken about my feelings of grief, I haven't kept them to myself, so how I am in my grief is in line with how I am as a person. But this instance of behaving out of character is the one place where that rule doesn't seem to apply, in my experience. Reflecting on losses that I have witnessed others experience, out-of-character behaviour isn't restricted to me and my visit to a psychic. I think that with regard to whatever out-of-character behaviours anyone engages in after loss, what matters first and foremost is that people are safe and that they do no harm either to themselves or to others. Second, what matters is that we forgive ourselves and allow for the fact that these things happen. It doesn't mean we are now a wholly different person, it just means that the grief squeezed us out of shape in the raw period of the immediate aftermath of the loss. We are still the self-same person.

Stepping out of life and away from people after the end of my dream of being a mother would also have been out of character for me, as I've always been a sociable person. Even from my school days I was someone who joined in, engaging in activities from school plays to trips abroad, anything that would have me connecting with my schoolmates. I continued in the same vein in college and alongside my academic work I thoroughly enjoyed a life rich in social and sporting activities. It was the same when we were married, we went out with friends, we travelled, we got busy living. Reflecting on the time after the loss of motherhood, I can see now how I retreated, something I have spoken about earlier. I stepped back from my wider circle and I also withdrew from activities that I loved to do, such as boxing and kettlebell workouts and running. As someone who had been active and sociable my whole life, these decisions were out of character. I had not really got back into being social or active again when Dara died and my marriage ended, so while I probably have not observed a huge difference with regards to uncharacteristic behaviours following the loss of my marriage, I can see now that I hadn't been myself for a while even before that.

I suppose the slow move towards acceptance of what has been lost is part of the process of returning us to ourselves. Yes, the loss is imprinted on us for ever, but we do move from those extremely heightened grief emotions, during which we can sometimes be a stranger to ourselves, towards the point where we can live with the grief. For me, as I said before, part of that process of acceptance was facing up to what had happened by seeking information about the crash and by reclaiming Dara's belongings. There was another moment that was similar to that at Dara's locker in the base and that also helped me to confront reality. I received a call from Garda Sinéad Barrett, the FLO based in Belmullet garda station, County Mayo. She informed me that Dara's helmet had washed up on a beach in the local area near Blacksod. I wasn't expecting to hear anything like that and it caught me offguard, knocked me off my stride for a moment. I pictured that empty cubby-hole with Dara's name on it at the base, and then her helmet lying on a beach, in the wrong place, out of place.

I had already been focused on getting to Mayo as soon as possible. First, and most important, I wanted to support the other families involved in this tragedy, especially as they were still waiting for news of their missing loved ones. I also needed to see for myself where Dara had died and to find out whatever information I could about what had happened to her that night. When I received the news about the helmet, I was anxious to get over there. I know other people would use this time to rest, to reflect and to sit with the numbness before confronting the hard facts, but I felt I would cope better when I had seen everything for myself. I needed to confront Dara's last moments in order to process them.

Two days after Dara's funeral I made the journey with three search and rescue pilots who had been so supportive to my family since the crash: Captain Mark Donnelly, Captain Cathal Oakes and Captain Tony O'Mahony. We took the road west and some hours later we reached Blacksod Lighthouse. Cathal drove us up to a viewing point nearby, from where we would be able to see Black Rock Island, the godforsaken rock on which the helicopter had crashed. I don't know what I expected, but it caught my breath when I set eyes on Black Rock for the first time. Out in the distance it rose up out of the water almost like a Skellig, puncturing the horizon with a deep purple hue. The car fell silent as we just sat and looked. This was the place where Dara had taken her last breath, where her life had ended. Even now I find it difficult to put into words what those moments were like, as reality hit home once more. It felt as if time stood still as I looked out into the distance and felt what it was like to be in that area where Dara had died, breathing the same air that Dara would have breathed. It was a silent sadness, deep to the bone.

After we had seen Black Rock Island for the first time I went to meet members of some of the other families and had an opportunity to extend my condolences to them all. I was so conscious that Dara had been found, her body recovered and returned to us, funeral rites completed, yet they were still here at the shore's edge, waiting for news of their loved ones. It was a living nightmare and my heart went out to them all. It's so hard to find the words for such tragedy; being there is all we can do.

The following day, Mark and Tony took me out to the beach where Dara's helmet had washed up. It took us time to find out the exact location from locals because there are several beaches in the area and we had a few false alarms before we found the right one, but we got there. While Tony walked in one direction and searched over the rocks for any crash debris that might have washed up, Mark and I walked out towards the water. There was no one else on the beach at the time and we stood side by side, not saying a word, just looking out on the ocean as it roared. The noise of the water took me by surprise, it wasn't a gentle lapping sound, there were loud crashing reverberations as huge waves collided. It was what I would describe as an angry sea and it was very hard to look at it and know that Dara had been in it. It seemed to be such a vast expanse of ocean and all I could think of was how small Dara was and how tiny she would have been as she was buffeted about on this huge body of water. I didn't know the details of her death at that point, but as I looked out over the Atlantic waves I couldn't get an image out of my head: Dara in the water that night, alive, in the dark, alone, frightened, aware of what was happening to her, crying out for her child and for her family. That was the single most terrifying thought for me, and the possibility that this was what she had suffered brought abject fear. Thankfully, I never permitted myself to dwell on these thoughts. Each time they came up, I escorted my mind to different, more useful thoughts and asked of myself to deal only in facts. In confirmed information rather than speculation. That was an important coping mechanism in those weeks of raw emotion.

Mark and Tony let me stay on the beach as long as I needed and when I was ready, we headed to the lighthouse. There I met lighthouse-keeper Vincent Sweeney and his family, and I also got my first view of the intended landing site. For me this was an important meeting because as a family we owe Vincent Sweeney so much. On the night of the crash his sharp instincts would not let it pass that the helicopter had not landed at the time he expected them to land. He didn't say, 'Ah sure, it'll be okay,' he didn't wait to see what happened next, he called it in right away, which meant the search for the crew of Rescue 116 began not long after they had crashed. That in turn influenced Dara's body being recovered from the water. There was a chain of people whose actions contributed to us getting Dara back, and Vincent was the first link in that chain. Therefore, it was a big deal to me to meet this man. It was emotional to say the least and I was very grateful that he agreed to see me.

Sitting around the kitchen table in the lighthouse with Vincent and his wife Doreen, a mug of hot tea pressed into our cold hands, the Sweeneys told me that although it had been a good many years since she had last been in, over the years Dara had sat around the same table in the middle of the night or day when she and a crew had stopped there to refuel. Vincent noted that she would sit in the same seat that I had chosen, her back to the window that faced out to sea, her hands wrapped around a big mug of tea as the heli crew and the lighthouse crew chatted. Knowing that when we were all asleep in our beds and Dara was at work that she was met with warmth and home comforts by the Sweeney family was such a lovely thing to hear. It was truly heartwarming and I was grateful that both Vincent and Doreen felt comfortable enough to tell us about those times, even if they upset and comforted me in equal measure.

Death and grief are uncomfortable subjects and many people simply cannot find the wherewithal to be around those who are newly bereaved. This can be magnified when the death is as a result of a tragedy. My experience is that whenever I do find myself in the presence of someone who is able to be with me while I'm in pain and engage in a conversation with me even while I might be crying, frightened, or even angry, I welcome both them and that opportunity with open arms. I feel grateful to not have to sweep pain under the carpet, but instead to be allowed to feel it while I talk. That's such a gift to give to the bereaved. It really helps them to survive the feelings, to cope with the pain and to start accepting that this is real.

That said, it isn't easy to bestow this gift on a person because the emotional pain of loss is palpable and can be quite difficult to be around. Even as a psychologist, it took time for me to learn to be okay in the presence of someone else's pain, to understand that sometimes people just need to be in pain and to feel it and express it. Think about how many times as a child we were all told, 'Hush, don't cry'. This was clearly well-intentioned and sometimes perhaps was necessary to soothe a distressed child, but it also unwittingly perpetuated the sense that pain is bad and that it should be held back, pushed down, stopped. Once I began working as a psychologist, I learned that while emotional pain may be uncomfortable or distressing to experience, it's part and parcel of the human condition. It is necessary. As such, we need to be okay with being in the presence of pain; indeed, because it is from this point that someone can move on to a place of peace.

This is very difficult for some people, understandably, and they avoid having those real conversations and instead stick to the shallow stuff, or even avoid those who have experienced loss. They may not be sure how to handle being in the presence of someone else's pain and worry about what's the 'right' thing to do. What do I do if the person becomes angry? Have I made things worse if I say something that makes them cry? That's the fear that some people have, that they will somehow make it worse or add to the pain. This is quite a common reaction, so someone who has had a miscarriage or whose child has died or whose spouse has left them or who has received a diagnosis of a serious illness might find themselves short of people with whom they can really talk, people who allow them to feel their feelings. They might rarely have someone tell them that they had met their child at school before she died and how she was so friendly and lovely. They might rarely have someone tell them that they just heard about their diagnosis and that cancer is shit and ask them how they're feeling today. They might rarely have someone ask them the name of their stillborn baby. If a person doesn't know what to say, they can often decide to say nothing at all.

There's a lesson in this for all of us. I have been on both sides of this. I have gone to wakes and funerals and although psychology taught me to be comfortable with emotions, I have still at times wondered if what I have said to the bereaved was welcome, if I could have said more, or could have asked more. And now, I've been the person standing beside the coffin as visitors come in, the look of dread hidden behind their eyes and their soft smiles as they wait in line to approach me. I have experienced the people who say nothing, turned inwards and paralysed by a fear of saying the wrong thing, and the people who have looked at me and talked to me and invited me to talk freely. I know now that any well-intentioned interaction in the aftermath of death is welcome, that the truth is that it is an extremely uncomfortable situation and some people waiting to sympathise will not have experienced loss in their own life. Yet they stand in line and wait to see me. That's the part that matters. The desire to help and comfort is always there, we just have to push aside our hang-ups and worries and let it come to the fore. The very best thing you can do for the person who is grief-stricken is to give them that gift of freedom to feel, freedom to cry, freedom to talk.

Vincent and Doreen were just such brave, kind souls. They gave me that gift and I was so grateful for their chat and their memories. Afterwards, Vincent took Mark, Tony and me out to the helipad where Rescue 116 had been due to touch down for refuelling. Looking at the square stone walls along the boundary of the patch of concrete next to the lighthouse, the big H in the middle of the circle on the helipad, was a strange feeling. It looked so ordinary and yet it was also eerie because the crew had never made it. I just stood and looked, there was nothing else to do and nothing to say really.

Leaving the lighthouse, we went to the community centre in Eachléim, a few kilometres away from Blacksod. This Irish-speaking townland housed the community centre that for many weeks served as the hub for those involved in the search for both the missing crew members and the helicopter. We walked into the centre and to say that I was amazed at what I saw would be an understatement. It was set up like a restaurant, with tables and chairs, food stations and Burco boilers dispensing a steady stream of hot drinks. The hall was fairly full that day, but I could still see that the walls were stacked shoulder-high with supplies donated from around the country – tea, coffee, biscuits, all sorts of non-perishable food items lay waiting for use as the crowds of searchers kept coming and needing to be fed. I saw a wall plastered with letters, cards and handwritten notes tacked onto it and on the table below was a photo of the four crew, a candle lit beside it. I walked over to the wall and began to read the correspondence and I saw that it was cards and letters that had accompanied donations given to the community centre so that they could continue to feed those involved in the search effort. Letter upon letter from all over Ireland explaining why someone had donated either money or food supplies, and the sense of grief at the loss of life came off the pages as I read. School children drew pictures of helicopters that they sent alongside poems and notes; businesses attached details of cheque donations; one elderly lady even wrote that her group at the nursing home had done a whip-round and were sending what they could to help the efforts. A little girl said that she had nothing to give except some cupcakes, but she was sending them and hoped that they would help. It was humbling and heartening to read the respect and love for the crew among the sadness.

As I stood there reading the wall from one side to the other, I think that some of the women working there spotted my red hair, which gave away that I was Dara's sister. Some of them came over to me and they just pulled me into hugs. Before they had uttered any words, those hugs said it all, they said that I was welcome, that they were *so* sorry for my loss and that whatever they could do to help me, they would gladly do. When we talked, they wanted to know how my mother was holding up and how Dara's little son was doing. Their kindness, concern and welcome, particularly when I was away from home and from my own family, meant so much. It is true that genuine human warmth and kindness makes the grief burden feel just that little bit more bearable.

The next day some of my family arrived, my father, my brother Johnny, my cousin Stephen and my uncle Peter, and we all prepared to go out on the Irish naval ship, the LÉ *Eithne*. Ship's Captain Brian Fitzgerald had offered to bring us out to Black Rock Island to see the site of the crash. The trip had originally been planned for the previous day, but weather and sea conditions meant it had to be postponed. We were told that conditions were still not ideal, but that it was safe to travel and that we would return to shore if conditions deteriorated. It was only when we drove towards the pier that I realised there was no steady gangplank onto the ship. It was anchored offshore and there was only one way out to the vessel, and that was on a RHIB (rigid hull inflatable boat). I'd had a few unpleasant incidents with water when I was young and while I can swim, I prefer to stay on dry land. I can say without hesitation that if the trip on the RHIB had been for any other reason than to go to Black Rock Island, I would have declined. But I wanted to see where Dara died more than I feared the water. Indeed, after what we had gone through, I wasn't really afraid of anything. The worst that could ever happen had already happened and I had survived that, so I reckoned I could tackle this trip on the sea.

After a briefing on the pier and being fitted for life jackets we went down the steps and climbed into the RHIB. I can remember that the one I was in was the first RHIB out to the ship and that it was piloted by a Navy Seaman called Craig, it's funny the details that stick. Craig put me sitting up beside him in the front and my family sitting behind us and we set off for the ship. The water was choppy and over the noise of the waves Craig shouted that he would do his best to keep us dry. Despite his best efforts and smooth driving, as the craft left the cover of the harbour and skimmed out into the open water a rogue wave washed over the sides, drenching us completely. As the spray spattered across my face, I just sat in my seat with my hands tightly clenched on the bar in front of me, focused only on staying onboard. Chatting as a family earlier, we had spoken about how Dara would laugh her head off at the very idea of us getting onto this RHIB in the choppy waters of the Atlantic to travel to a Navy ship, that it would have given her a right giggle. Sitting there like a drowned rat, I pictured Dara with her head back, laughing out loud at her sister whose hair is usually perfectly blow-dried and who hates water, clinging on for dear life beside Craig-the-Navy-guy who was looking cool as a cucumber. She would have teased me mercilessly about being so far out of my comfort zone!

Once at the ship, the RHIB was winched up from the sea to the top level, where we disembarked. The crew welcomed us aboard and brought us through the narrow corridors until we came to a deck that had a portion inside under cover and a portion outside, and it was between these two that we spent the journey out to and back from Black Rock Island. Noticing my soaking wet hair, one of the female crew members kindly brought me to her quarters and lent me her hairdryer so that I could dry off a bit, which was a welcome relief.

The other RHIBS soon arrived and with everyone on board we set off on a round-trip journey that would take a few hours. Captain Fitzgerald and his crew were most hospitable and on the way out to the island we had some lovely chats with them. I even chatted to some crew who had met Dara as over the years they had been involved in dunker training that she had completed. This is where search and rescue crews are put into a simulated helicopter that is then dropped into a huge tank of water and turned upside-down, with a rain and wave machine on and the lights turned off. Disoriented, the crew have to find their way to the exits and out of the helicopter and back up to the surface. Some of the Navy crew had met Dara at some of the dunker trainings and we talked about it because Dara had just completed her dunker training about ten days before the crash. Indeed, during my last conversation with her we talked about the dunker. It's a pretty terrifying experience and she was glad to have it done and over with for another while. I'm no expert, I'm just a sister, but I did wonder if having dunker training so fresh in her mind had helped Dara to escape from the helicopter, that was my thinking anyway, and so we chatted about that for a while.

There were others on the trip out to Black Rock Island, so I won't give any details about what it was like when we got there. That should remain private for those who were onboard. But I will say that when we reached the area around the rock, Captain

Fitzgerald pointed out to my family where Dara had been found by Rescue 118. I had seen on a map where they had located her, but to see it in person was different. Again, as with the day on the beach, the ocean felt so big, so powerful and so vast, it made it all the more horrifying to think of Dara in those waters. But I personally needed to know where she had been found. I needed to see it with my own eyes. I felt that the more I knew about and understood what had happened to Dara and the less speculation in my mind, the better. For me, knowing is better than not knowing, so coming back to shore later that day I felt that the trip on the LÉ *Eithne* had been a tough day but also a good day because it had yielded more understanding.

That evening there was a candlelight vigil for the crew down beside the graveyard overlooking the sea, with Black Rock Island out in the distance and the backdrop of Achill Island across the water from us. It was sad and yet also comforting, there was such a sense of community from the huge numbers in attendance and I was glad that I went. My family were so grateful for the support and care shown to us.

We also got great support over those few days from many of Dara's colleagues as they had come from the four search and rescue bases to help with the search. They were staying at the hotel that we were in and we would sit in groups over breakfast and dinner, talking about our day and, of course, talking about the crash and about the crew. I was able to get answers to some of the questions I had about Dara's job, different questions that came into my head every now and then. Mindful that everyone else around me was grieving too, I kept a watch on my emotions, but sometimes while talking I did get quite upset. Never once was this an issue with Dara's colleagues, whether they knew me or not they let me cry and then they answered my questions, quietly and clearly, helping me to understand terms like waypoints and top cover. It was immense kindness from these men and women, who had lost four of their colleagues and friends and were in mourning themselves, that they gave me their time to help me to try and understand some of the elements of the tragedy.

It might seem strange that there can be a need by the bereaved to both hear and tell the story of the death over and over, but each time we tell that story and go over the details involved, it does something in terms of helping both our head and our heart process the most important detail, which is that the person we love is not coming back. The repeated telling feels to me as though it can be about understanding, processing and ultimately healing. It's not done to be maudlin, it's done to be real and to face what has happened. When a bereaved person wants to tell you the story of their loss, if you can, stay quiet and listen. It will help them to wrap their head around what has happened, which can help to process the trauma of loss.

After an emotional few days in Blacksod, confronting the reality of Dara's death and our loss, travelling back to Dublin I felt very glad that I had gone to Mayo and seen it all with my own eyes. My decision to travel to Mayo was made because of a desire to support the other families, for there were three crew members still missing. I knew also that I had a need to travel over to the crash site for myself, but I don't think I knew back then just how beneficial doing so would be in terms of my own grief journey. Reflecting on it now, I can see that although it was really difficult to do, being there and seeing where Dara died was a healthy way of grieving for me. It's different for everyone, of course, but that process of gathering information and facing the truth were important factors in my grief journey. I think I subconsciously knew that if the 'what ifs?' took hold of me, I would be in trouble, for ever tortured, my mind wondering about all sorts of things and aimlessly going over it all again and again. Standing up and looking at death and the circumstances surrounding it straight in the eye turned out to be the best thing that I could have done to help myself. I learned that I was right to follow my instinct, even if some people might have questioned my decision and wondered if I was doing the right thing, if I was upsetting myself for no good reason by travelling to where Dara had died. But I didn't doubt myself. I may not have consciously known all the good reasons at the time, but I went with what felt right. I think that's the best thing we can do when faced with loss that upends us. I work hard at my mental and emotional health by paying attention to how I feel and by understanding that there is validity in those feelings, thus they need to be expressed in some manner, and action is often needed too. It wasn't easy getting through many of those days, but some days I leaned into the grief and let it wash over me and other days I felt more able to function, but always I was gentle with myself and trusted myself to keep putting one foot in front of the other. Looking at the three losses in my life, I can see now that the way in which I approached those early weeks after Dara's death was that I listened to my gut instinct. This is important to do so that we are not swallowed up by the advice and opinions of stronger personalities. I made sure to feel the feelings, even the ugly ones, validating everything I experienced both cognitively and emotionally. I cried, I raged, I talked. I listened both to those who could advise me and also to my own head and heart. And I did what I needed to do, what was right for me.

By virtue of the fact that it occurred at the same time, these were also strategies that I employed in surviving the early weeks after the end of my marriage. With regard to both of these losses, I feel the better now for that approach then, in that I think the honest, open, raw expression of my grief in those early weeks was the right approach for me because it put me on the path towards a healthy grief. I want to be very clear, again, that there is no 'right' or 'wrong' approach overall when it comes to grief, this was just what worked for me. Every person is different and every loss is different. However, I think that respecting our own feelings is essential because it respects our uniqueness and that of our loss.

I can also see with hindsight that my approach to surviving the early weeks after the loss of motherhood was somewhat different, although there were elements of the strategies I utilised to survive the early weeks after Dara's loss and the end of my marriage, but they were much more faint versions of those tools. I know now that this is because I never recognised it as loss, never named not being able to be a mother as grief. Had I known then that I was grieving, I would have realised that this was a significant loss in relation to the life that I thought I was going to have, and I would have sought professional help to process that loss and guide me towards acceptance. I did listen to my gut instinct and I did give myself permission not to have to be in the midst of christenings or children's birthday parties for a while, and I also allowed myself to feel the ugly feelings of resentment towards those who have children. I cried. I raged. But I didn't really talk about the loss at all, a fact that now seems unbelievable to me. And I can see that what was missing was that outside voice, the qualified and trained professional who could have helped me to understand the depths of this loss, for that would have helped me to grieve. Acknowledging that my inability to be a mother was life-changing, that it required a complete re-route on my life sat nav, would, I think, have facilitated me processing that loss in a healthier way. It might have resulted in me not retreating for quite such a long period of time both socially and in terms of engaging in life's activities. But sometimes we don't know what we don't know. We can only do our best, making better choices when we have a fuller picture.

One of the things often said to those in mourning after the death of a loved one is that they ought to keep busy. Get back to work, get back into the daily routine, fill the hours with distraction. Again, I heard that advice and I deliberately chose not to take it. It didn't feel right to me, so I didn't force myself into it. In those six weeks when I wasn't working and striving to be 'normal', it granted me the space to do things like travel to Mayo, spend time with my family and lose hours and days to crying and talking. Some people might shudder at the thought, but I simply occupied the grief space and shut out any pressure to return to 'normal life'. I'm very glad now that I did so because the space and time afforded by those 'abnormal' weeks were really important in helping me to survive that awful raw period after Dara died.

The other gift those weeks gave me was some very special days that I wouldn't have experienced if I'd been sitting at my desk. On one of the trips to Mayo during that time, I was sitting in Blacksod Lighthouse with my mother and my brother, Johnny, when we were told that Rescue 118 was coming in to land on the helipad. Without uttering a word, my mother, brother and I simultaneously rose from our seats, grabbed our jackets and went outside. We watched as the helicopter came into view, the small dot in the sky visible in more detail as it got nearer. The three of us stood outside the lighthouse, still not a word shared between us, looking up into the sky, watching the approach, no one else around except Vincent Sweeney as he made preparations for it to land. We never verbalised it, but we had an overwhelming need to see that journey completed and watch the helicopter land where Dara and her colleagues should have landed that night. Getting to experience that sight served to close a circle in some ways. There was an inexplicable comfort in having been there to witness the completed journey. It facilitated a further release of emotions and I cried a lot that night, but it provided a moment of emotional shelter in the grief storms of those early weeks.

Another day that also brought tears and comfort in equal measure was a day that I called 'the best worst day' – worst day because all those early days were so awful. I was invited to a wreath-laying ceremony for the crew of R116, hosted by Dunmore East RNLI in Waterford. Neville Murphy is Winch Operator on Rescue 117, the Waterford-based Irish Coast Guard helicopter, and he is also a volunteer with Dunmore East RNLI. He secured permission to invite me onto the lifeboat so that I could lay the wreath for Dara myself. Dara had lived in Waterford for 11 years and any trips I made down to that city were usually to see her, so when I drove into Waterford to go to the ceremony, it was the first time I had been in the city for a long time. I felt really emotional at the physical kick in my chest at the sight of the signs indicating that I was in Waterford. I suppose it's because any other time I had driven this road, I was driving to Dara's house to see her.

Memories flooded back, places where we had done the big fun stuff together, but also places where we did the normal, ordinary stuff together. As I drove my car into the city I wept. Dara was gone and it was just shit.

I drove to Dara's house, where I sat outside a while, thinking about the times we had all shared when she'd lived there. It felt like a parallel universe: six Sundays earlier Dara was alive and now I was sitting outside her Waterford house, having attended her funeral and burial only weeks before. I wasn't even sure what I was doing there, I only knew that I had to see the place where she had lived for many happy years, just to be there. I know now that my need to be there that day was part of that urgent desire for any connection possible, anything that will be a link to the person who has died. I suppose I had nothing else left but those links and my memories. That's why I sat outside Dara's house and I had a cry and I remembered her and our lives together.

Before going to Dunmore harbour, I drove to Waterford Airport to visit the Rescue 117 base for the first time since Dara died. We had been on the base with Dara many times over the years, and only a few years earlier the company held a family day and we went up in the helicopter with Dara and the crew. I have some lovely memories from that day and both the Waterford base and many of the crew stationed there felt familiar to me. When I walked into the base, the smell and sounds of the building, walking along the ground-floor corridor with the photos and awards up on the walls, looking into what was Dara's office when she was Chief Pilot, it all had an added edge to it this time around, the same with walking into the hangar and seeing the helicopter. On the way to the crew room I saw a book of condolence for the crew of Rescue 116 with a candle lit beside it, a reminder of the loss of colleagues and friends felt by those working in this building.

After a catch-up with the crew I headed with some of them to the harbour in Dunmore East, where we were met with an incredible sight. The harbour walls were lined with crowds, people as far as the eye could see, covering almost every inch of the pier, sometimes several deep along the barrier wall between the harbour and the open water. It was estimated that almost a thousand people had turned up for the ceremony to honour the crew of Rescue 116 and to pay their respects. I should have anticipated it because given that it's a coastal area with a big fishing community, the southeast of Ireland has a strong connection to the Coast Guard helicopter crews. Along with the volunteer crews from the RNLI, these are the people who come to the aid of those who encounter difficult times on the seas around the coast, the people who get out of their beds in the middle of the night and go out in all weathers, 365 days a year, to help others whose names they don't even know. It's no wonder that people talk about the rescue helicopter with affection and respect – they even refer to it as 'the helicopter' as if there were only one – so it made sense that the crowd would be big. I just wasn't expecting it to be quite so big. But then, even though Dara was a Dub, as Chief Pilot of R117 she was an important member of the community and they had made her one of their own. That became very clear to me over the course of that day and it was a solace and a source of pride.

A lone piper led a procession from the lifeboat station to the water's edge, where we boarded several boats involved in the ceremony, including RNLI lifeboats from Dunmore East and neighbouring areas. The flotilla of boats moved slowly through the harbour and as we passed the harbour entrance, a fire engine was parked at the very end of the pier. Beside it, the crew were lined up solemnly, saluting the flotilla in a gesture of solidarity and respect for their fallen colleagues. The boat cut through the waves until it got into position less than a mile out, still visible to the crowds lining the walls. The other boats circled in close to us so that we were all near to one another. A priest led us in prayers to remember the crew of Rescue 116 and also others who lost their lives in rescue missions: Coast Guard volunteer Caitríona Lucas, who died in 2016, and the four crew of the Irish Air Corps Rescue 111 helicopter that crashed on the way back from a rescue mission in 1999, Captain Dave O'Flaherty, Captain Mick Baker, Sergeant Paddy Mooney and Corporal Niall Byrne.

Neville guided me towards the lower step of the lifeboat and held on to me as I lowered Dara's wreath into the water, followed by others who laid wreaths for the other three crew. I had never laid a wreath at sea before and I wasn't prepared for how emotional it would be to see the wreath drifting away from me. Once all were laid, we went back up onto the deck of the lifeboat and after a minute's silence, four flares were set off, one for each member of Rescue 116. When the flares went off it all became too much and I put my head in my hands and covered my eyes. But Neville wouldn't let me. 'No, look up, you have to see this,' he said. When I did look up, I saw four bright white lights in the sky above me. Dara had flown these skies for a significant portion of her career and now she was represented in that same sky by a brilliant white light that faded into the distance as it went higher and higher. As we stood side by side, both Neville and I had a cry, joined, I was told later, by most of the people on the harbour walls after the flares were set off and the strains of Sarah McLachlan's 'Angel' played across the harbour and out to sea.

Then came the familiar sound of the rescue helicopter approaching and Rescue 117 from the Waterford base did a fly-past, passing over the lifeboats several times, with a winchman lowered down on the end of the winchline as the aircraft crossed the bay on the last pass. Some of the crew that day had flown with Dara for a long time and it was lovely that they were the ones to do the fly-past for the four crew of R116, including their long-time colleague and friend.

Those darkest days, in the early weeks after Dara died, have been the worst days I've ever known in life, but this was a day that helped me hugely. It was such a sad day, so poignant and full of sorrow and regret for lives lost far too soon. But the intensity of that sorrow gave release to emotions that needed to be expressed. The experience of being on that boat and feeling the support from the RNLI crews and the other emergency services, as well as from the crowds of locals on the pier, not to mention the wall of warmth and support from Dara's colleagues from Rescue 117, all came together to make it the best of those worst days. What helped was the ritual of it all: the ceremony, the remembrance, the strong sense of community. All the tears I cried that day helped me, and that's an important lesson to pass on.

Back in Dublin, while I had already retrieved Dara's phone and laptop from her locker at the base, we still had to clear out her belongings from her workplace and remove her car. I will admit now that this was a task that I was really dreading. The very idea of clearing out Dara's work clothes and driving her car away from the base one last time brought towering waves of emotion roaring down on top of me, and I found that I couldn't speak each time I tried to talk about it. I think these emotions were linked to the thought that clearing away her things would be another part of Dara's presence on this Earth slipping away. When someone dies, they leave your life bit by bit, their presence in your life slowly ebbing away, like footprints on the beach washed away by the tide. First, they are physically gone, there one day and gone the next. For ever. Then, as life goes on, things happen that erase other parts of their presence from your life. They aren't there to call when you reach for the phone to tell them something. Their image in your head becomes a still snapshot. It gets harder to picture them precisely. They become more memory than flesh and blood, losing their realness. These losses cause waves of grief as well, not as big as the initial waves that pound you in those early weeks, but they lap around you, triggering tough emotions as you register each one.

The thing is, we desperately don't want the presence of the person we love to end up like a faint outline on the sand. We want them to rest in peace, but we also want and need for them to always have a presence in some way, otherwise it's as though they never existed. That just *cannot* happen. We often hear the word *lost* when it comes to death: 'I'm sorry for your loss,' or 'I lost my sister last year.' But we know that the person isn't lost, they aren't missing, they're dead, their body turned to dust and their soul gone from this Earth. But they are lost to us. We no longer have their physical and emotional presence in our world, we can't hear their voice, see their lovely face, speak to them and listen to their thoughts and advice; we can no longer sit together around the table and chat for hours over a leisurely weekend brunch, we can't drive them to the airport when they're going on holidays, see a film with them or walk the dog together on a blustery autumn day. All the normal things that we do with the people we love are gone, they are lost to us, hence when I say to someone that I'm very sorry for their loss and when I say that I lost my sister, that's what I am referring to, the loss of their life and of their presence in a person's life.

This is why the idea of the visit to the base was so difficult, because it would be one more ebb of Dara's life away from us. I acknowledged this to myself and I reached out for help. The night before we were going to the base, I sent a group message to a few of Dara's work colleagues, just saying that I was struggling with this and asking for advice. Within moments my phone pinged over and over with messages of support and guidance from some of the people who I believe to be the bravest of the brave. The responses were as varied as the people. Some sent reminders of my own words at Dara's funeral, telling me to remember to 'Do a Dara' and find that inner toughness and bring it with me. Some sent silly jokes or pictures to make me laugh (which they did!). Others told me that Dara would be there with me in spirit.

Winch Operator Neil McAdam from R117 in Waterford rang me right away and said that he had done a similar task before in his own life and he talked me through his experience. Mac, as he is known, told me that going through someone's clothes and personal effects and clearing out their locker was a savagely difficult job to have to do and he said that it was okay to cry my way through it, if that's what happened. In telling me his own experience, he quashed any hopes I had about a way for this to be anything other than harrowing, but that was a good thing. It became clear that I didn't have to 'cope', I just had to get the job done. I decided there and then that if I needed to, I would just 'pack and cry, pack and cry'. No matter how much I cried, I was just going to keep packing Dara's belongings. Sometimes in life we need a signpost, a point towards the right direction, and I got that guidance from Mac that night when we talked. It was enough to settle my mind so that I felt I had my focus back and that I was ready to go, with my family, and bring home Dara's belongings.

At the base the next morning, we were greeted by a number of Dara's Dublin colleagues. Also there was Mac, who had driven up to Dublin from Waterford early that morning to be there when my family and I arrived to do this hardest of tasks. The kindness in that gesture – I was stunned. Again, I saw the best of humanity in the worst of times. We all chatted together for a while, sitting in the kitchen that Dara had sat in so many times over the years, hearing stories of her at work, how she would raise her eyebrow at the lads each time they put their cup in the sink instead of in the dishwasher. One crew member told us that now, every time he goes to put his cup in the sink, he thinks of Dara. I'm not sure if that means he also puts his cup in the dishwasher, but it's nice to know that he thinks of her. Captain Anne Brogan then brought Emer and me to the women's changing rooms and she stayed and helped us as we cleared out Dara's locker. Anne and Dara were great friends, so that can't have been easy for her, but she was so kind to us and having her there really helped. When we finished gathering Dara's personal items, we collected her car and, with thanks and hugs to the crews on the base, we headed home.

I know that I'm beginning to sound like a broken record, but despite having dreaded that task, I was very glad afterwards that I had done it. It was another confrontation with reality, not allowing myself to somehow look away from the most important detail, which is that Dara isn't coming back. I found that each time I did something that brought reality into the room, it turned out to be a time that was intensely emotional but that helped me to accept. It was worth the pain.

Even in those early days of loss there is space for the shoots of acceptance to begin to grow. When I knew for sure that I would never be a mother, what helped me survive those early days and weeks was physically packing away the paraphernalia related to, first, the IVF and then the adoption application. In the former, it meant appropriate disposal of medications and needles, removing pencilled-in further treatment schedules from my diary, leaving space in my fridge, in my cupboard and in my timeline where these aids to hope once were. When the adoption application came to an end, again I physically removed from my sight both the hard and soft copy files of paperwork that housed the hope of parenthood, letting my head and heart know that there was an end to this dream. When I knew for certain that my marriage was over, I removed my wedding ring, the public symbol of the love that I had vowed to uphold years earlier. I had removed the ring on occasions over the years, of course, as anyone does, maybe when painting or at the gym, but this removal was different. It was an acknowledgement to myself that the marriage was truly over. It was one thing to wear this ring when we were in trouble, but the moment I knew in my heart that there was no coming back for us, I knew that I had to stop wearing it. When I did take it off, I realised that this small act alone helped me to acknowledge both the truth of where we were and also the loss of that relationship.

I had asked for help from Dara's work colleagues when going with my family to clear out her locker and now it was time to ask for a different kind of help. I went to see a psychologist, to get that safe space to work through the overwhelming emotions I was feeling about my marriage and about Dara. Grief is not an illness and we don't need to pathologise it; many people will grieve perfectly well without professional support. Indeed, without the additional elements I was facing at the time, I expect that I might well have been able to handle my emotions. But I was dealing with the sudden death of Dara under traumatic circumstances and the end of my marriage on top of a re-emergence of feelings around motherhood that I had dealt with years before. It was just too much and I buckled under the weight and needed help to stand up again and that's okay in my book, it's human and it's understandable. A dentist doesn't pull their own teeth, after all; we all need help from others at times and going to see a psychologist was the best thing I could have done to help myself.

I had received professional support in an informal way from Dr Eddie Murphy in the days following Dara's death, and of course my family and friends had been a wonderful support as well, but it was now time for formal sessions, to work through what was going on in more depth. My first appointment with Clinical Psychologist and trauma specialist Mark Smyth was a month or so after Dara's death and I continued to attend for talk therapy regularly for about five months. I have remained in contact with Mark and I intend to return for another batch of sessions once the final reports into the crash are issued. I have had to hold so many emotions around that grief admin and I know even now that I need that safe space to freely express those feelings. This need will be even greater if there is media debate and discourse over the findings of the report, as happened with the interim reports.

It's an important thing to acknowledge that I asked for help, because so often people feel embarrassed or ashamed about asking for help. They are afraid of reaching out and saying that they need some support to be able to cope. They valiantly try to carry the burden alone, but that's not always the healthy or sensible thing to do. I think when it comes to the all-consuming feelings that surround loss, it is better to listen to our own true needs and to ask for help when needed. I certainly found that to be the case. When I texted Dara's colleagues for help in clearing her locker, that was the right thing to do. I made an honest request for help and advice that I felt I needed, and I got exactly the help and advice I required to get through that horrible task. There was no shame in reaching out like this. Similarly, when I asked for professional help, I see no shame in that. Instead, I see strength in understanding that the demands of this situation called for reinforcements. Even though I am a psychologist myself, I never expected to be able to deal with such significant and indeed traumatic loss on my own. Even now I can remember the feeling of relief when I read Mark's reply to my initial contact, offering me an appointment; the cavalry had arrived. A problem shared is a problem halved, as the saying goes, and it does lighten the load to express your thoughts and feelings aloud and let others respond and help you. This holds additionally true for therapy work with a skilled professional, where the person listening is qualified and experienced in their responses.

While I never asked for help at the ultimate end of the dream to be a mother, after our adoption process came to an end, I did seek professional help from a counsellor specialising in fertility matters when our IVF journey was moving towards the point of needing to make some decisions. Those talk therapy sessions were invaluable in providing a safe space for me to explore my limits with regard to assisted fertility, for there comes a point when you need to decide whether to go on to further types of treatment or stop altogether. Enmeshed in those decisions are immense feelings of fear, both of going on and of stopping. The work of my skilled counsellor helped me to work through those feelings until I knew what felt right for me personally on this journey. Similarly, when my marriage was in trouble and heading towards the possibility of ending, I attended for therapy sessions with a relationship therapist. The prevailing emotion at the potential loss of my marriage was anger. I was so furious that we had got ourselves here, to this endpoint, so those sessions were about working through those feelings until I could see and think more clearly. In each instance of loss, speaking about the feelings I was experiencing was of huge benefit, even those ugly and unpalatable emotions had a space where they could exist, from which I could start to process the loss. Especially in relation to these two losses, of motherhood and my marriage, I had thoughts and feelings that I would not have wanted to share with family or friends, but in the neutral space of the therapy room I was supported in bringing them from the dark corners of my mind out into the light, so that in time they no longer had a grip on me.

In April, we observed the traditional Catholic marker of the month's mind mass, held four weeks after Dara's funeral. We held a mass in the church where we had held the funeral and it was packed to capacity. I hadn't given much thought to this tradition before then, but once I experienced it, I realised that it's actually a very helpful thing to do. It reassures the family that their loved one is not forgotten and it allows the community to gather round once more, now that the full reality of the situation has sunk in and support is needed. For me personally, I drew solace from the fact that I had survived four weeks in this world without my sister. I wouldn't have thought that was possible, but I had done it. It made me feel that I could possibly survive this, that I did have it in me after all to keep going and, although it was a long way off at that point in time, to eventually, one day, find a way to live in peace.

The month's mind mass was lovely, allowing us to remember Dara and her three fellow crew members. We are a close family and that includes being very connected to cousins and aunts and uncles. It's a big gang, and they all turned out to be there for us and to remember Dara, whom they loved so much. There were also a large number of Dara's colleagues from the four search and rescue bases, who, along with our neighbours and friends, had returned once more to honour her and support us.

That evening, we all adjourned to Johnnie Fox's pub in Glencullen, which is right next to the church. We shared some stories and checked in with one other to see how everyone had been doing over the past month. Among those around my table were some of the rescue crews, one of whom was Winchman Conal McCarron, who had been on board Rescue 118 on the night of the crash. When alerted that there was a problem with Rescue 116, Conal and crew were in the final stage of their long-range medical evacuation and they immediately returned to the Blacksod Bay area and began to search the area around Black Rock Island. They located Dara in the water, and it was

Conal who was winched down on the end of the line to try and recover her. However, the weather and sea conditions were atrocious that night and Conal had been injured during the medical evacuation, so after several attempts, during which he got within an arm's length of Dara, they had to call in the RNLI's Achill Island lifeboat to recover Dara from the sea. One night soon after the crash, I had a long conversation on the phone with Conal, when he talked me through what had happened, not an easy thing for him to do, but he was kind and generous with his time. It was information from another important source and it filled the gaps in my imagination and let me know the facts, which is all that mattered.

I had never met Conal in person, so I was delighted to get to shake his hand the day of the month's mind and talk to him again. Also present that night were Captain Ciarán Ferguson, one of the two men who had stayed with Dara in the mortuary until we arrived to bring her home from Castlebar; and Captain Mark Donnelly and Engineer Eoin Murphy, the two men who had volunteered to deliver the awful news that the helicopter was missing to our family just one month earlier. It was a special group of people, to say the least. They are some of life's truly good people and my family and I owe them a debt. After all we had been through over the previous month, it was good for us all to be able to have that time together and chat in a relaxed setting, not talking about the crash but just chatting about ordinary things in life. It felt good. It felt normal. And it was needed, I think, for everyone's sake.

The first weeks after a loss of any kind are particularly difficult and tough to get through. Yes, the numbness does provide a buffer at first, but there is no avoiding the new reality that is your life with that loss. What I found was that surviving that time was a matter of fronting up to the truth and trying to accept it. Acceptance, to me, is letting go the hope of things being any different than they are, and that is terribly painful in the face of any loss. The pain is in the 'was': Dara *was* a lovely person; I *was* going to be a mother; my marriage *was* going to last. The waves of grief do come crashing down on your head in those first weeks, but there are ways to steady yourself and survive those waves.

Everyone is different and will have their own coping strategies, but for me it was all about feeling the feelings, speaking the feelings and forgiving myself for having the feelings. I had to do a lot of work to achieve that, but I was greatly helped by my family and friends and the support network provided by Dara's colleagues. I also sought professional help so that I could work through the grief as messily as I liked without worrying about burdening someone else. I didn't really know what I was doing at the time, it was like feeling about in the dark for a light switch, but I knew enough to trust my own instincts and follow what my head and heart were urging me to do. As a result, I was able to give thanks at Dara's month's mind mass – thanks that I had made it through, my family had made it through and Fionn had made it through. We had survived the first hurdle, and I was comforted by the idea that Dara would have been proud of us for that.

CHAPTER NINE

GRIEF IS PHYSICAL

While I would have expected to experience grief emotionally when it came to Dara's death, I was taken by surprise at the way it impacted me physically, at how my body responded to loss. Perhaps because bereavement grief, especially following sudden bereavement, hits in a unique way, I had no prior experience of the physicality of loss. It hadn't attended those earlier losses of infertility and marriage breakdown to the same level. In the moment when I realised that I would never be a mother and when it became apparent that my marriage was over, physically I just felt hollow, there was no other response from my body other than an infinite sense of emptiness in my chest. On reflection I can see that I did have a physical response to both losses over time, but in that moment of impact all I felt was hollow. My body responded very differently to the loss of my sister, however. Reflecting on bereavement grief, I think of it on two physical levels: how grief impacted my body at the moment when I heard that Dara was dead; and how I have experienced the physical impact of loss in the weeks, months and years since her death.

The first thing I experienced when I heard that Dara had died was a bodily response: my heart immediately felt heavy, my breath seemed to catch in my lungs, my stomach sank like a stone; it was a body blow, an actual physical impact, a visceral reaction. It seemed to me that I felt the emotional pain of loss in my physical body even before I had uttered a word or had a thought to express that pain. The physical experience of grief was instantaneous, a combination of fright, shock and grief.

Any death will bring a grief response, but a sudden death may also bring a shock response, where the body moves into the Fight, Flight or Freeze mode as the sympathetic nervous system is activated in the face of the traumatic news. Neither loss is greater than the other, it is simply that anticipated loss and sudden loss are different in nature and may therefore evoke different responses. Of course, each situation is unique and the individuals involved are unique, so someone hearing about the death of an elderly loved one who has lived with a terminal illness for a long time may still experience shock when the news finally comes and reality hits. But in the case of a sudden death, when there is no time to prepare, it is understandable that the body responds to such horrifying news in the same way that it responds to danger: a surge of adrenalin powering up our physiological and psychological systems, readying us to deal with threat. In the instance of traumatic loss, the threat is not to our physical but to our emotional survival. In those first seconds, both the fear and the enormity of the loss are overwhelming. We are staring into the deepest darkness of the abyss, and it is utterly terrifying. We experience physical symptoms in the wake of such fright: the heart pounds, respiration rate quickens, muscles tense, blood moves towards the bigger, more useful muscle groups like legs and away from the less vital extremities or the face, the skin can go cold, all of which are signs of hormones essentially screaming at every cell to wake up, rousing them to recognise the danger, assess the situation and take action.

In our situation, I suspect that the circumstances of Dara's death and the sense even then of the horror of her last moments added depth to the trauma and intensity to the shock. To know that your sister lived through such unspeakable terror as her life came to a close ... I almost have no words. Knowing that fact is the most frightening and horrifying feeling that I have ever experienced in my own life. Those initial physical feelings as my body registered Dara's death did not last long, perhaps minutes, but the sense of shock did last. It is worth noting that those suddenly bereaved find themselves dealing with shock first, before the other layers of grieving emerge. It is an added layer to deal with, if you like.

Also interesting to note is that this physical response to loss has remained to this day. Even now, as I type the words that Dara is dead, I can feel an empty feeling in my chest, as though I'm physically hollow. A bit like the Tin Man from the *Wizard of Oz*, if you tapped on my chest, I wouldn't be surprised if you heard an echo back. That hollow sensation feels as though someone has scooped out my heart with a spoon, roughly, leaving jagged edges on the wound. I don't know how it's possible to feel empty yet to feel pain in that empty space, but that's how it feels to me. I see these sensations as a physical manifestation of sadness, my heart literally feels different because of the sorrow. My experience is that the physical grief response brings changes that are distinctive. It feels as though my body tenses and braces every time I think, hear or read the words *Dara is dead*. My head knows that she is not coming back, but my heart contracts in pain again each time I hear it.

Within minutes of that initial physical reaction to the news that Dara had died it was as though I received a shot of anaesthetic into my arm because my body began to feel numb. After that huge physical shock, it was like I shut down and I could feel nothing physically. I can see now that I remained more or less like that for that first couple of weeks after her death. If someone had sliced a knife across my hand, I'm not sure that I would have felt it, if that makes sense. I had neither appetite nor thirst, I was exhausted but didn't feel impacted by the exhaustion, it was as if it was happening outside me. In all ways I didn't feel fully present physically, almost in that looking-from-the-outside-in-on-yourself perspective. My body was going about the daily tasks of living but somehow I couldn't actually feel anything. I would describe those first weeks as feeling neutral from a physical perspective. I was like a greyed-out version of myself, slightly anaesthetised, but functioning nonetheless.

As the weeks, months and indeed that first year went by, I began to experience a range of different physical symptoms that I now know to be characteristics of grief. For a long time I had problems sleeping and would find myself lying in bed at all hours of the night, eyes wide open, staring at the ceiling, my body showing no interest in sleep even though I was completely exhausted. Those first few weeks and months were a frantic mix of long days, travel to the far side of the country, meeting so many new people, trying to get to grips with new terms and understand new information, making decision after decision, as well as trying to somehow bring some sense of routine into our lives, especially for Fionn. I was also dealing with the end of my marriage, so it was a time of complete change and chaos in my life and I expect that this additional loss contributed to the problems with sleep.

Then there's the matter of the sadness element of grief, which is like the Dementors from *Harry Potter*, sucking the life out of you. It is *exhausting* feeling so sad all the time, so between that and the lack of sleep I found grief utterly, achingly, mind-numbingly exhausting. It wasn't at all helpful that sleep evaded me just when I needed it most. But in this instance, I knew what to do. I understood that if I let it get in on me that I wasn't getting quality sleep, I would simply be creating a long-term issue. My bed didn't need to be an anchor for distress, so when I found myself awake after only an hour or two of sleep, I used to listen to music or just lie there and tell myself that I would rest my eyelids, that I didn't need to worry about sleeping, I need only consider the concept of rest. I accepted that I had experienced an emotional shock and that the impact of the traumatic loss of Dara was immense and my body needed time to find its way in this new normal. Accordingly, I didn't add a layer of stress about it to the situation. I knew that in time, when I had processed things a bit more, sleep would probably come.

When I did manage to sleep, I sometimes had nightmares that would wake me up with a jolt. I hadn't had nightmares since I was a child, but they were a regular feature of those first few weeks after the crash. The days were so busy that I was fully occupied until darkness fell, then the world went quiet and provided both space and opportunity for my mind to run riot. I saw awful scenes in my head that I don't even want to repeat here. Perhaps it was an unconscious attempt to work through the horror of the facts that I was facing about Dara's death as I tried to come to terms with this unimaginable end to her life. When I began the psychology sessions with Mark Smyth, I found that talking about the circumstances of Dara's death and the loss of her life not yet lived, as well as speaking about her loss from my own life, contributed to the fact that the nightmares soon disappeared and, in time, normal sleep patterns returned. However, no matter how much sleep I got, the truth is that I never really felt rested in the first three years. I felt as though I was dragging myself around, like wading through mud or walking in waist-high water, things felt such an effort.

Exhaustion is a definite effect of grief and has been a constant companion in the past three years, with a level of fatigue that has been both immense and unprecedented. I found this was a factor in all three losses, in fact. When my dream of being a parent ended, I didn't connect the exhaustion I was feeling to grief. It wasn't as intense as the exhaustion that came with Dara's death, but it was there nonetheless. Similarly, when my marriage was in trouble and I began to countenance the possible loss of the relationship, I found myself feeling depleted no matter how much I slept. I can see now that in both instances my mind and body were trying to process the actual loss of infertility and the anticipated loss of my marriage, huge voids in my life requiring immense work to process, hence the exhaustion.

Since Dara died, I have known exhaustion at a whole other level. I'm talking here about bone-deep tiredness, the kind that makes you feel like you've been running uphill with weights on your legs, in savage heat, with no water or rest, there's just nothing left in the tank and you feel utterly emptied out. When you're feeling this type of tiredness everything feels slow and laboured, doing anything takes longer than usual and you have an aversion to being physically rushed, you need to be able to go at your own pace, at least that's how I felt. My theory on it is that there is such an amount of work to be done emotionally to process the loss that it takes all your energy, with little left for much more than everyday functioning, and sometimes not even enough left for that. This aspect was a dimension of loss that was surprising to me. Now, when someone I know loses a loved one, I know to support them but also to give them space. I tell them not to worry about replying to my texts or when we might meet because I know that most likely they are so exhausted that even just functioning is a challenge.

There is also a long-term aspect of the physicality of grief in that I have had a compromised immune system since Dara died, regularly experiencing colds, flu and chest and throat infections. I have been on more courses of antibiotics and steroids in the past three years than in the previous ten years. I just kept getting sick in that first winter after Dara died. However, because I was preparing a mortgage application to be able to buy my ex-husband out of our house and I'm self-employed, I had to keep going so I could show a good set of books to the bank. That wasn't ideal. I was relying on my meds to get me through, but what I really needed was a decent period of time off to fully rest and recharge and heal a bit. This is always the advice I give to friends who are experiencing bereavement and who ask for input. I recommend that, where possible, they reorganise their lives so that they can take care of themselves properly.

I kept going through that first winter and into the new year, and I went to Blacksod for the first anniversary of the crash. There was a vigil on 14 March, the date of the crash, and a ceremony on the helipad the following day, during which it rained constantly, that cold rain that trickles down your neck and makes you shiver. By the time I got back to the hotel after the ceremony I was exhausted, cold, wet, tired and emotional. Anniversaries can bring all the feelings of loss right back up in intensity and it was a tough couple of days. I had a hot shower, got dressed in dry clothes and that was the moment I've described before, when I checked my emails and received confirmation of the mortgage from the bank. Even though I felt like hell, this raised a small smile because I felt Dara Fitz was looking out for me.

Within twenty-four hours of getting that email I had a cold, and within days the cold had developed into a chest infection that wouldn't shift with medication. A couple of weeks later I was still very unwell and ended up at a doctor's surgery on a Saturday morning, after which I was swiftly sent to hospital with suspected pneumonia. I was indeed quite ill and was admitted to hospital right away and spent several days on a ward, with heavy medication and lots of monitoring. I don't think it's a coincidence that I became sick after securing that mortgage. It's as though my body had done what it needed to do in keeping me working until I was able to remain in my home, near Emer and Fionn, and once it was safe for me to stop and rest, the sickness ensured that I did stop as I had no choice in the matter.

I was off work for several weeks before I began to see clients again, and while I was never again as ill as I was when I was in hospital, over the next eighteen months I got regular chest infections and steroids and antibiotics were a constant in my life. It would be a long time before my body felt well again and in that space of time I had to cancel various pieces of work that I was scheduled to do because I wasn't well enough. That was understandable, but it really bothered me as I pride myself on being reliable and it goes against what I stand for to let people down. This was an impact of loss and grief that I definitely wouldn't have imagined.

On top of the issues with my immune system I also found myself dealing with a previously diagnosed endocrine issue from years earlier, as well as coping with the hormonal turbulence that comes with being a woman in her late forties. My poor body was a mess. At the end of my thirties I was in great shape, both from a health and a fitness perspective. I worked out with a trainer regularly and I loved to box, kick-box, run and strength train. Over the next few years we underwent fertility treatment and I never seemed to get my body back after that. I struggled with sleep issues and tiredness and with both blood sugar and energy levels. All of this took a toll, so by the time Dara died I was already depleted physically. Add grief into that mix and it's clear that in the time after she died and my marriage ended, physically I was dealing with an awful lot.

It's not like nature says, 'I know that you're dealing with grief, so I'll hold off on this hormonal stuff for a while.' And grief certainly doesn't say, 'I know that your body is out of balance hormonally, so I'll go easy on you with the grief for a while.' Not a chance. Both hit me at once and hit me hard, so while I was handling the emotional aspect of loss reasonably well, physically grief floored me. In fact, it is probably where it has had the most destructive impact. For example, one major effect of physical grief for me was losing my hair, which was shocking to me but apparently is not uncommon after trauma or loss. Over time I spoke to some of the other women impacted by the crash of Rescue 116 and when I told them about my hair falling out, they said that they had experienced the same thing. I hadn't encountered it before, so it came as a shock, and of all the physical effects of grief, it was the one that hit me hardest emotionally.

It started maybe nine or ten months after Dara's death. I was in a changing room trying on some clothes when in the bank of mirrors behind me I noticed a flash of pink scalp on my head. I put my hands to my head and I could feel a difference in the volume of hair. I had been noticing hair in the shower tray each morning, but with so much else going on it hadn't registered fully. I had also noticed that when I tied my hair up the bunch was becoming smaller in density, but again it didn't register. But when I saw and felt the sparseness of the hair on this day, my brain put it all together and I almost shrieked in fright when I realised that my hair was falling out. I remember saying to myself in the changing room, 'You might be a bit chubby, but being fat is one thing, fat and bald is *not* an option.'

I might have tried to have a sense of humour about it, but I was distraught at the idea of losing my hair. I don't think that it was a vanity thing, though. I wouldn't say that I'm an ugly duckling, but I've never been one of those women who is known for her looks. I was always the girl who was the friend of the hot chick rather than being the hot chick. Dara was one of those women who was a hot chick; when we walked into a bar, men's heads would turn as she moved across the room. She never even noticed it, but of course we used to tease her about it. And while all eyes were on her as she walked past, I was more the person who was the right height to lean on while ordering a pint at the bar! Anyway, my (slightly rambling) point is that while I do care about how I look, it has never been a selling point for me, so that wasn't what bothered me most about the idea of losing my hair. The real reason was that as my hair is red, like Dara's and my other sisters', it felt as though losing my hair was somehow letting go of another part of her. I have described how we can lose our hold on our loved one little by little, through the loss of small connections. This was one of those connections and there was no way I was going to lose it.

At home, I sent a panicked email to Dr Rosemary Coleman, an excellent dermatologist I had seen before. She contacted me immediately, asking for photos. My best pal, Tara, got the job of trying to take images of my scalp while I was mid-freakout. We sent off the photos and Dr Coleman agreed that I should come in to see her after the weekend. The fact that I had an appointment, a plan of action, let me relax a bit. Even the fact that she didn't tell me that I was imagining things was a help. I knew my body and I knew my hair and I knew it was different from how it normally was. I didn't let my mind go down the rabbit-hole, but I did wonder what I would do if she told me that my hair wasn't going to grow back and would keep falling out. I even played around with putting hats on, to check out my face shape without hair. I decided that I'd prefer to shave it all off and wear a scarf or hat, rather than having unsightly bald patches. The fact that I faced up to the worst-case scenario and created a Plan B, even though it was highly unlikely I would need it, made me feel better and able to cope.

I attended the appointment, and my quick action in seeking help was the best thing I could have done. After an examination,

Dr Coleman was immediately able to diagnose telogen effluvium and I left her office with a multi-pronged plan of action. Telogen effluvium is a form of hair loss that is usually temporary and can occur after a shock following a traumatic event. It's the body's way of saying that it needs to direct resources to what is needed to survive the traumatic event, and as having hair is not necessary for survival, the systems that support hair growth cease to function. Telogen effluvium can also occur when living with major stress or significant hormonal changes. Given that I ticked the boxes for all three of those, Dr Coleman referred me to see a doctor to look more closely at the hormonal situation and she also gave me advice and treatment from a dermatological perspective. The diagnosis and plan let my mind settle, which was vital given that stress was a big player in this condition. Thankfully, Dr Coleman had got me on to the right track in terms of the hormonal consult and the dermatological treatment plan and in time my hair started to grow back and stay put. I now have a full head of hair again, with no need for any extra help. I still look like Dara and my sisters, which is a comfort and a relief.

It is now three years since Dara died and I have finally found my way through the issues with my immune system and my body feels as though it has healed. I have even achieved a balance hormonally and for the first time in over a decade I feel on top of this side of things. I feel also that I have found my way through that initial exhaustion that comes with grief. I'm still very tired, but that's wholly understandable given all I've had to cope with and process, so I'm kind to myself about it.

There is one physical aspect that I haven't addressed fully yet, which is to get fit and lose the weight that I gained in the midst of grief. I'm aware that might sound like blame deflection, trying to point to grief rather than greed, but I'm currently a couple of dress sizes bigger than I would normally be and I know how I gained the weight and the factors that contributed to piling on the pounds. First, following the bout of pneumonia just after the first anniversary of Dara's death, I stopped moving. I was constantly sick and constantly exhausted and there was just nothing left in the tank to use for exercise. So for about eighteen months, apart from getting out for the odd walk, I wasn't moving to any great degree. I embarked on an exercise plan what feels like seven hundred times, but I was never able to sustain it. Every time I got a few weeks into a schedule I got sick again, with yet another chest or throat infection, and I had to stop exercising until I'd finished the latest batch of antibiotics and steroids and cleared my body of infection. It also felt as though I was having to do so much movement cognitively and emotionally to survive that I just wasn't able to move physically. I had run out of battery, having been worn out by the head and heart stuff with the cumulative grief for my sister and the conclusion of my marriage.

Second, to combat the fatigue I did what is probably the worst thing I could have done: I reached for sugar to prop me up. Sweet foods, sugary coffees, anything that resembled a simple carbohydrate and gave a short-term boost. Of course, those choices had long-term consequences. The combination of sugar in my diet, a lack of exercise and hormonal imbalance thrown into the mix for good measure was a perfect recipe for going up a couple of dress sizes. My body also appears to have produced a significant amount of cortisol over the past few years because when I did gain weight, I gained it around the middle, something I had never really done before. As the stress hormone cortisol is one of the contributors to weight gain in that area, it seems to have been a factor in my case. Understandable, but also interesting given the work I did around looking after my emotional state.

I'm a reasonably smart and very motivated person, but up to now I just haven't been able to tackle my fitness and get in shape again. The physical impact of grief is a bit like the app on your phone that drains the battery and leaves nothing left to make the phone call, that was me to a T. I just had nothing left to give, so the energy wasn't there to make the required change in terms of food and exercise.

Some people might look at my body and say that I should have known better, given my profession, and that being out of shape means that I didn't cope and wasn't in control as much as I could have been. Maybe they're right, there could be some truth in that. Being overweight and unfit certainly doesn't fit with being a psychologist who has a handle on life. But the way I see it, these have been extreme circumstances, the darkest times in my life, and they have taken me to my knees and nearly broken me, but I'm still here and whatever shape I'm in, I live to fight another day. While I should have known better than to let my physical body become unfit, I'm a human before I'm a psychologist and I dropped the ball. If I were to go back and do it all again, during those times of complete exhaustion after illness, I would tell myself that even a ten-minute walk outside in one direction and a ten-minute walk back would be great for both my head and my body. I would have kept my body moving, even in small ways, until I was well enough to move in more significant ways again. I would also have prioritised finding small ways to rest when I was exhausted, rather than reach for sugary foods to prop me up. But I let exhaustion dictate the pace and influence decisions and that was the wrong thing to do. I got it wrong and I ended up with a heavy body to match my heavy heart.

I have wondered, of course, if on some level I used food to fill the emptiness of loss. Was it a psychological prop? Was I trying to fill the space, the void left in me by such significant loss? I've given this some thought and have asked the hard questions of myself in that regard. On reflection, I really don't think that it was emotional eating that brought me to weight gain. It feels that I covered the emotional aspect of loss quite comprehensively, seeking out both professional and personal help to navigate the emotional rollercoaster of grief. I am glad to have looked into it as a possibility, but it doesn't feel that it was a factor in my case. The problem wasn't that physically minding myself wasn't at the bottom of the list; it never made it on to the list at all.

But there is another aspect to this as well, which is that when we are facing grief, we have to go easy on ourselves and not ask too much of our bodies or minds. I think that getting through the hard times isn't about being perfect, it really doesn't matter if it looks pretty or messy, what matters is that we keep going, picking ourselves up each time we fall. It's about being good enough, a concept that is under-valued, in my opinion. By this I mean that when we are grieving, we need to base our expectations on what is currently possible, not on what is normally possible. When life is anything but normal, we can't expect to think, feel and act as if everything were the same as before. It would be unrealistic to expect our best to be the same as it was before life-changing circumstances came to visit, and we need to take that into account and allow for it. I'm a great believer in self-compassion, especially after experiencing a loss. For me, one aspect of getting through the hardest times of loss is about getting the job done, day by day. It's about backing yourself and holding hope that one day you will feel human again. Allowing yourself to drop the ball and pick it up when you are able. No judgement. No criticism. Just kindness and learning.

It came as a shock to me that grief had a physical impact on my body. It was also a shock that this physical impact lasted for so long. I thought the physical bit would be about tears and tiredness, which was largely the impact from the fertility journey and the loss of my marriage. Those losses were more emotional, I think, more centred in my brain and heart. The bereavement grief was a different animal entirely, hijacking my body as well as my head and heart, holding them all hostage.

Physically, I feel as though I have been put through the wringer, bashed about and spat out the other end. At times, I felt it would never end, that I would never own my body again or feel happy in it because the imprint of traumatic and cumulative loss was imprinted so deeply on my physical self. But thankfully, time does bring change. I hung in there, refusing to let my mind go into hyper-stress over what was happening, and now I can say that I feel that I have turned a corner in this regard.

It's been a long time coming and I'm not fully there yet, but I'm so grateful to feel like I'm heading towards that feeling of being back in my own skin again. I enjoy reasonably good health now and am no longer floored by constant infections; my hair is healthy and shiny; my energy levels are good; I sleep soundly and wake rested; the physical journey will be complete once I have shed the excess weight, which is an ongoing project. Key for me in navigating the physical impact of grief was working on keeping my stress levels down, which is really important in that grief state. It can be hard to focus on such things, and indeed it can be hard to give attention to yourself. I managed to do this emotionally but failed at it physically, so it's worth making a big effort to learn from my mistakes and do the things that I got wrong: to get out for walks, to breathe deeply, to prepare good food that will nourish my body. Nourishment. That's an essential concept when we are suffering the physical effects and the emptiness of grief. It's a time for a bit of self-love, a lot of self-understanding and a bucket-load of self-patience.

CHAPTER TEN

GRIEF IS COGNITIVE

t probably seems obvious that loss and grief have a mental impact and effect, but it can still come as a shock to realise the extent of those effects. If we don't allow for this aspect, we can expect too much of ourselves and castigate ourselves for not being 'better', for not being 'normal'. The truth is, we aren't normal during these times, we aren't our best selves and there's no point piling on the pressure by asking ourselves to achieve that. Our brains are affected by loss and grief, including our decision-making skills, our self-awareness and our ability to think with perspective. These effects will differ depending on the loss and the circumstances of the loss, but they are real and it's important to be aware of them and make allowances for them.

I found that I was relatively unscathed mentally while I was going through the initial fertility testing and investigations, it felt like I took it all in my stride and got on with it without too much cognitive impact. However, investigations complete, the understanding that I did need to undergo assisted fertility took a while to mentally come in to land. Throughout the exploratory operations and tests, I think I must have unconsciously assumed that it would all work out fine because being told that in fact IVF was recommended almost took me by surprise. Living in that world of assisted fertility brings a preoccupation with all things pregnancy- and baby-related and your previously balanced mind is taken over with thoughts of the world of parenthood. I found that I was hyper-aware of the bumps and the buggies, with other aspects of life fading into the background of my consciousness at that time. Then, before we started the first IVF cycle, I had to get my head wrapped around the idea of injecting myself and of keeping to a strict schedule of appointments for scans, blood tests and medication. It was a sizeable cognitive load.

During each cycle of treatment I used my mind to help me handle my emotions as the cocktail of drugs played havoc with my mood, as my hormonal system was being shut down and ramped up again. Whenever I felt a powerful surge of irritability, I used to say to myself on repeat, *'It's not me, it's the drugs.'* This small strategy let me step away from the feelings a bit by acknowledging that whatever was annoying me was not really annoying me, it was a function of my pharmacological state rather than my psychological state. This meant that the medications did not have the psychological or behavioural impact they might otherwise have had. It was an effective plan, because people who only heard afterwards that I had been taking those injections and medications observed that they would never have known that this was the case as my moods remained stable throughout. That was no mean feat because there was something about those particular medications that felt like they brought a lifetime's supply of irrationality and rage to my door over the course of a few weeks.

When the first cycle of fertility treatment failed, I found my mind moving towards 'what if?' thoughts: *'What if it doesn't work?'*; *'What if it never works?'* I knew from my psychology studies not to let myself dwell on such thoughts, so I would simply observe them, notice them, sit with them and let them be. Then I would take a breath and remind myself to come back to the present and deal with what was in front of me.

When the time came and it was confirmed that fertility treatment had not worked, I think that having the adoption route still to be explored provided some sort of emotional safety net to a degree, although it brought other challenges mentally. Adoption is something that I would have always considered doing, but when you find yourself going through an adoption process there is a lot to think about and absorb. The rigorous nature of the assessment forces you to think really hard about parenthood and demands that you are sure that this is for you; probing, checking, assessing your readiness for this most important job. When you have gone through assisted fertility, that readiness has already been tested. You simply would not endure all you have to endure on that route if you were not wholly sure that you wanted to be a parent. Although it is understandable and necessary to have those checks as part of the adoption process, it was tough to revisit that cognitive space again. I found the adoption process enjoyable nonetheless, but it certainly took up almost all the space in my head while we were doing it.

I can see now that it was when the adoption journey ended that the full force of grief for lost motherhood came crashing down on me. That is not to say that adoption was in any way a fallback option, because it had long been a choice that attracted me, but when that journey ended in a cul de sac, I was sad for us both for not being parents. I was sad for me for not being a mother. I was sad for the children we might have raised and nurtured to adulthood. I did not identify it as grief at the time, as I have said, but that's what it was nonetheless. It was during this time that I had more work to do cognitively, as I began to dismantle my concept of my future, re-routing and re-imagining life not being a mother. I had to ensure that I saw myself as multi-faceted, not simply as someone who was supposed to procreate. I had to consciously give value to other roles in life besides motherhood. I had to be mindful to look for the joy in places other than mothering. I had to begin to think about having a relationship with both those adults and children in my life that I had avoided during the journey towards parenthood. As mentioned before, I did not think to go back to the counsellor I had attended during the IVF, so I did this work by myself, and it's safe to say that, without the benefit of objective perspective and reflections, I made quite a long journey out of that. Having a trained, objective eye to help me work through my thoughts and feelings on this loss would have brought me to a place of acceptance of the loss and vision for my new life sooner, I think.

Looking at the loss of my marriage, the cognitive impact of that was also significant. When the marriage was floundering, rather like when we were going through the fertility journey, it was all I could think about. It was my first thought in the morning and my last thought at night. *'What if we cannot make this work?'* I used the relationship therapy sessions to express and explore my thoughts, and that helped hugely to clear space in my head. When the marriage did eventually end, it was at the same time that Dara died, so my sessions with psychologist Mark Smyth provided space to continue that exploration. Nonetheless, the end of my marriage and our failure to preserve what had been a really lovely relationship occupied so much of my head, vying for attention beside Dara's death and the aftermath of that loss. The admin around becoming legally separated, buying the house and so on, all served to keep the loss of my marriage in a central space in my mind. It was only when the admin was completed and we could each start our new lives as single people, amicable but apart, that I noticed it starting to take up less space in my mind.

As with the physical impact, I think bereavement grief brought the greatest cognitive changes as my mind registered the effects of the shock, trauma and loss. The first impact I noticed was a difference in my ability to concentrate. I would tend to be well able to focus, I can stay in the present moment and I would be sharp enough to pick up on things going on around me fairly easily. I work with athletes on the area of concentration, helping them train to be in that zone where they are fully focused on the game and on the task at hand, so I'm well aware of how to maintain concentration. Despite all that, a few weeks after Dara died I noticed that there were times when I was unable to concentrate. I was absent-minded, forgetful, easily distracted and I missed things that I would normally pick up on. I would put something in the fridge that should have gone in the oven or vice versa. Or I would boil the kettle and put the teabag into the pot but forget to put the boiled water into the teapot. Or in a social conversation I had to ask someone to tell me again something that I knew they had just spoken about. I just wasn't mentally present or sharp. I'd be doing one job and then find myself on a whole different train of thought doing another job. I might begin to put the bins out and halfway through I'd start taking something out of the freezer for dinner, forgetting to finish doing the bins until I noticed them tied up by the back door. I would put something somewhere safe and forget where the safe place was. I'd inadvertently throw out a piece of paper with information on it that I needed and then have to root through the bin to fish it out. This definitely wasn't how I was before, so I became aware of this change in my mental processes pretty much immediately.

I wasn't worried about this change in my capacity to focus, because I knew it was the result of shock, trauma and loss. I just put it down to grief and didn't even try to force myself to concentrate. I went with the flow and trusted that I would be back to myself mentally when I was ready. I understood that my mind was trying to process a significant amount in terms of the scale of the loss, and also in terms of the massive volume of information that we were having to take on board at that time. As the point of contact for my family with the Gardaí in Dublin and Mayo, as well as with the Air Accident Investigation Unit, I was receiving details of the investigation that involved many new terms, references and concepts to be absorbed. Mentally, that was challenging, especially to a brain that was already reeling from the impact of grief. So the way I interpreted my lower levels of concentration and attention was that my brain was overloaded, so it was understandable that I wouldn't be myself on occasion.

Similarly, I found that I kept forgetting things and small tasks slipped from my mind, only to be caught wanting at a later date. Again, I decided to see this as a natural effect of the grief and I gave myself a break in that regard. It was helpful that I was having therapy sessions with psychologist Mark Smyth at that time. I remember he made an insightful observation one day when we were talking about not getting lost in all the information that was coming at me. He said: 'All those details are important, but don't forget to give time to the most important detail, which is that Dara is not coming back.' He was correct; that was really the only detail that I had to remember. Emotionally, it was vital that my mind grasped that truth and that I didn't allow all the other details to keep me from processing and remembering this. If I forgot to do small daily tasks, it didn't really matter. I knew that I was remembering the one thing that I needed to remember at that time.

In that first year I also noticed that I wasn't great at making decisions and when I was asked to give input into a decision it sometimes felt like overloading a plug socket. I know that it was a time when there were lots of decisions coming at us, but even when the volume is high I would normally be sharper and more capable of assessing something and making a call on it. But it's as though grief takes up all the space on your hard-drive and there's no memory left for new data to be saved, so your mind just doesn't have the capacity to do much thinking, planning or deciding. Even those small, non-urgent life admin tasks get pushed onto the long finger as you find you can't make a decision on whether to shred, file or reply. So when anyone asks about supporting someone through grief, I always suggest to avoid giving someone who is recently bereaved a lot of decisions to make because more often than not they just aren't ready to make them and so it will only add to their stress. It's also for this reason of diminished cognitive capacity in those early times of grief that it is advisable not to make any big decisions. When we are grieving we are capable of working well and of living well, but sometimes we just aren't in a place where we can widen out the lens and take in all the information necessary to make a fully informed decision about something big. We can also be in that 'live only for today' mindset when initially bereaved, so making a decision about something that will affect us in the long term is not a good idea until that settles down a bit and balance is achieved. In my own situation, some people queried the end of my marriage coming so soon after Dara's death, but the reality is that the decision had already been pretty much made by both of us. Losing Dara simply brought clarity into our lives and made it apparent that it was the right decision. My experience is that this sense of being overloaded and unable to commit to things or to make decisions lasted about two and a half years. I really feel as though I'm only coming out of this now, and I'm tackling the extra emails and piles of paper that need my attention.

I also noticed the cognitive impact of grief when it came to reading. I'm an avid reader, both personally and professionally. It might be cheesily predictable for a psychologist, but my bedtime and holiday reads tend to be mostly psychological thrillers. On a two-week holiday I read a lot of books, getting lost in the pages of a novel for a few hours each day, so that I've been known to have read ten books by the time I get home. From a professional perspective, I buy psychology books like others buy shoes and each week I sit on the floor in my attic, where I keep all my psych books, and I dip in and out of a few texts, keeping up to date with what's going on in my profession. Books of all kinds are a big part of my life. However, in that first year after Dara died I found that I could push myself to read my psychology texts and extract learnings from them, but when it came to fiction I simply could not take in more than a few words on a page before my mind zoned out. I had no interest in reading in the first few months. The days were busy and full and by the end of each one I would just get into bed and want to lie there quietly. I had lost my desire to pick up a book.

I missed reading. I missed the smell of new books after a haul at one of my local bookshops. I missed the feel of a shiny new novel in my hands. I missed the quiet companionship of a good book. I missed losing myself in the story, turning the pages with eagerness to find out whether the fictional killer would be caught before they killed again. I missed the mental recharge that reading a novel delivers, that sense of having had a cognitive rest, like a spa break for my mind. When we grieve, our brain is trying to process and come to terms with *such* an incredible amount of data: it's trying to deal with the trauma of loss, as well as the facts of the loss, the emotions around the loss, and the new life as a consequence of loss. I suspect that being unable to read my beloved books of fiction was down to that sense of being overloaded by life at that time, as my mind worked hard to process everything. I also wonder if there is something about not having an interest in other worlds when your own world is in such emotional chaos? Perhaps while my own cognitive, emotional, physical, behavioural and social worlds were going through such flux and change, the other worlds that I might encounter in a work of fiction simply held no interest for me?

It took a long time for this to change. One day I happened across a book by an Irish writer and something about it caught my eye, so I sat down to read and found that the characters grabbed my attention and I wanted to find out what happened to them. I kept reading, and almost a year after Dara's death I managed to finish a novel. It was a real comfort to want to and to be able to read again. I wouldn't say that I have returned to even near my previous capacity, but I now have the desire and the capability to read again and that feels good. I think that in among all we lose when someone we love dies, we also lose ourselves, and feeling the urge to read again felt like I was finding a part of me again.

Even when it came to writing this book, the cognitive impact of grief put in an appearance on occasion and I found myself at times staring at a blank screen, paralysed by sorrow and unable to put any shape to my thoughts. I felt this particularly badly around the second anniversary of Dara's death. It was as though cognitively I was switched off and I was just a bundle of sadness, nothing more than a shell consumed by emotion. Week after week I sat down to write but nothing was coming out, like a tap with no water in the pipes. I tried writing different chapters or just writing down some of the facts and not trying to describe anything. I stayed relaxed about it and patient with both the process and with myself. Then one day I had a client who said they were struggling to cope with what was going on in their life and one of the things that I wondered aloud as a conversation opener with them was whether it was that they couldn't cope, or if it was that they just had too much to cope with at that time. When we wrestle with handling life's challenges, sometimes we can be very quick to jump into that place of blaming ourselves for the stumbles. But in the context of a healthy mental perspective, it's shortsighted to assume that when we struggle, it is because we are less than we should be, that we are flawed and to blame. Sometimes the struggle comes from the plain fact that life is asking too much of us. Rather than underestimating the demands placed upon us and automatically assuming that we must cope, it is useful to stop, take a breath, and assess whether the demands are reasonable. There are times when we do have to simply dig deep and work our way through what is asked of us, but there are other times when we need to jettison some of the demands because there are too many. Sometimes the best course of action is to make allowances for the situation we find ourselves in and give ourselves a break. After that particular session, each time I sat down to write, those words I had uttered to my client came to my mind again and again and I realised that the concept applied to me as much as it did to my client.

I felt as though I had a lot to cope with at that time and while I was coping emotionally, I had no space left for writing because coping was taking up all I had. I felt like I was back in surviving mode. That wasn't a bad thing. It was just a fact. My brain was consistently silent when I sat down to write because it was too busy just trying to get by. As the anniversary date approached, all I was thinking was, 'This time two years ago she was here, Dara was with us, she was walking and talking and living.' Like a movie show reel, my mind replayed the images of the last few weeks and months of our lives together and that was what occupied my head when I wasn't working. As I had done before, I reached out for help and spoke about this problem. I explained the situation to my editor, who told me to put the book down and take as much time as I needed and that when I was ready to start writing again, that was time enough. The sense of relief when I got that response was enormous. I stepped away and let myself feel what I felt without any judgement, and sure enough in time the desire and capacity to write came back. I just had to let it come when it was ready.

Although writing this book has been unbelievably tough cognitively, emotionally, even physically (sixteen chapters is a *lot* of writing hours when you are wading through grief and moving as slowly as I am), it has also been unbelievably cathartic. Many times I was asked if writing was keeping me in the throes of grief. In fact, it has been quite the opposite. Writing this book and reflecting on my experiences of grief and loss, holding a magnifying glass up to my thoughts, feelings, physical experiences and behaviours and noting the learnings along the way has been freeing and healing. Whilst it represents one more of those 'most difficult things I have ever done', it has also undoubtedly been one of the best. I would highly recommend writing or journaling to anyone who feels that it could possibly help after loss.

What was interesting was that, having said all of the above, the one area where I noticed no negative impact of grief from a cognitive perspective was in my therapy work. Bizarrely, I would almost say that I have been cognitively sharper than I had ever been before in this environment. I am usually pretty sharp, but on return to work I felt laser-focused. When I had a client sitting in front of me, I was able to tune into them, to focus on them fully, I could remember details from previous sessions without any bother and I could keep my train of thought without difficulty. I'm aware that this sounds odd and contradictory, but I think that I gathered up all my capacity to engage mentally and brought it to my work, but outside of that I reverted to what my overall capability was at that time, which was near to zero. I can't really explain it, but again I think it's that thing of sometimes needing to just step up and do what life asks of us. It forces us to reach into the reserve tanks and to find an extra hidden reserve tank way at the back. We can usually do more than we think we can.

CHAPTER ELEVEN

GRIEF IS EMOTIONAL

Humans are emotional beings. By this I mean that we are capable of both conscious and unconscious states of feeling. Encompassing a wide range and influenced by what is going on both around us and within us, we experience basic emotions from anger, to joy, to disgust, or sadness and beyond, as well as higher-level emotions such as empathy, embarrassment and pride. Our emotions are linked to our brains and our bodies and are experienced across both, which means there is a tangible element to emotions that we don't often think about when we use the word. When we feel the first waves of romantic love, for example, we feel it in the flutter of our heart or the flush of our cheeks at the mention of our beloved's name. Going out onto the sports field to play, we may experience confidence in the lengthening of our spine as we stand up tall and draw our shoulders back, ready for battle. Any emotional states we are experiencing engage both our bodies and our minds, making themselves felt in both.

Emotions and their accompanying mental and physical effects also signal when something is wrong and requires our attention. I've said that I see them as being like the lights on the dashboard of a car: they alert us to something that we need to turn towards and look at more closely. Although some emotions may be less pleasant and less palatable than others, they are all part of our intricate system of communication and, as such, are all welcome, in my opinion. What we need to watch for when it comes to our emotions is that we do turn towards them, with support if we need it and when we are ready. It is important that we do not ignore the flashing orange light, afraid to see what it means, and by doing so leave ourselves vulnerable to orange turning to red and the car grinding to a halt.

I have known many 'big' emotional states throughout the years. Love: for people in my life, for passions that I hold dear, for experiences that I have been privileged to have over my five decades on Earth. Fear: when I encountered bullies in my younger days and change in my latter years. Pride: for work well done and for playing my part and doing what life asked of me. The feelings I experienced during the loss of motherhood and the end of my marriage were also big feelings. Disbelief. Fear. Confusion. Anger. Sadness. Loneliness. These feelings were strong, powerful, overwhelming, all-consuming. And yet none of them could have prepared me for the emotions I felt when I was suddenly bereaved by Dara's untimely death; that felt different altogether. It was like every emotion I have ever felt in my life multiplied and experienced at the same time.

My own theory is that when it came to the loss of hope around having a family and the loss of my marriage, I had warnings of some sort, the tiny buds of realisation that grew slowly over time. Such as when I sat in the GP's surgery and had the chat about fertility. When I sat in the consultant's office and had the discussion about an exploratory operation. When I sat in the fertility clinic and had the conversation about assisted treatment options. When I sat in the classroom with other couples and individuals and we discussed the particular needs of an adopted child. Each time I sat in one of those chairs, even though I always remained hopeful, I can see now that some small part of my mind began to consider the possibility of this loss. In this way I was introduced to it slowly, piece by piece. It was the same with the end of my marriage. Mine was not one of those cases where one spouse just ups and leaves one day, leaving the other one behind in a daze of confusion and hurt. The dawning realisation that our relationship was not working happened over time, and as with the loss of motherhood I was introduced to the possibility of the loss of my marriage slowly, piece by piece.

When Dara died, having been lulled into a sense of comfort and security about her job because she had been safely flying search and rescue missions for twenty-three years, news of the crash came without warning of any kind. It was like an emotional equivalent of the civilian recruits on RTÉ's television programme *Special Forces: Ultimate Hell Week*. The recruits are removed from their beds in the dead of night, blindfolded by a cloth bag placed over their head, hands tied behind their back, marched across a freezing cold yard to a second location. Blindfold ripped off their head, they sit dazed and disoriented, eyes blinking in the brightness of the overhead lights in the darkness of the room. Across the table sit two former members of the Army Ranger Wing, ready to interrogate them while they are vulnerable, having been woken from sleep and dragged from their beds without warning or explanation. It sounds so dramatic to equate our experience with something like this, but that is honestly what it felt like that morning when I was woken by that pre-dawn phone call. The circumstances and suddenness of Dara's death were so shocking, so unbelievable, so unlike anything I had ever experienced before in my life that it added layers to the loss and the emotional response. Whereas the loss of motherhood and the loss of marriage were the end of hopes and dreams, there was life still, a different life but life nonetheless. But Dara's death was the ultimate end. The end of her life. The end of the life she was supposed to have with her son and her family and friends. The end of our family life as we knew it. The end of Dara in my life as a sister and a friend. Her death felt so final, and I think that contributed to having a different emotional response to her loss than I had to the other two losses.

My immediate emotional reaction after hearing that Dara had died was shock and, as I've described before, rather than the huge wave of sadness that I would have expected to feel, I felt numb, empty, hollow. This was a mirror of what I was feeling physically: I felt nothing. My emotional brain went into shut-down. I was in a state of emotional shock. All I seemed capable of was thinking the same thought over and over and over again: 'How in God's name are we going to live without Dara?' I wasn't yet able to feel emotions about something that was entirely unbelievable. I felt almost disoriented by the feelings that coursed through me and nothing could have prepared me for the range and intensity of those emotions, nor indeed for how much they would change over the weeks, months and years that followed. Grief is emotionally exhausting for many reasons, not least of which is that I found I could go from sitting, staring at a wall, to sobbing, to wanting to slam a door off its hinges all in the same day. It was like going from being Eeyore to the Incredible Hulk within a twelve-hour period. The Irish have a lovely phrase that's said gently of anyone who's suffering emotionally – 'She's not herself at all'. That's how it felt, that I wasn't myself any more, that I had become separated from me, like watching myself in a film. It was a dislocated and disturbing feeling.

The day before we got that news, the night before, the hours before that 6.00 am knock at the door, life had been normal, we were all going about our business, living our lives. We'd had a brilliant Christmas, all together as a family, everyone moving into my parents' house over the festive season where we had lovely long chats over breakfast and long, cold walks together. We even had turkey sandwich-making competitions to see who could come up with the best combinations, with big discussions about whether to toast or not to toast! At that time we were also really looking forward to my brother's wedding, which was coming up in June. It was just normal life. Then that life disappeared in an instant. The landscape as we knew it changed and we became different people because part of you dies when the person you love dies, you're no longer whole, there's a bit of you missing. At least, that's how I feel.

In the initial couple of weeks after Dara died the main feeling was confusion and a sense of bewilderment. Each morning, there would be a second or two when I woke up before my mind would remember that she was gone. And then it would hit, the realisation that this was not a nightmare, that this was reality and that Dara was gone and not coming back. The confusion in those moments was terrible. It really messed with my head to have to have that, 'Oh God, it's real' moment each day over and again until it sank in. Over time, though, the more I processed what had happened, those bewildering and confusing moments left me and became a thing of the past.

One thing that I discovered through this was that while I experienced a wide range of emotions related to grief and I can see that there is a process or evolution of some sort in there, grief has not in any way been about stages. I know this is a popular idea, a myth that I addressed at the start of the book, and perhaps it comforts some people to think of it as a linear progression through stages they can tick off, but it wasn't remotely like that in my experience. For me, grief feels more jumbled, not clean-cut or neat in any way, but more of a lurching messily from one emotional state to another and back again, repeatedly, often without warning. I found that it is about being okay with forwards and backwards. Being able to accept that you feel some version of okay one day, but not expecting that to be an indication of how you will continue to feel from now on. You may. You may not. Either way, it's normal. You aren't 'losing your mind' or 'doing badly' at grief if you feel slammed down by a wave of grief one day, having smiled the day before. It's about not thinking that you've got a handle on grief today and expecting that to automatically slide over into the next day. I found that grief plays by its own rules and may well make up the rules as it goes along. In fact, there may even be no rules at all. Grief is an animal all in its own category, so allow for your experience to be to-and-fro, up-and-down, confusing, bewildering, lurching, oscillating. I think that is entirely okay given that you have lost from your life someone you love and, in that loss, you have also lost the life that you were living and the life that you had planned to live. Expect chaos.

As time went on and I developed my ability to carry the loss, I found myself feeling slightly altered emotionally. Perhaps a bit like finding that I can walk 10 km in a faster time after a block of consistent training, I think that learning to carry loss happens in stealth mode. All of a sudden, I realised one day recently that I felt stronger in carrying my grief, and that's when I felt more stable emotionally. When I was a child, my grandparents had a cuckoo clock and when we stayed with them that cuckoo clock woke me up every hour on the hour, night after night. Then one night I slept through, habituated to the sound. I think that grief is kind of like that. When faced with it every hour of every day, we get used to the pain of loss and we learn to live again, alongside the pain.

It's perfectly okay that this processing of grief and developing acceptance takes time – perhaps a very long time. I had to let myself have that time, without judgement or impatience. Losing a sibling is hard. At the time she died, Dara had been my sister for forty-five years and aside from my twin and my parents, she's the person I've known the longest in my life. We share our DNA, our childhood and our history and as adults we also shared our lives. Then all of a sudden, she was gone, decades of being sisters wiped out in a heartbeat, this person who is woven into the fabric of my life since childhood taken from my life overnight. That is traumatic loss. And there isn't even a term for losing a sibling, which given the magnitude of that loss seems strange to me – all these overwhelming emotions and no word to describe someone who has lost someone who shared their life from childhood. That's why it felt like I lost a bit of myself the day Dara died. I am beginning to feel like a person again now and I do know that I will be okay, but I haven't felt completely whole since Dara died and I honestly am not sure that I ever will.

When the news was released that Rescue 116 had crashed and the crew lost, naturally the media covered the story extensively, the shock of the nation mirrored across news bulletins throughout the day. I was already known to people behind the scenes in radio because I had a weekly segment on Neil Delamere's show on Today FM, *Neil's Sunday Best*, so I was contacted on the evening of the day Dara died by journalists asking if my family would like the opportunity to tell people what Dara was like as a person. We were still in shock and weren't thinking straight, and by that I mean that we didn't really give it the lengthy consideration that we might have done under other circumstances. We knew, though, that we wanted to take that opportunity to talk about Dara, so we agreed to the requests. Between my parents and myself, we did two radio and one television interview on the morning after Dara died. In each of the interviews, while my voice was emotional and sometimes broken, I was able to focus on what I was asked and to speak coherently and lovingly about my sister.

In the coming weeks, when speaking about the first radio interview, two people commented separately to me that they were surprised that I could be so 'clinical' in that moment, so soon after learning of Dara's death. I don't look for criticism or for places to find offence, but there was perhaps a sense of judgement in that comment, a sense of wondering why I was not grieving 'properly'. Could I be wrong about that? Of course, but I sense that I am not. It was the way it was said and the use of the word 'clinical'. I can fully understand why someone would wonder why I wasn't sobbing and unable to speak during those interviews that morning, so I don't take it personally. I have spent a lot of the past three years sobbing and unable to speak, but on that particular day, less than twenty-four hours after I had been told that Dara was dead, having driven the whole way across the country to see my sister laid out in a mortuary and stayed up all night with her so that she was not alone, I was dazed, I was exhausted, caught up in a life that I didn't even believe was real. I was also fully aware that I had one chance to speak to those journalists about Dara and that I needed to get it right and do justice both to her and to my family, so I got myself together and I got the job done. There is no 'proper' way to be when a loved one dies, and there was a whole host of things going on that day that the people who made the comments didn't know about. So when we see someone after the death of their loved one, it's kind to take a step back and observe without judgement, appreciating that some things in life are just not as black and white as we might imagine.

The reason I was able to do those interviews so soon after receiving the news of Dara's death was largely down to shock. As I said, I was in an emotionally and physically zero state – utter nothingness. There was also probably a bit of my professional training kicking in. I think the years spent working as a psychologist in high-pressure situations such as at the Olympic Games or All Ireland Finals and the years working on radio stood to me and helped me to remain composed and able to think on my feet. But really, shock was the main state I was in that morning and that's why I was able to do it.

There was probably another factor, too. The country was hearing about a pilot, a rescue services crew member, an employee of the Irish Coast Guard. But we had lost a person. A person who was in the middle of our world, whose presence was felt in our everyday lives. Dara was a mother, daughter, sister, cousin, friend and sister-in-law. So when we were asked by the media if we would like to talk about what kind of person she was, we took that opportunity with gratitude. It was a chance to talk about Dara the person, as opposed to Dara the pilot. It was surreal, though. That day after she died, I found myself standing outside the mortuary at Mayo University Hospital, with Dara lying in a coffin on the other side of the wall, while I spoke to RTÉ radio. Afterwards, my parents and I talked to RTÉ television and finally I spoke to Today FM, the radio station where I was a contributor. I was told later that the interviews were well received, but I have no recollection of them. I can remember things from over forty-five years ago, but I cannot remember these interviews from three years ago. I do remember vividly the kindness of all three interviewers, the gentleness with which they asked the questions they needed to ask. And I remember that while they were professional throughout, I also had a sense that this tragedy had impacted them on a personal level. But still, those interviews remain a blank in my head. I literally have no recollection of them and cannot remember what I said. They are all a blur, like someone else did them, not me.

For the next few weeks I swung between that emotional state of shocked numbness and full-on breakdowns where I cried as I have never cried before, with sounds coming out of me that I didn't recognise. On some occasions I had to be physically held up by friends or family during some of these moments, such was the overwhelming and overpowering nature of the sadness. I found myself halted mid-sentence by a wave of sadness and I would just burst into tears, unable to stop weeping, unable to do anything but let the wave wash over me and cry it out. I know for some people, this would be horrible and perhaps embarrassing, but I'm okay with it, I was then and I am now. Emotions are part of being human and we need to feel them when they come. Indeed, a breakdown can sometimes be a breakthrough. I found this to be true because each of those huge waves of grief brought me further along in the process, like a tide moving towards shore. Those tears came from a place of pure pain, a raw, howling acceptance that Dara wasn't coming back. That acceptance is very painful, but it isn't a bad thing. It is only once we accept the truth that we can begin to deal with it.

We can be very hard on ourselves to grieve privately and hide the emotions we're trying to deal with, and it can also be the case that other people are hard on us – whether consciously or unconsciously – if they feel our grief is 'too much'. We can carry notions of grief that we don't even realise until we're in the thick of it. If we deviate from those notions in our feelings and behaviours, it may cause us to feel negatively towards ourselves. This isn't helpful. Grief is individual to us all. We each have to let our grief be what it is, without apology or embarrassment or shame. I saw a water safety campaign once with the message that drowning doesn't always look like drowning. It was warning against ignoring a person in the water just because they weren't shouting or waving. Drowning doesn't always happen in the way we might picture it, or the way it's shown in films. When Dara died, I soon learned that grief doesn't always look like grief. It might not show up as sadness, it can visit us as anger, hopelessness, frustration, bewilderment, confusion or loneliness. There is no single grief state. It's a kaleidoscopic collision of many different emotions and there's no predicting how it will take shape. All we can do is keep going, keep feeling, keep trying, without grabbing at it, to reach acceptance.

Some emotions were prevalent in the early days after Dara's death and then disappeared, others put in an appearance now and then, while others remain to this day. As grief has so many parts to it, it's understandable that it fluctuates continuously. The anger part of grief made an appearance early on, but my psychology training taught me the importance of expressing anger but not getting stuck in it, because it could consume me. I tended to lean into the feeling when it came, but then take a breath and ask myself if it was useful to remain focused on the things that were driving the sense of anger. And when I use the word 'anger', you can also read rage and fury, by the way. I experienced anger on the full range of the spectrum, which was a first for me in my life.

The anger came from a few aspects of Dara's death, the first being the sense of waste. Dara should have died when she was ninety-eight, in a warm bed, with her family around her, when she had done all the living that she wanted to do. Instead, she died alone in the Atlantic Ocean, midway through her life. It is such an awful waste of such a good life. It feels so unjust and is especially hard to take when there are so many people who commit crimes and live terrible lives, terrorising others, yet they get to live on. Dara lived her personal life with kindness and she chose a profession in which she helped others. She loved the flying aspect of the search and rescue work, but she also loved helping people, bringing people home. Most times, thankfully, that meant bringing them home alive, but sometimes her job meant recovering a body and bringing them home to a family to bury. She certainly met a lot of sadness in her work, but even in that sadness there was a knowledge that they were helping people and Dara loved that aspect of her job. So the fact that she would get out of her bed in the dark of night and go with her colleagues to the aid of someone who needed help and that they would then not come home themselves is so unjust and such a waste. I definitely felt anger around that. Dara was robbed of her life and she had so much living left to do.

I was also angry that we never got to say goodbye, that we were robbed of Dara and of the chance to know that our last moments together were our last moments together. But we had no clue, of course, and so on that Sunday before she died when I said goodbye to Dara, it was just a normal, casual goodbye. What would it have been like to have known that it was the last time I would ever see her alive? After a lifetime together, a chance to say goodbye feels like it's deserved, but it turned out to be a luxury that we would never know. For a long time I felt real anger about that.

However, I do see anger as being an aspect of grief that I processed fairly well, largely due to giving myself the space and time to express my feelings in the sessions with psychologist Mark Smyth. Now I can talk about anger in the past tense rather than the present. I do still get angry about it all, but I feel that from the start I had that element of grief under control. Anger can be useful emotion of course, but it can also be a destructive one, so it was important to bring some influence to this emotional state, in particular, and psychology was a great help to me in this regard.

Conflict is another part of grieving and I noticed its presence in a variety of places. For example, an ordinary question that has been a perfectly normal one for the previous forty-eight years of my life became more complicated when I was asked it after Dara's death: 'How are you?' I really struggled to find a reply that sat well with me because I felt conflicted when I was asked this question. I didn't want to say that I was okay because I wasn't okay, yet at the same time I didn't want to be a moan and say what I was really feeling, which may have been angry, lonely, sad, or all three. In the early days I replied by saying things like, 'I'm taking things a day at a time and putting one foot in front of the other' and that covered it all. It alluded to things being challenging, but it also didn't fall into the 'being a moan' category. I probably gave that as my usual response for about the first twelve to eighteen months and after that I unconsciously changed it to 'I'm getting there.' Once again, this simply alluded to the fact that grieving is very much an ongoing state and not one that has a conclusion or endpoint. Then, about two years after Dara died, without thinking I began to reply, 'I'm okay, thanks.' But the real truth is that again I found it conflicting because part of me would scream inside, 'I'm *not* okay!'

Bit by bit, I'm learning to live with this loss and I know for sure that in time, for the most part, I absolutely will be okay, I have no doubt about that. I even *want* to be okay. But I also know that there's a part of me that will never be okay, a broken part of me that will never knit and heal, that will never again be the same. Hence the internal conflict when I hear myself saying that I'm okay. I do understand that when some people ask how you're doing they just want you to say 'fine' or 'grand' or whatever. I get that it is more of a greeting than an enquiry into my state of wellbeing. But grief changes the rules of the game and I find that my capacity to give a throwaway reply to this question has reduced and my need to tell the truth has increased, which drives the conflict. So now I strike a balance by saying something like, 'I'm good, thanks, good days and bad days, but I'm doing well at the moment.' If I were feeling particularly sad, I might say something like, 'Good days and bad days, today's not great, but thankfully there's always another day around the corner.' That sits well with me and doesn't scare people off by being too intense.

When Dara died, it took me a while but I got my head wrapped around the fact that I wasn't okay and couldn't be expected to be okay given what had happened, so I never really made any demands on myself to feel normal or even any approximation of normal at that time. In fact, with this new life without Dara and with the end of my marriage and all the fallout from that, the world as I knew it was a new normal, so what else would I be but distressed, out of sorts and not feeling like myself? Rather like one of those little quicks on your nail that hurts but you get used to, I suppose that it soon began to feel familiar to feel not okay. But then, when the time came that I began to feel emotions other than the ones that are not so pleasant, I was caught off-guard in some ways and I struggled a bit with the fact of feeling okay. It took me a while to realise that it was okay that I wasn't okay, but it also took me a while to realise that it was also okay to someday feel okay. I had to give myself permission to feel happiness, joy, contentment. Maybe I even had to forgive myself for feeling those feelings.

That may sound a bit daft and you might wonder why I wouldn't have been happy to feel more pleasant emotions after experiencing sadness for so long, but when you're missing someone who has died, those moments when you feel happy can feel wrong and you can be so conflicted, almost like a form of guilt. There is a psychological concept called *cognitive dissonance* and it describes the conflict we can experience when we hold two or more contradictory beliefs. Our mind likes congruence and we can feel psychological stress when our concurrently held beliefs are incongruent. It felt to me that this is what was going on at the time: I felt distress at holding the belief that I could be grieving for Dara at the same time as holding the belief that I could experience a moment of happiness. They felt incompatible. I think that, for a long time, some part of me has needed to hurt, as though it dishonours Dara if I'm not hurting. Part of me never wanted to let go of that pain because the pain keeps the connection to her, if that makes sense.

My brain couldn't get around what it would mean if I were able to feel joy again. Would it mean that Dara's life was worth so little if I were to feel something other than pain less than three years after she died? Intellectually I know that it is possible to hold two apparently different emotions at once, and I know that joy and grief can co-exist in our lives, so logically it would be possible for me to feel contentment or happiness and at the same time respect Dara by feeling grief at her death. But emotionally, that message took much longer to get through and I felt conflicted about this for a long time. If I'm being honest, it still doesn't sit fully right with me yet and sometimes, when I share a happy time with friends or family, there's that whisper in the corner of my mind, 'But Dara's not here, how can you be really happy?' It is sadness, sitting on a chair at the far end of the room, always making sure that it is in my line of sight, not yet ready to leave the building. My feeling is that this is entirely normal, so I don't worry or feel guilty about it. I take a breath and remind myself that I can fail an exam and pass my degree, I can make a mistake yet make progress, and I can also feel sorrow at Dara's loss yet happiness at the joys in life. Grief is not either/or and in time, when we're ready, we can feel both sadness and happiness. It's a welcome understanding when we reach this point.

Another emotion that has presented itself is loneliness. From the moment Mark Donnelly and Eoin Murphy elected to come in person to deliver that awful news on the morning of 14 March, as a family we were supported and that support has continued to this day, which has been both heartwarming and indeed life-saving. However, my observation is that even with that support, the truth is that we grieve alone. There are some things in life that we must do alone, some bridges we must cross by ourselves, even though others are nearby. Birth. Death. Grieving. They are experiences that are ours alone. No one else can carry our loss for us. I think of grieving as being like having a bag of rocks thrown at you and having to carry them up a hill. Well, the loneliness would be like your neighbours and friends trekking up the hill with you, but they aren't allowed to carry your bag of rocks for you. They can walk beside you, they can encourage you and tell you that where you are on the path is normal at this juncture, they can feed you and put your hood up when it rains, but they cannot pick up that bag of rocks and carry it for you, you must do that yourself. You had your own unique relationship with the person who died and you will have your own unique grief for that death. Therefore, it can be quite lonely as we each figure out how to carry the pain of loss in our own lives while we move along that journey towards acceptance. This in no way takes away the benefit of support. I, for one, would not have got through this time without the support that I've received. But it is interesting to note that there is still an unavoidable element of being alone on the journey of grief.

I found, too, that grief changed my capacity for absorbing both happiness and sadness and I am emotional around both in a way that I never was before. Imagine I had a glass in front of me, a glass I've had all my life, and the glass is me and the level of liquid in the glass reflects the level of sadness in my life. Up to now the liquid level in my glass was always well under a quarter, leaving me plenty of space to be able to comfortably absorb sadness or distress without spilling over the top of the glass. But after Dara died the emotional onslaught of sorrow was so great that my glass was immediately filled to the brim, remaining at that level. Now, whenever I hear anything sad or distressing it tips me over the edge, which means I cry at things that I wouldn't have cried at before. I can no longer absorb even a drop of sadness without it affecting me. I can do it in a work context, of course, but even there I need to keep a good check on my emotions because I sometimes find my eyes welling up if a client is talking about their own loss. It doesn't interfere with my capacity to work, and in some ways it brings even more humanity to the therapy space, but I do watch it carefully in that environment. What's interesting is that happy news has the same effect, in that it tips me over into tears. I could be watching a home makeover programme on television and when I see the joy of the homeowner when they see their new home for the first time, I cry. It happens in lots of different situations, like hearing someone is pregnant after years of trying or seeing someone showing kindness to another person. It's not big, heaving sobs or anything, but a few quiet tears, and there's nothing wrong with it, it's just that I never would have responded in that way before. Grief has changed me in that regard.

My experience of grief after my marriage ended was also an emotional rollercoaster and grieving for the loss of that relationship brought sadness, anger, loneliness, regret and a whole host of other feelings. However, mourning the loss of my marriage has felt like a more straightforward and less complex set of feelings than the grief for Dara, and I can say now that I'm in a good place and that my emotions around the end of my marriage are more stable of late. After the house became my house instead of our house and my ex-husband had moved out, I was so sad that it took more than eight months before I was able to put anything in the wardrobes and drawers on his side of the bedroom. For a long time I couldn't even stretch over onto his side of the bed, I just stayed inhabiting my own space. There's a famous photo of actress Nicole Kidman that is said to have be taken as she left her lawyer's office after signing the divorce papers ending her marriage to Tom Cruise. Her sense of relief and release in that moment was palpable even from the photo. Of course, we don't know what was actually going on in her life and if relief for that particular reason was what the image captured, but I imagine that many people would feel a sense of relief when a marriage that was not working has finally ended and they have their own space. I didn't feel anything like that sense of relief, though. I felt an intense sadness that what was once a lovely relationship was gone and that we hadn't managed to make it work. As a result, shelves were bare, drawers remained empty, hangers had no clothes draped on them; the physical emptiness of the house mirrored the emptiness I felt in my heart.

And then one day I felt differently, and it seemed like time to begin filling those spaces. So as I changed emotionally, I also changed practically and was able to live in my home as if it were my home, rather than a space with someone missing from it. I've also got used to the fact that this man who I saw pretty much every day for twenty-one years no longer features in my daily life. We are in contact from time to time, but not regularly, and emotionally that took a bit of getting used to, even though it was helpful at the same time, as it allowed space to heal. As with the grief of bereavement, the distance of time creates a space for change. I have changed and can now say that I feel the period of grief for the ending of my marriage has ended. The emotions around that are now stable and soft.

Of all the emotions that have been triggered by Dara's death, sadness is the one that feels embedded in me for ever, it has been there from the start and remains present today. In the early days, as the numbness began to lift and I began to process the loss of my sister, I started to feel a sadness that was acute. In those first few weeks I was so sad, I couldn't even get through a normal conversation with someone without saying that my sister had died recently. I *needed* to tell people that Dara had died, even random strangers. It was like a compulsion. On one level it seems so strange now when I write that I did this, but in another respect it makes perfect sense to me. The loss of Dara was such a heavy weight and I was only new at carrying it and hadn't yet developed the mental and emotional muscles to be able to cope with that weight. I couldn't carry the bag of rocks – it was much too heavy. Over time, I developed the muscles that allow me to carry those rocks, but in those early days I was crushed by the weight of the sadness. People told me that they could even see the sorrow in my eyes. I think that's why I needed to tell people that Dara was dead, I had to explain why I was so clearly sad and weighed down.

I think this is usually the case when someone dies; there is a need to tell their story. The person you love has no physical presence on this Earth anymore and there's something about this that makes you want to say their name and tell their story, even to strangers. There is a quote attributed to the artist Banksy that describes it very well: '… they say that you die twice. One time when you stop breathing and a second time, a bit later on, when somebody says your name for the last time.' I think that the need to say Dara's name and the need to explain the sadness emanating from me in those early days contributed to me wanting to tell everyone I met that she had died. I still have a need to say her name today, but I am now able to have conversations without disclosing that my sister has died.

Sometimes people ask if religious belief gives me solace. I was raised a Catholic and I do believe that I will see Dara again. Maybe I truly believe that or perhaps I just need to believe that because the idea of never, ever seeing her again is so completely horrifying that I can't even contemplate it as an option. But what if I never see her again? What if there's no afterlife and if this is it? Dara gone from our lives for ever, ripped from us in the blink of an eye without ever being afforded a moment, even in an afterlife, to say our goodbyes after a lifetime together. The cruelty of that would be savage. I don't think that I can even consider that this may actually be the truth, it's just too awful.

I really don't know which it is, but I do tell myself that some day we will be reunited, and whether that is a deep-down belief or an attempt to soothe myself, I'm okay with it. In the meantime, however, whenever we are all together as a family, I feel so sad that Dara is somewhere by herself rather than with us. I *really* hate that thought. My parents had a little girl who was stillborn, so an obvious way to think about it would be that my baby sister and my adult sister are together, and to some extent I do see it that way. However, Dara was the only one of the two sisters who spent time on Earth with us, so I miss her presence in a way that isn't the same as with my other sister. It feels more wrong that Dara is not there in the middle of us when we're all together, and I feel a huge sense of sorrow that we're all here and she's not. Losing a sibling while I was a child and losing another as an adult, I've noticed that the loss feels different. I was ten years of age when my sister was stillborn, too young to under-stand the concept of loss, and as I obviously hadn't met her, the truth is that it wasn't a loss that I could feel directly. It was more about grief for my parents and an awareness of their loss than it was a loss of my own. I think that this is why I feel a sadness at Dara's absence that is different from the feelings I have about my baby sister.

That sadness came with me wherever I went and it was a big presence in those early days after Dara died, different from the quieter presence that it is today. I remember on several occasions literally crying my way around the supermarket as I did the weekly food shop, wiping my eyes at the end of each aisle after having sobbed as I walked down it. The staff were so kind: when they spotted this weeping woman in their shop, they just asked me if I was okay or if they could do my shopping for me, or sometimes they gave me a hug to settle me a bit. The kindness was really appreciated and it did help, though in the first few weeks I would often be soothed and continue on to the next aisle only to cry my way down that one, too.

This, then, is the largest and most lasting emotion from the loss of Dara: sadness. And I find that the sadness has many layers to it. When I examine it closely, it has layers reaching far down, like a huge cave with hidden paths and pockets that I stumble into randomly, multiple levels of sadness that exist within me. These are what I must accept and live with for the rest of my life without Dara.

I'm sad that Dara's life ended when it did and how it did. That she never got to kiss her son's little face or feel his little toddler arms around her neck once more. Or to hear her own mother's voice one last time.

I'm sad that her career ended the way it did and she never got to have that retirement party and celebrate her achievements over more than twenty-three years working in search and rescue. There's sudden loss, traumatic loss, anticipated loss, natural loss all linked to the completed life and the uncompleted life. Dara's was an uncompleted life, she wasn't finished living, she had so much more to do and her untimely death halted that living in its tracks.

I'm sad for Dara's little son who woke one morning to find that his mother was not there and she was never there again. I'm sad for my parents who had to go through the trauma of it all and who have now buried two of their six children. I'm sad for my siblings that we've lost a friend as well as our sister. The five of us loved hanging out together and we spent time together because we wanted to, not because we had to. I'm sad for my cousins and extended family because Dara was a central part of our big, noisy family group.

I'm sad that I can't fix any of their pain, that I can only be there with them as they learn to carry it themselves. You've lost one of the people you love most in the world and then you have to see the other people you love most in the world in pain, it's awful. When you see your parents or siblings upset, you can't make them feel better because when it comes to grief, feeling better isn't the goal, it's not even possible. Instead it's about learning to absorb the loss into our lives so that we can one day find that balance between remembering and living, letting the dead rest in peace and us live in peace. While I know intellectually that it's part of the process, when I see one of my family visibly upset, my own sadness is acute.

I'm sad for the loss of the life that we all had, a life that we appreciated while we had it but was there for a such short time. I miss the innocence of that life, replaced by the stark reality of this new normal that we're in. Death makes you acutely aware of the fragility of life. We tend to think that we have any amount of time to say what needs to be said or to do what we want to do, but we don't. We never know when the sands of time will run out. There's a positive side to that, of course, as we appreciate life in a different way and that's a good thing, but there's also sadness to it because it brings the loss of an innocence about life and about how long we have got on this Earth.

I'm sad for the little things that you wouldn't think would make you feel sad. Like the fact that we all used to roll our eyes up to heaven each time someone asked one of us four sisters within minutes of meeting us, 'Are you the pilot?' No one will ever ask us that again. Or when my mother and sisters are each sitting in our own homes watching *Strictly* on a Saturday night and we throw our thoughts about the show into the WhatsApp group, hearing the silence of Dara because she's not part of our chat any more, knowing she would have had lots to say about the dances and the costumes. Or when my sister Orla cried when she watched *Master Chef* for the first time without Dara, because it was their thing and now isn't a thing anymore. I'm sad each time we reach the end of those little things that we shared with Dara, like the bottle of Liz Earle cleanser she bought as a communal one to be shared on overnights. When that bottle finished, Dara would not be buying another one. Even something as little and ordinary as an empty bottle can bring such sadness.

I'm sad for Dara's colleagues, many of whom were also her friends. They are the people who go out in all weathers, at all hours of the day or night, to rescue those who are lost, yet they endured the biggest loss of all with four of their own gone overnight, an unspeakable sadness. I'm also sad for their families because the events of Tuesday, 14 March 2017 brought to their doorstep and into their homes a fear and a worry that might have hovered in the background before then, the reminder that there is risk and danger in this job. I've met many family members of Dara's colleagues since her death and I always feel for them when we meet because I think that in some ways my family is a walking reminder of their worst fears. We're always met with warmth, kindness and solidarity from both crew and their families; indeed, some have become dear friends, and I don't necessarily think that they would see us as reminders of what they don't want to think about, but in many ways I wouldn't have blamed either the rescue crews themselves or their families if they hadn't wanted to be around us after the crash, because as a family we are living their worst nightmare.

I'm sad for some of the awful things that we have had to hear about what Dara went through before she died. There are things we know that we can't un-know and there's a bone-deep sorrow that comes with that.

I'm sad because I miss Dara. I will miss her every day for the rest of my life. As long as I have breath in me, I will miss her not being in my life, in all of our lives.

I'm sad because as a family and an extended family we spend time together frequently because it's important to us. Looking at photos from family gatherings, Dara is there in the middle of it all, bringing her famous chocolate roulade to the birthday dinner, making the rest of us sick because her birthday presents looked good even on the outside – she could wrap like a pro, tying her hair up to go outside and play football even in her glamorous boots, whatever we all did as a group, she was always right there with us. Now it feels as though Dara is left out, as if she is somewhere on her own while we are all together. That thought … no, that image, brings waves of grief two hundred feet high washing over me. I cannot bear the idea of Dara on her own.

I'm sad because the person who went to bed on Monday 13 March 2017 is gone, I'm not the same person any more and I can't ever go back to how I was. Even though I had experienced difficult times in my life, there was an innocence about life before that date, so I'm sad that I had to let go of my old self and also my old life and get used to a whole new self and a whole new life.

I'm sad because as time marches on, I have to work harder to be able to hear Dara's voice in my head, the sound of her feels so far away in my mind now, fading a little more as time goes by. I'm sad that her image has become still in my mind, like a photo, a snapshot of her smile in a moment in time. I don't see her in motion in my mind straightaway, the way I do when I think of my other siblings, and after forty-five years of living life together, that's just heartbreaking. It's like death robs the person and time tries to rob the memories. But I'm not going to let it. From time to time I watch videos I took of Dara on my phone, or I call up RTÉ's *Rescue 117* documentary programme online and I watch clips of her talking, moving and living her best life.

I'm really sad because in coping with all that came in the aftermath of the crash, my family and I had to become the best versions of ourselves. We have harnessed our strengths, faced our fears, found our courage. We are kinder to ourselves. We hold hope. But Dara never knew this version of those she loved. I find that so sad.

Possibly the saddest, and definitely the hardest thing of all has been my brain beginning to truly comprehend that Dara is dead and that I will never see her again in this life. I can hope and believe that there is an afterlife, a place and time where we will meet again, but that remains an unknowable hope. Whatever may happen in that respect, what I do know is that I have lived my last day of being able to talk to Dara and hear her voice as she replies and shares her thoughts and feelings with me. I know that the silence is for ever. That she has truly gone from my life in terms of her physical presence. It has taken time for that truth to seep into the farthest crevices of my mind. Now when I feel that sadness, it's no longer accompanied by big sobs, but by a single quiet tear rolling down my cheek. I think this is a tear of acceptance that this is the way things are now. And that, to me, is the rock-bottom sadness. I know that acceptance is a good thing, that it's emotionally healthy and hugely helpful in that grief space, that we need to accept that they are gone rather than fight against that truth, but nothing with grief is simple and the other side of that acceptance journey is that it can also be excruciatingly painful. When it comes to the feeling of sadness I've experienced since Dara's death, it seems to me that grief is as awful as love is wonderful. What I mean by that is that when a loved one dies, the fierceness of our grief matches the fierceness of our love. They are equals. That's why it hurts so much.

The presence of sadness is the truth about grief from an emotional perspective, but the other truth is that this is normal. The sadness has been like nothing I've ever experienced before and emotionally I felt at times like someone else was inhabiting my body because I didn't feel like me. I felt sometimes that I was 'losing my mind' because I was all over the place. But then, of course, how else could it feel? It was the worst shock, the worst pain, the worst sadness ever. But I survived. Whatever else goes on, remember that truth as it's the one that will provide the pinpoint of light at the end of that dark and long tunnel.

CHAPTER TWELVE

UNDERSTANDING GRIEF

Throughout the losses I have experienced, I always had my work to fall back on, which was very lucky for me. As a psychologist, I help others to work through their feelings, their motivations, their desires and fears. In order to be able to do that, I study the human mind, emotions, mental health, ill-health and optimum performance and I listen intently when a client is describing their inner life to me. The skills I have gained from psychology stood me in good stead when I was the one who felt like they were falling apart. As I've described, I descended into the depths of grief and sorrow, but I always felt the plumb line of psychology beneath my hand, a guide back to the surface. I was grateful for that.

When I left school, I wanted to study law and become a solicitor but I was short by a few points in my Leaving Cert, so I decided to do an arts degree and make my way towards a law degree that way. I randomly chose three subjects for my arts degree: English (because I love language and I love to read), psychology (because I was always fascinated with people and how we work) and philosophy (because I was told that it was an easy third subject). What I did not bank on was that I would fall in love with psychology. It felt like coming home, and I realised very quickly that this was what I was supposed to be doing.

I graduated with a BA in psychology and went on to do further study in both clinical psychology and sport psychology and gained a master's in both. Since then I have worked with clients in the areas of mental health and also optimum performance for sport. While my psychological knowledge, skillset and toolkit could not prevent me from feeling the feelings of the losses in my life, I think what I have learned along the way in my profession was of some benefit to me when I encountered loss. It is vital for those of us working in the field of psychology that we walk the walk, that we know ourselves, understand our emotional states, have the courage to explore our cognitive experiences, that we live what we teach. So I suppose that over the years, through continuous learning and skill development, as well as attending for talk therapy myself, I have learned to do those things and to navigate my way through the trials and tribulations of my own life. I can see a rationale behind the saying that *'youth is wasted on the young'* in that it is only now, in my latter years, that I feel as though I have really come into my own in this regard. It feels as if it is all coming together now because the mix of experience and learning is a powerful teacher.

Over my lifetime I have undoubtedly struggled with my own emotional life and made mistakes along the way, but I have found that, by and large, I've enjoyed a good life from that perspective. I think I had a solid base to work from when I encountered loss in my forties. I am the type of person who values information and understanding and I tend to seek both to help me process whatever I am feeling in the big emotional times in life. I will reach for a book, or I will reach out for guidance. I am not afraid to identify whatever I need in order to help me understand what's going on.

When facing assisted fertility, for example, I adopted what I would call an emotionally pragmatic approach. I felt the fear and the other emotions that we experience when we cannot have a child, but I decided – and it was very much a conscious and deliberate decision – to take the view that we were lucky that IVF was an option for us. I had read up on the topic and I knew that many couples are deemed not suitable for one reason or another, but we had the luxury of at least getting to try. So even while I was buffeted about by the more unpleasant emotions around infertility, having that as my cognitive and emotional starting-point was helpful. My approach wasn't about thinking positively, not at all; it was about thinking in a way that was helpful, choosing to look at this situation in a way that would serve me well. Later, when the big decisions came along when the treatment had not worked, I knew that it would be useful to seek professional help and get some support and guidance while I figured out what my own limits and boundaries were. I didn't see that as being weak or stupid or a sign that I was not able to cope. I viewed it as being a smart thing to do and that mindset served me well and helped me onto a good path.

Thinking of the end of my marriage and whether I helped myself with a good mindset, on reflection I can see that it took me much longer to achieve that with regard to this loss. I was so angry with us for not making it through that I probably took longer to process the truth and make helpful choices about how to view it. As a result, more time passed between realising there was a problem and seeking relationship therapy. I was much quicker to go for fertility counselling or sessions with a trauma specialist when I needed each. The anger clouded my judgement, perhaps? Not unusual, really. We often make our best decisions from that sweet spot of a balance between emotion and logic, so it is quite common for our judgement and decision-making to be compromised when we are influenced predominantly by intense emotions. Anger is a response to pain (physical or emotional), so there are other emotions hidden beneath. When we are angry, it tends to be true that there is also a lot else going on. Anger, in many ways, can be a handy way to disguise our true feelings from ourselves and others. I had to work through that anger around the separation before I could access and process the more central emotions, like regret and sorrow. However, once the separation admin was complete and we began to live separately as single people, I was then more able to bring that emotional pragmatism to bear. Once that happened, I feel that I moved quite quickly in terms of processing the loss from that point onwards, not that speed is a goal.

When I was faced with the overwhelming emotions that followed from Dara's death, I once again turned to what I knew best and began searching for information to help me understand my own feelings because they felt too huge to manage on my own. I came across the work of Megan Devine, a psychotherapist whose partner drowned right in front of her eyes during a holiday in 2009. After this tragic event, she quit her psychotherapy practice and began to work in the area of grief, creating a space for open, honest, real and accurate conversation. Her book title perfectly explains her approach to this conversation, *It's OK That You're Not OK: Meeting Grief & Loss in a Culture That Doesn't Understand.* Devine has made a significant contribution to our understanding of this subject and her work is often cited as a useful resource in the field. Initially, in that cycle of searching and reading, I read a sentence of hers that made such sense to me, I stopped searching because I had found my first step in understanding grief: 'Some things in life cannot be fixed. They can only be carried.'

I instantly understood that this was not something that could be made better, that the loss of Dara could not be fixed. Therefore, I shouldn't try to fix it. Nor was this about trying to find a way to be okay. The pain we felt at Dara's loss could not be fixed either. Therefore, I shouldn't try to be okay, I shouldn't try to fix that pain. Instead, it was about learning to carry the loss of Dara and the pain of that loss. That one sentence from Megan Devine removed a weight of expectation from my shoulders because it framed the context of what I was dealing with, moving me away from that instinctive desire to soothe and calm and towards a more appropriate approach of accepting the pain of loss and grief by sitting with it. That made so much sense to me, even at that point in time, which was just six days after Dara died. The enormity of her loss both in our lives individually and as a family was hard to fathom and I hadn't even come close to understanding how we would cope, but now I knew that the starting point was sitting with the pain. Letting go of the need to put our world back upright after it had been turned upside-down was helpful. It meant that I used what precious little energy I had on surviving, trusting that in time I would learn to carry this loss that I couldn't fix.

Given that I am a psychologist, it might be expected that all my sources of information and understanding would come from academic texts and materials but, being honest, at that time they didn't really speak to me. I needed more. I needed warmth and understanding and real-life, first-hand experience. So instead of burrowing into my psychology books, as I would normally do when researching a subject, I cast the net much wider in searching for words that would speak directly to me. That's how it came about that my next source of understanding about grief originated from a somewhat unusual place, which was a response to a question on the online forum Reddit.

Someone posted on Reddit a simple statement: 'My friend just died. I don't know what to do.' A response came from someone who went by the name 'G. Snow' and described himself as 'an old guy'. That response was a beautifully articulate and accurate description of grief that resonated with me. He used the analogy of the sea and likened death to a shipwreck. He said that when the ship is first wrecked, you're in the sea and you're drowning, debris is all around and you're trying to hang on, to somehow stay afloat and stay alive after your life is torn to pieces. Then the waves of grief come and at the start they are huge, towering above you and washing over you, coming so fast, ten seconds apart, leaving no time in between for you to even catch your breath. All you can do is stay afloat and try to survive the waves. In time, the waves arrive at intervals, giving you some time to catch your breath in between, time to function, and you eventually begin to live again in between the waves of grief. Over time the waves reduce in size and you can even see them coming, you know that they will hit at times such as at Christmas or anniversaries. They still knock you down, but you come out the other side of the wave, gasping for breath and hanging on to that wreckage with your fingertips, but surviving. He said that grief is like learning to survive the waves and to keep coming out the other side every time they hit.

Reading this description not long after Dara died gave me a sense of the form that grief might take. It was hard to read G. Snow's analogy given that Dara died by drowning and he was talking about waves and wreckage. Indeed, it is only recently that I have been able to read it without crying, given the images that it conjures up in my head. But it was well worth reading, even through the tears, because I found it useful to have a sense of what I could expect with grief. When I read it first, I was in the hundred-foot-high wave stage, with grief coming at me so quickly that I couldn't catch my breath. It was so intense that at times it felt like I was being dragged under by those overpowering initial waves of emotion. G. Snow's own experience told me that what I was feeling was okay, that it was normal. When you're grieving, anything that helps you know what's normal is welcome, because everything feels so alien at that time and you're not quite sure what's going on.

Now, three years after first reading that description of grief, from my own experience I would add to G. Snow's account that it is important to expect rogue waves, ones that will appear out of nowhere, knocking you off your feet when you least expect it, even when the water is calm and there is no obvious trigger. As you become better acquainted with the characteristics of grief you develop a sense of what to expect and you learn to identify the things that will trigger a big wave, but you can also be caught off-guard and floored by a powerful rogue wave of grief. It's about knowing that those moments are normal, that even the rogue wave will recede and that you can survive it.

I find that rogue waves often hit me when I am out and about doing basic life chores. On one occasion I was in a pharmacy, talking to the pharmacist, when something sparked off a chain reaction and a wave of grief washed over me and swept me off my feet. I began to cry and I couldn't stop. The pharmacist was wonderful, she quietly passed me a tissue and stayed with me as I cried. I told her about Dara and she just let me cry it out. I dried my tears, made my purchase and with a big thanks to her, I left the shop. When I looked into the paper bag as I walked up the street, she had put in two small packets of tissues along with my purchases. Naturally, her kindness made me cry again and I wailed all the way to the top of the street. Especially in the early days, but even now for some reason, I cry in department stores, bookshops and other retail outlets, they seem to be the places where these rogue waves of grief wash over me. Perhaps because in that environment I'm just going about the daily business of life and I'm among strangers, so I have no reasonable expectation of grief being triggered. When someone does say something kind to me or asks me something that brings Dara's loss to the surface, that wave washes over me and the tears can come to the top on occasion. I think this is both normal and understandable and over the past three years I've become quite adept at crying and still managing to talk, so it really doesn't bother me if I do cry in public. It's an expression of love and of sorrow and there's nothing wrong with that.

Another book that has come into my collection is Sheryl Sandberg's *Option B: Facing Adversity, Building Resilience and Finding Joy.* Sandberg's husband, Dave, died suddenly while they were on holiday, leaving her a widow with two young children. A few weeks after his death she was chatting to a friend, discussing a father–son activity, and they selected someone suitable to stand in for Dave. Sandberg was upset at even the thought of this and she said to her friend, 'but I want Dave'. Comforting her with a hug, her friend replied, 'Option A is not available. So let's just kick the shit out of Option B.' I found this *such* a powerful concept because the only world that we had known was gone, Dara was not coming back. I would give anything to have all my family together again, but that's Option A, it's not available. It's never going to happen, except in my dreams. So what happens when the life you loved, which is the life you want, is gone for ever? How do you wrap your head around that so you don't sink into the depths of despair, never to return? For my part, I agree with Sandberg's wise friend: eventually you have to accept and work with Option B.

I'm aware that this concept of Option B won't apply to every loss and neither will it appeal to everyone. Perhaps, indeed, it can be applied more readily to losses in life other than bereavement. It works well to apply Option B thinking when that much-longed-for family will never be yours. Or when your body is altered for ever by life-changing injuries. Or when the person you love doesn't love you back. Or when the years of hard work don't end in the success that you so badly want. With any loss in life, be it the loss of the life we had or the loss of the life we want, we must face it and find a way to accept it as our truth. One of the things that can help in this regard is knowing that one day, when we are ready, there is an Option B out there for us. That even though we cannot see it at the time, there is a life worth living around the corner. Or maybe around ten corners, it doesn't matter. We only need to know that it exists and that while Option A is the optimum, Option B is not the opposite, that there are some great parts to our Option B life, parts that stand up on their own merit.

Irishman Mark Pollock is a powerful example of someone who has had to face his Option B several times in life. In fact, he describes the life he is currently living as his third life. The first he says, was his life before he lost his sight at the age of 22. The second was his life after blindness, adapting to a world without the use of his eyes. The third life, the one he is living now, is his life dealing with both blindness and paralysis after he lost the use of his legs in a fall. When you listen to Mark speak (he has talks available online, such as *A Love Letter to Realism in a Time of Grief* by Mark Pollock and Simone George), you are listening to a man who is the epitome of how to embrace the existence of an Option B in life – or even an Option C. He is searingly honest about his journey. His embrace of his Option B did not happen immediately, not by a long shot. But he got there and now through his organisation, the Mark Pollock Trust, his *'mission is to find and connect those people worldwide, to fast-track a cure for paralysis'*. For me, Mark Pollock leads the way in pushing the boundaries of adaptation to a new life, different from the one we imagined ourselves having, different from the one we wanted.

In my own situation, when I look at a life without children of my own, it would be easy to focus on what I don't have (a child to love and nurture and teach) and won't ever have (membership of the parent club, grandchildren). While those things are true (although I am in the very lucky position of being a guardian to Fionn, so it's a bit different for me), it is also the case that a life without a family of my own brings other opportunities. I choose to embrace Option B, which means focusing the lens on the flipside of this coin, such as a greater level of freedom and spontaneity in life, greater disposable income and being able to spend time alone if I feel like it, without having small children with me 24/7.

The same applies to being single. I can choose the focus of my thinking on this unexpected development. It took time, but I am now kicking the you-know-what out of making my own decisions and living alone. I choose to enjoy the fact that I can make decisions about my life or my home without having to consult another person. I chose the paint, the furniture and the finishings for my recent renovations by simply looking at something and deciding if I liked it. If I did like it, I said yes to it, there and then. No need for the to-and-fro that is part of being in a couple. There's nothing wrong with that to-and-fro, of course, and it's lovely to have a home that has parts of you both within it. But I've now learned that it also feels lovely to hand over my credit card and say on the spot that I'll take that chair or that the grey paint would work well with the light in the hallway. It feels very freeing doing it all by myself and I like it. I embrace it.

As I said above, the Option B philosophy works very well in these situations, but naturally embracing an Option B in life without Dara has been much more difficult. In some ways, though, that made it much more important that I worked to hold the possibility of this in my mind. After she died and her life ended and life as we all knew it ended, it would have been *so* easy to sink into the depths of despair, indeed so understandable and so tempting. But the way I look at it is that if I were to spiral down into that abyss, then I would die while I'm living and that would be tragedy on top of tragedy. Death has taken Dara, has it not taken enough? I knew that when I was ready, I would need to consider the concept of an Option B and to contemplate making something of the new life that we now have, going after it with determination once the time was right, honouring Dara in the process. It would be quite a while before I would be able to take this idea off the shelf and dust it off, but it certainly was a warm blanket when I needed it in those early days of grieving.

One thing to note about *Option B* is that Sheryl Sandberg mentions the word *resilience* in the subtitle of her book. It's different for everyone, but for me grief is not about being resilient and by mentioning this book I don't want to suggest that it is. In my experience, grief is about feeling the feelings of our loss, learning to carry that loss and, in time, finding a way to live with the pain of loss, with the emphasis on living as opposed to just existing. In many ways, for me grief is about survival, and that survival period can last a long time. As a result, there is something about the word resilient that just doesn't feel like a fit in my own conversation about loss and grief. There are myriad possibilities, of course, but when I think of resilience, I think of things like an athlete bouncing back from a failure, extracting the learnings and finding their confidence and getting back out there on the playing field. I think of the candidate who didn't get the job dusting themselves off, getting feedback, learning the lessons and applying for other jobs. I think of the business that failed because it grew too fast taking on solid advice, rewriting the business plan and opening up again, only this time sticking to one store rather than a chain. Perhaps it is that the term feels as though it involves a time frame: when we act with resilience, we bounce back quickly. That concept does not apply to grief. There can be no timeframe or expectation around how we grieve; there can be only understanding and kindness and compassion and getting to where we want to go when we are able to do so. So that is why, while I like the concept of Option B, I don't see resilience as a feature of grieving and so I do not subscribe to that aspect.

I do acknowledge, however, that enduring a marriage breakdown at the same time as grieving for my sister required some level of resilience in the sense of withstanding the blows. Ending a marriage is complicated, emotionally, legally, financially and practically, there's a lot to do and most of it is not easy. All that side of things happened while I was in the throes of those very early days after Dara died, so I was dealing at the same time with the admin of grief and the admin of the separation. All this while I was distraught, depleted. So for a long time I felt as though I was on a tennis court, but instead of an opponent at the other side of the net there was a ball machine, firing tennis balls at me so hard and so fast that I had to respond to the next ball when I had only just hit the previous one. With each additional demand that arrived, I was absorbing a blow that felt like it would fell me, but taking a breath and whispering gently to myself, '*Get up and carry on, just one last effort*', even though I had asked myself for 'one last effort' three efforts ago. Sometimes in this hectic juggle I didn't have the luxury of taking my time and feeling my feelings. There were days when I had to dry my tears and dust myself off after reading a report on Dara's death and go into a meeting about my mortgage application or marriage separation; it's just how it was. In this way, resilience has been a necessary factor in my life of late, as it is in all our lives, to be fair, but I want to be clear that I see it as being very much separate from grief. The idea of resilience brings with it the idea of overcoming and pushing past, and I can't align those notions with how grief feels and how the grief journey unfolds.

As time went on and I got back into normal life, or at least what was now normal, I kept reading and searching and I came across a TEDx Talk by Nancy Berns called 'Beyond Closure'. Berns discusses the mythical issue of closure after death, the idea that we grieve and then somehow arrive at a place of closure, whereupon we finish grieving and rejoin life. She rightly debunks this myth and talks instead about the idea that grief and joy can co-exist, that we don't have to finish one before we can experience the other. During her TEDX Talk, Berns stands on one side of the stage and marks this space as *grief*. She walks to the other side of the stage and calls this area *joy*. She uses these two spaces during her talk as she takes the audience through the truth as she sees it, which is that we can at the same time grieve and feel joy, that we can grieve for our loved ones and bring that into our lives rather than feeling that we need to leave it behind. Adding this understanding to my learnings about grief enabled me to handle that re-entry back into real life and I still watch her TEDx Talk to this day as I find it useful.

Sometime later, someone sent me a link to a series called *BBC Stories: Like Minds*. Episode 12 was called *Grief: It's not something you have to 'get over'*. In this episode, a psychologist explains what happens to grief over time. She draws a circle and says that within that circle is our life. When someone dies, grief impacts every area of our life, and to represent this she draws lines over and back across the circle in black marker, touching every side of the circle in the way that grief touches every part of us. She explains that the thinking used to be that over time, this area of grief became smaller, until it eventually disappeared. But the thinking now is that the area of grief stays the same size, but we grow our life around it. To represent this, she draws another circle outside the first one, showing how in time we begin to live again, with other aspects of our life fitting in around our grief. However, when we encounter birthdays, anniversaries, Christmas and so on, that outer circle reduces down in size momentarily as we dip back into the grief and it takes over again as the biggest and most important part of our life. When the birthday or anniversary passes, we then go back to the other areas of our life and the outer circle is activated again. The grief remains ever-present, but our life expands to allow space for other things alongside it.

From these and various other sources I came to understand a little of what grief is about, including a vital truth, which is that grief isn't about trying to fix things or feel better, it's about learning to live with your loss. I was lucky enough to have learned this truth early on after Dara died, which meant that I had a reasonable expectation for myself from the start and I never chased the idea of feeling better. I learned to sit with the pain of loss, to absorb it into my life. I also learned what can feel like a painful truth about loss, which is that there *is* life after loss and that when we are ready, we can grow our lives around grief, we can find that Option B and embrace it fully. We can honour the person we love by living our best life. One of the biggest truths that I discovered is that grief is not about seeking closure and then getting back to life, it's about allowing grief and joy to co-exist. I hate the expressions *moving on* or *getting over it*, neither sits well with me because when you love someone and they die, you don't *want* to move on or get over it. How on Earth could that be okay? It makes no sense to me. Understanding that grief and joy can co-exist and that we can hold the sadness for the person we love and at the same time we can feel joy again in our life has been my antidote to the moving on/getting over it thing. I can feel both.

One of the things that we sometimes do as humans, and that makes it much harder to work through difficult emotions, is that we layer problems one on top of another. I see it all the time in my work, and indeed in life, whereby people end up with feelings of shame on top of a failed effort or feelings of anger on top of a miscommunication and it makes a situation harder to handle. It's far more helpful if we can deal with the initial situation without adding unnecessary layers of secondary emotion on top: *if you can't make it better, at least don't make it worse.* This is not necessarily easy to do, but it is possible. When it comes to grief, there are many ways in which we can inadvertently add layers of difficulty. For example, we can spend all our time in the 'if only' space, going over and over again how things would be different if only one factor in the situation had been different. But it wasn't. It isn't. Things have happened as they have and wishing that they were different, although understandable, is not helpful. It serves only to build a layer of anger or perhaps depression on top of the grief. Another layer sometimes added on top of grief is that of guilt, built up as we go over how we 'should have' behaved. All of these are wholly understandable, but they leave us with an additional layer of pain to deal with and my feeling is that in the face of loss, we have quite enough to be dealing with without inviting more pain. I was fortunate in that I was aware of this tendency from my work, so I was conscious about avoiding it. I tried hard to ensure that I never made what was already an awful situation even worse by my expectations or thinking.

The first thing I did in this regard was that I decided early on that I would only deal with the facts, and that when it came to details about Dara's death I would neither speculate nor assume. I wouldn't worry about things that might have happened, I would deal only with what had actually happened. I also decided that I wanted to hear the facts from relevant parties, and that I wasn't going to engage in idle chat with anyone and everyone. These two decisions meant that I never let my mind go down the rabbit-hole of 'what if?' scenarios around Dara's death, which meant I never layered anxiety on top of grief. Of course, from time to time, especially in those early days, I had thoughts about the things I feared most about Dara's death. Thoughts and images around her last moments of life. Whenever this happened I acknowledged those thoughts and accepted they were there, but reminded myself that they were just words or pictures running across my head, they weren't facts yet and might never be, and therefore they weren't useful. Then I moved my attention and focus to something else, usually something in the present moment. I found with this approach that I was able to remain pretty much with the facts most of the time and that I didn't drive myself into a greater state of distress than I was already in.

I also made a choice early on to focus only on what was in front of me and not to look too far ahead. I did get caught with this sometimes, like the time I got upset wondering how I was going to get through my brother's wedding even though the wedding date hadn't arrived yet, but in the main I remembered to keep my focus on whatever step was the one I was about to take and to deal solely with that. The onslaught of information coming our way after the crash, along with the volume of tasks, was significant, never mind also trying to get my head wrapped around the emotional task of accepting Dara's loss, so it was essential that I took it one step at a time. What we faced was huge and there was plenty of potential to be overwhelmed by it all, but by deciding to be disciplined and only look to the next step, I protected myself against that. So I didn't think about clearing out Dara's locker until the night before we had to do it, for example, and I didn't think about Christmas until Christmas week. This way, I remained largely in the present and I can see now that it helped me greatly.

In addition, I also broke things down into small, manageable chunks and didn't fall into the trap of being unrealistic with what I expected myself to be able to handle at once. I focused on taking one day at a time, especially in the early days, using that micro goal I identified after my first conversation with Dr Eddie Murphy: that I would only ask of myself to keep putting one foot in front of the other, rather than worrying about how I was going to handle the bigger picture of Dara's death. Her loss from our lives was quite simply too big for me to consider at that point. Focusing on small baby steps and allowing myself to deal with things in manageable pieces was key in my own experience and prevented me from slipping on the banana skin of expecting too much of myself.

I also helped myself by remembering that even in the horror of this nightmare, I had a choice about what I focused on and how I behaved. In order to keep that uppermost in my mind, I put both Viktor Frankl's and Edith Eger's books on a shelf where I could see them, to serve as a reminder of people who'd made positive choices under the most appalling conditions imaginable. I'm not saying that everyone can make choices about what they can focus on in all situations, only that I know that it is possible sometimes, and that was enough to be of help to me. Four months after Dara's death my birthday came around, my first without her. I'm a twin, and I remembered that the previous birthday there had been a little situation that morning where I'd got into a bit of a nark with Dara and the result was that my twin Orla and I didn't see Dara that day. So on what turned out to be our last ever chance to be together on our birthday, my stupid, snippy behaviour robbed both Dara and Orla, and indeed me, of that day together. It was the kind of regret that could mark you and stay with you for ever. But Frankl's reminder that 'the last of the human freedoms – to choose one's attitude in any given set of circumstances, to choose one's own way' helped me to realise that I could either let that go or I could let it sink me. I could feel guilt or regret or anger about it, or I could choose to think about the many birthdays over the years that we had all been together for. The choice was mine to make. I chose to remember the many happy birthdays that we had together, instead of one that we didn't.

The realisation that we have a choice in these matters is really important. After a sudden death, it is easy to focus on the regrets, like the arguments, the words said or not said, the missed opportunities. After the ending of a marriage, it is easy to focus on the anger, to deflect blame away to the other person, to hold on to jealousy and sometimes even hatred. After the loss of motherhood, it is easy to focus on the sorrow, on what's not in your life, on the empty spaces that should have held the children you thought you would have. All of these reactions are completely normal and understandable, and I've felt many of them myself. But if we get stuck inside those emotions, if we nurture them and focus on them, then we risk being swallowed up by grief, anger, resentment or any one of a whole host of other emotional states. That brings loss on top of loss, tragedy on top of tragedy. In the face of loss, it's useful to assess our situation honestly and realistically and, in whatever capacity we have available to us, work to choose the best perspective on it for our well-being.

Another way I helped myself was to allow people to help me. I didn't expect that I should be able to cope with such significant loss by myself and I wasn't too proud to ask for or accept help. I've talked to grieving people who say things like, 'Everybody else can cope on their own, I just need to get on with it,' but working as a psychologist for three decades I've met enough people to know that, despite some differences, deep down we're all the same in many ways. We all feel sadness, worry, fear and anger sometimes, but we don't always show that side of ourselves to the world. As we stand at a distance and look across at others, we can make assumptions, but as the saying goes: *don't compare your inside to someone else's outside.* We don't really know what's going on with someone else unless they specifically tell us, so it's not helpful to make assumptions and to compare our grieving with others. We're all human and part of that is needing help from others sometimes. I see that as being not only okay but necessary. As a result, I asked for and took all the help I could get without shame or guilt.

Grief doesn't have a date-stamp, nor is it one-size-fits-all. I gave myself permission to go at my own pace and to grieve in my own way, rather than conforming to what others might have expected of me. Putting the weight of expectation into a box and leaving it there has been useful as I was never burdened by that sense that I wasn't grieving as I 'should' be grieving. I hear others talk about how they feel bad because they think that those around them expect them to be 'better' than they are. I think it has been freeing to not have this as a factor at all.

A helpful concept that I borrowed from my sport psychology work is the idea of *controlling the controllables*. We often talk about this in sporting circles and the term refers to focusing your energy and effort on the aspects of the situation that you can control. An athlete cannot control the weather, the ground conditions or even the result, but they can control their work rate, their response to a mistake and their composure. I found this really useful in keeping me grounded, because for a long time I was juggling many things at once and, especially when it came to the marriage separation and house sale, I felt at the mercy of others regarding some of the biggest changes in my life. But while I couldn't control the speed at which the wheels turn in the worlds of banking and the law, I knew that there were things that were within my control, such as where I chose to focus my attention or what I spent my time doing. In the midst of the heavy days of to-and-fro with mortgage and legal documents, delays, obstacles and downright frustrations, there were some days when it felt as though all I could control was my breath. So that's what I did, I controlled my breath. I had a couple of meltdowns, of course, in those moments when it looked like the house sale might not work out, but other than that I kept focusing on what I could do and I didn't worry about what I couldn't do because that would have added a thick layer of difficulty to an already difficult situation.

Grief is not an illness, as I have said before, so we don't need to pathologise it, but the complexity of my situation meant that there was a mountain of feelings to work through and I couldn't do it on my own. I figured that I was already living with difficult emotions and that talking it out would assist me in processing them, which is why I chose to see a psychologist. This decision stopped me making things worse by bottling it all up and imploding. It confirmed my choices, as set out above, and helped me to stick to them, and it added greatly to my understanding of loss.

The area where I fell down and where I made things worse for myself was the area of self-care. I most definitely added layers of pain to the demands of grief by not taking care of things like getting sufficient rest and hydration and good nutrition. Being self-employed and working towards a solo mortgage meant that I worked myself too hard at a time when I needed to take the foot off the gas. Between the admin of grief and the admin of separation, I was chronically overloaded. This impacted my immune system and led to eighteen months of constant poor health. I think I had a laser focus on remaining in my home and I was goal-oriented towards achieving that and in doing so neglected the cornerstones of health. My gratitude now for having my home is off the charts, so on one level I don't regret it. I did what I had to do and I achieved what I needed. However, the cost was very high in terms of my health and it will take me some time to get fully back on track in that regard. Reflecting on this, I made choices that made things worse and added an extra layer of difficulty, and that would have been preventable if I had been more tuned into the broader picture in which I was operating.

The truth is that bad things happen in life and there are times when we can't make it better, when nothing we do will make it okay. But it's also true that during those times we need to do what we can to not make it worse. This isn't easy, but it is worth remembering because it can mean the difference between a healthy journey along the path of grief and getting stuck somewhere on that path. When we mention the dead, we often use the expression 'rest in peace'. It is important for those of us left behind to be able to *live in peace*. I think that for me, understanding these truths about loss and grief let me lean into the feelings rather than fight them and that has been a key factor in not getting stuck in grief. I don't feel personally that we move through grief, it doesn't feel to me as if there is an out-the-other-side element to grief. It feels like we absorb loss and grief and they become part of us, remaining as a presence in our world as we live on without the person we love. I'm okay with that. It feels that this way it honours Dara, while at the same time letting me live and, in time, thrive. I think that she would want that for all of us who have survived her.

CHAPTER THIRTEEN

RETURNING TO WORK

Returning to work after a loss signals the time when we rejoin the world again after those early days of raw grief. Depending on the nature of the loss, colleagues may know about what has been going on in our life or they may not. If a parent dies, it's likely that work colleagues will know about it, and some may even have been at the funeral. But someone who is going back to work following a miscarriage or a failed IVF cycle, for example, may walk back into a workplace after only a couple of days of annual leave, perhaps tagged onto a weekend. As they sit once more at their desk, there might be no clue as to the loss they are carrying. Or someone could have moved out of the marital home over the weekend and return to work on Monday with no one any the wiser as to what they are going through, perhaps bearing silently the loss of seeing their children only at weekends now that they are not living in the same house. We can feel ready to rejoin the world in the aftermath of such loss, or woefully not ready.

Whether a secret or a public grief, returning to work after loss brings different challenges. If you are bereaved, the worry can sit centre-stage in your mind around what will happen when you go back into that environment that is so familiar but now feels so different. Because everything feels so different to you now, life is changed for ever. You're going back into the same place, but you're not the same person. Does work even matter to you now? You're struggling to concentrate, so will you be able to perform at your job? What if people ask how you're doing? What if they don't? What if no one says anything and it's awkward? How are you going to sit through the coffee break chit-chat when you already found the office gossip challenging and it seems so meaningless now? Or one of the biggest fears, what if you cry? What if you lose control of your emotions and weep in front of your colleagues? You might also be consumed with thoughts about your new responsibilities. Will Mum be okay on her own at home now that Dad has gone? Or, how am I going to get out of work on time so that I can get back across the city to my folks' house and have tea with her so that she is not eating alone all the time? These worries can run through your head as the day approaches when you re-enter the workplace after bereavement.

If the loss is a private loss, such as miscarriage, a failed assisted fertility attempt or, perhaps, marriage breakdown, then as with a loss through bereavement your worries can centre on fears of an ability to concentrate and perform and also on the fear of breaking down in public, especially when that might give away the feelings you are trying to hide. Secret grief also brings additional fears, such as what if someone announces that they are pregnant? Or tries to show you photos of Mary's new baby? Or, worse still, what if Mary comes into work with her new baby to introduce him to everyone? When you are already depleted and distraught with grief, these layers of worry and stress add to the load you are carrying.

Even before Dara died, I could never quite decide if the fact that life goes on was the kindest or the cruellest thing for the bereaved. I'm not sure even now if I have that figured out, but whichever it is, the fact is that life does have to go on. Food needs to be bought, cups and plates need to be washed, clothes need to be ironed and bills need to be paid. We need to keep living when someone dies, even though we kind of don't want to. So it felt like an important milestone when I felt ready to take those first steps back into the world of work and to begin to live my life again. Of course, this particular loss was extremely public – the whole country had followed the aftermath of the crash, the search mission, the funerals, our grief. I was in a position where I knew I would have to address it and that people would talk to me about Dara. But I was also in the position that my marriage had ended as well and not many people knew about that. Therefore, I was carrying a private loss and a public loss when I returned to work, which felt like a double load. I wasn't sure how I would feel in the workplace again, but six weeks after Dara's death I knew I had to rejoin that space.

The first task I decided I was ready to take on workwise was the Agony Aunt segment on Today FM, with presenter Neil Delamere. I spoke with my colleagues at the radio station and we decided that rather than just going straight back and doing a normal segment, it would work better for Neil to interview me about how I had coped with the previous weeks. I was glad to do it this way because I was worried about how I would manage my grief in that space and other people's reactions to me. I had met Neil and some of the team at Dara's funeral, so I knew that seeing them again in the workplace would be okay, but the listeners were aware that I was Dara's sister and I couldn't just ignore what everyone knew was the reason for my absence from the show for those weeks. Therefore, an interview to tackle it head-on felt like a good approach. It also felt good to get the chance to talk about Dara's death and my loss of her from my life out straight, so that listeners could relax and feel comfortable around me and not be wondering if I was okay or up to the job.

Since I'd begun doing the Agony Aunt segment seven years earlier, Dara always texted or called me after each show to give her thumbs-up (or not!). She was an honest sounding-board and would tell me if I was speaking too fast or not getting to the point quickly enough. This would be the first time I did my radio segment when Dara wouldn't hear it either live or on playback, the first time I wouldn't get that text or call to give me the straight-talking thoughts on whether or not I was hitting the mark. There's a line in the Snow Patrol song that we played at the crematorium: 'Even if you cannot hear my voice, I'll be right beside you dear.' Given the link between Dara and my radio work, that line took on new meaning for me as Neil played the song as an introduction to my piece. It was fitting and beautiful, even if emotional.

The interview went very well. In response to Neil's gentle and sensitive questions, I spoke about what life was like after our lives had been turned upside-down on 14 March. I talked about everything, from hearing the news of Dara's death, to the wave of emotions that had rolled over me since that day, to the things that I was struggling with. I talked openly and honestly and we covered a lot of ground in that I got to speak quite a bit about what loss and grief felt like to me in those early weeks after death. I remember feeling shaky and needing a lot of water because my throat kept getting dry, but I was okay and we got the job done. We had a free-flowing and real conversation about loss, grief and the cacophony of emotions that I was feeling, and we also discussed some of the things that I felt were helping me along the way. I was proud of myself for how I handled it and I left the studio contented that my first day back at work had gone well. It really was a milestone.

At this point I hadn't yet done normal things like going out for an evening. All of that ordinary part of life had fallen away in the weeks after Dara's death. Again, while it felt like a big step, I decided I was ready to try. I had tickets for a comedy gig and had almost given them away. Life didn't feel funny anymore, and I wasn't sure if I would be able to see the lighter side of things. But the tickets were for a Neil Delamere gig and given that I knew him personally and his shows are always excellent, I felt I might be able to enjoy it. In addition, given the interview that we had just done together on my first day back at work on the radio, there was something fitting about it being one of Neil's gigs that would bring me on my first step back into the real world from a social perspective. There was initially a bit of mental conflict in this decision, but in the end I decided to not feel guilty for feeling something other than complete sadness for the first time in six weeks. I went to the gig with some friends and we all laughed until our cheeks hurt. That night was a great gift, it was so good to laugh – not to forget, because I couldn't forget if I tried – but just to put down the sorrow for two hours and give myself permission to feel something other than pain. It was a good decision.

Soon after that I felt ready to return to my client work, which felt like another huge milestone. By that time, and after working with psychologist Mark Smyth to process what had happened, I was emotionally at a point where I was able to see clients and focus on helping them. Mine was a somewhat unusual situation in that, under normal circumstances, when someone goes to see a psychologist, they don't know what's going on in the therapist's life. But given that the crash of R116 had made news around the world, it was possible that some clients, new or existing, might know that Dara was my sister and thus what was going on in my life. It was vital, however, that when someone came to me for a psychological consultation they would feel able to talk freely about their issues and not be concerned if I was going to be okay, or indeed if I could be fully present for their consult. Mark worked with me on what to say to clients and how to address the elephant in the room and I felt prepared and able to do my job properly.

When I did sit in that therapist's seat once again, I could see the relief in clients' faces when I led the discussion about Dara and reassured them that I was okay, that I myself was very well supported professionally and that I was fully present and ready for their session. I could see their shoulders drop as they took a breath and the nervousness went out of the room. It was important to be honest and upfront about what had happened, because then everyone knew where they stood and the boundaries were safely put back in place once that discussion was over. That was important for me as well as for my clients.

Sitting back in that chair for the first time, I felt like I was coming home; this is my space, a place where I feel comfortable. I love my work and I love that it makes a difference in people's lives and I wanted to be back doing that work again. Life had been turned so unbelievably upside-down in the previous weeks, and I needed some sense of routine. I was, quite simply, ready to work again. I felt somewhat nervous on the morning of that first day, but equally I felt prepared given the conversations I'd had with Mark Smyth around planning for that day. There is something so comforting about knowing that you are properly prepared, that you have covered all bases and are ready for all eventualities, and then completing that task just brings confidence with it and that's how I felt that day. Slightly nervous, yet comforted and confident.

On their first sessions back with me, my female clients brought flowers on a scale that left me stunned. I could have nearly opened a florist some weeks with the beautiful bouquets and pots that I received. They came to the door with flowers and a hug, then we had our elephant-in-the-room chat and we got on with the task at hand, which was to work through whatever issues they wanted to address. It took a while to settle in and to get fully back into that mode of feeling like my working self again. What I mean by this is that from the very first session of that very first day back I was present and ready for work, but it took weeks before I stopped having to dry my eyes at the end of the day. I would see clients and teach psychological skills to help an athlete move towards optimum performance in sport, or help someone to reflect on and process whatever emotional pain they were feeling, but when the working day had ended it was as if a valve was released and I cried a lot. For the previous weeks, when

I was off work, I could cry whenever I needed, but I suppose that I was storing up those tears for Dara while I was working, and they came tumbling out at the close of the day. I was still doing the psychology sessions with Mark Smyth and they continued to provide a safe place for working through my feelings of loss as well as those around the trauma of Dara's death, and they also served to ensure that I continued to be in a good state to work and see clients myself. Similar to my return to Today FM, I was happy that I made an effective return to work.

I was back at work about a week when I was approached by Stephen Rochford, then manager of the Mayo senior county football team. At the time I had over twenty-five years' experience under my belt in the field of sport psychology, so as a name that tends to crop up reasonably regularly I receive a lot of enquiries about working as a psychological consultant to sports teams. Often it wouldn't feel like a fit, so I say no to more than I accept, but this enquiry intrigued me. I thought it was coura-geous of Stephen Rochford to even consider bringing someone into the backroom team who had been through the trauma that I had been through in the previous weeks. It had all happened on his doorstep in Mayo, so he clearly knew that I was Dara's sister as well as being a psychologist, and I admired him for even exploring that option. I had only been to Mayo perhaps once or twice in my life until Dara died, but in the intervening weeks I had become very familiar with the road to the west. The people of Mayo had been so good to us. They welcomed us into their county and minded us in the darkest times, they sent emails offering beds in their houses when we were travelling to Mayo, they told us that Fionn could play with their young children if he was up there with us and we wanted a bit of normality for him. The communities of Belmullet and Blacksod and the surrounding areas wrapped us up in kindness and care from the first moment they met us. Now the manager of the county's senior football team was seeking my professional skills and the first thing I thought was that this could be a chance to give back to these people, to use my professional skillset to help this county whose supporters are fanatical about their football and wanted so much to win an All-Ireland title.

I met with Stephen and we hit it off right away. As he talked through his plans I could see where he was coming from and what his vision was and I liked what I heard. My experience over the years has been that if you do it correctly, working as a sport psychologist with an inter-county hurling or football team will take over your life for the championship season. It's a huge job. There's usually a panel of about thirty-five players, plus a manager as well as a backroom team that can run to maybe ten or fifteen people, and my job would be to facilitate optimum performances from each of them, individually and collectively. It's a significant role with considerable responsibility and given the number of variables in the mix, it's a complex role. But when Stephen asked, I didn't hesitate for a second and I accepted immediately and became the sport psychologist to the Mayo senior football team for the 2017 All-Ireland Championship campaign. I'm not going to talk about the team in this book, I don't talk publicly about clients unless they specifically ask me to do so, as some have done in the past. I only mention Mayo in the context of loss, because working with the team from the county where Dara died brought an added edge to my work in this instance. That summer, the links between my professional and personal lives were significant and they overlapped in a way that I had never experienced before in my working life.

The first night I met the players, for example, was the day I visited the crew of the RNLI's Achill Lifeboat. I wanted to meet the crew who had recovered Dara from the water and had minded her until the rescue helicopter arrived to airlift her to hospital. I wanted to thank them, and to see if I could find out more about that night, and they kindly agreed to meet me. I went out to Achill and the crew patiently answered my questions. I learned that they had recovered Dara's body from seas of four-metre swells, that they had carried out resuscitation attempts under the extremely difficult conditions of a lifeboat moving around in those seas, before eventually making the difficult decision to stop attempts. After which, Dara was gently laid down inside the lifeboat and one of the crew remained with her at all times until R115 from Shannon arrived to bring her to the mortuary. Before that meeting, my mind had often thrown up an image of Dara alive on the open water after the crash, in the dark of night, on her own on those big angry seas, frightened and alone. That image haunted me whenever it crept into my head. The idea that Dara might have been conscious and have known her predicament and possibly her fate was for me the absolutely worst possible thought. I couldn't bear to think of my sister in that scenario. When the image came into my head, I used to tell myself that I had no idea if it was accurate or not and that I was going to pause that thought because, accurate or not, it was in no way useful to let it invade my mind.

It's not always an easy thing to do, but it is possible to influence what we focus on and I knew that I wasn't a victim of what I gave my time and attention to. With intrusive thoughts

I had options. I could simply observe the thoughts and notice that, *Today I'm feeling particularly impacted by this thought.* I could remind myself of what it is: *It's just a thought, a series of words or images in my head.* I could label it for what it is: *That's an intrusive thought/image and it's a function of the high stress situation that I'm in at the moment.* I could ask myself, *Can I be 100 per cent sure that this thought is true?* Or I could just realise that the thought or image would pass through my mind, it wouldn't stay there for ever. I used to play around with a mix of those strategies when I'd find myself seeing that awful image of Dara on the water and it would settle my mind and stop me from getting caught in a loop. I was able to notice the image but not stay with it, a bit like scrolling through the television channels and choosing not to click on the programme about snakes.

But that day in Achill, within minutes of talking to Coxswain Dave Curtis and his crew I knew that Dara was not alive when she reached the surface of the water. There was comfort in this knowledge, and the image that had tried to haunt me was banished for ever. We talked about what had happened that night in more detail and while it was one of the most difficult conversations I have ever had, it was one that helped me enormously. The information and knowledge I received filled in gaps and cut off the blood supply to most of the 'what if?' thoughts. I was quite upset during the conversation and I cried throughout, but the crew just let me cry and kept answering my questions, they weren't fazed by the tears. The weather and sea conditions on the night of the crash were horrendous and what Dave Curtis and his lifeboat crew had to endure, both physically and emotionally, was truly horrific, which made their generosity in giving me their time and going over the details of that night even greater. I am for ever grateful to them all.

It was later that same night that I met the Mayo squad for the first time, in Castlebar. That day turned out to be the first of many times where my professional and personal lives interlinked that year, as this county became such a significant part of my life. To this day, Mayo and its people hold a big piece of my heart.

It's quite a daunting thing, to walk into a room filled with a squad of players, management and backroom team, perhaps fifty pairs of ears listening to what you have to say, making up their minds about you within a short space of time. I'm quite used to talking to groups and I'm also passionate about the psychology of performance so, oddly, I tend to enjoy even those first meetings with a new team. I had done my crying back in Achill and had made sure that I took time out to clear my head after the difficult day, so that I could remain composed and get the job done that I was there to do. The meeting went well: I introduced myself, summarised my credentials, outlined the role that psychology plays in achieving optimum performance on the football field and spoke a bit about what I would be looking for from the players in terms of input. I knew by the room that the response was good, it felt well received. But towards the end of my talk, I also knew that I would have to have the elephant-in-the-room chat. There was no way that these players didn't know that Dara was my sister. The deaths of the four crew of Rescue 116 had occurred in their own region and it was known about the length and breadth of the county. I took a deep breath and ended by telling them that I had to address Dara's death. I assured them that I was receiving appropriate professional support myself and that I was fit for work. I also told them that some of the psychology skills I would be teaching them were ones that were helping me survive these early weeks after life changed for ever. I'm sure that my voice cracked a little during that part of what I had to say to the squad, but I remained composed and said what needed to be said. At the end of my session, one by one the players came up to me and kindly and gently expressed their condolences, but after that it was down to business and they trusted me to deliver despite my recent loss.

Like everyone on board that year, I worked hard and brought my A game to the psychology sessions. I threw myself into this role and in the sixteen weeks that we were together, from May to the last game against Dublin in September in the All-Ireland final, we became like family. These men are good men, I found them decent, hard-working, ambitious and honest and as a squad we were a tightknit group who worked well together. In our quest for the Sam Maguire trophy we made it to the semi-final in August, only to draw with Kerry. The replay was called for the following Saturday.

This presented an interesting moment as one of those professional–personal overlaps because I was already booked to go to a memorial charity concert for the crew of Rescue 116 on the Friday night, the night before the replay. It would be a unique event, held in a sort of Spiegel tent in County Cavan, with powerful one-off musical performances by the likes of singer Declan O'Rourke alongside the rousing drums of the Clew Bay Pipe Band. By all accounts it would be a poignant but also joyous musical celebration of the lives of the four crew of R116. I had a ticket, which was an achievement in itself because they weren't to be had for love nor money, and was looking forward to the night. When the semi-final replay was set for the following day, after the concert, there was no pressure whatsoever from anyone in the Mayo camp for me to attend the match, but I knew myself that what I both wanted and needed to do was to be with my team and help them prepare for this game. The concert was important to me as it would be the first time that many of those involved in the crash would be together for a happy occasion, but the Mayo team mattered to me too.

This is probably the first moment when I prioritised my 'normal' life ahead of something to do with Dara's death. I didn't have any sense of that at the time, but now as I reflect on it, that was in fact an important step on my grief journey, a step towards 'real life', if you like, and one that I wanted to make. The decision itself wasn't difficult, I was committed to Mayo and we had a job to do and the concert was going to go on whether my seat was empty or not. I toyed for a while with the idea of doing some work with the team on the Friday night in Dublin, then driving up to Cavan for the concert, and driving back to Dublin late that night to the team hotel. But I knew deep down that this was not really a realistic option.

The team needed every person to be at their optimum for the game, and that's something I work on a lot with players. I talk to them about having a rule-of-thumb when making decisions, with the question, *Will this help my performance?* as their guide. If the answer is yes, do it. If it's no, don't do it. If the answer is that you don't know if something will help your performance or not, then don't do it. I am fairly hardy, but there would be a drive up to Mayo and back that week already, and a trip up to Cavan and back midweek to drop off some things for the concert, so I was highly unlikely to be at my best if I added another late-night drive up and down the country into the mix.

Plus, even if I did manage somehow to bring my A game after doing that Friday night trip to the concert and back, there was something not right about me asking one thing of the players and doing another myself. That didn't sit right with me. Of course, I knew my family would be disappointed that I wasn't there with them all, but I also knew that they would understand the challenge of the situation I was in, and they did. I made my choice. I chose to miss the concert and be at the team hotel on the Friday night to do my usual prep work with the players in readiness for the game the next day.

While initially there was a sting in the tail to be missing the concert, on the Friday night I was happily with the squad, doing our normal pre-match prep that we did every other night before a game. Mayo brought a great game of football to the field that Saturday and we were victorious, beating Kerry by 2-16 to 0-17, which meant that we had earned our place in the 2017 All-Ireland final.

In the dressing room after the game, Stephen Rochford said a few words to the group and then the players began getting showered and changed. I was standing in the now-quiet warm-up room when I began to cry. These weren't small, subtle tears, these were full on choking, heaving sobs and despite my armoury of psychological tools, I couldn't stop them. While I had of course laughed since Dara died, this was the first time since 14 March that I had experienced pure joy. Seeing the faces of those players and backroom team as everyone spilled back into the dressing room after the match, arms around one another, big smiles on their faces, it was beautiful, pure and utter happiness. We had set out to give ourselves an opportunity to compete for an All Ireland title and we had achieved that. That feeling is immense and as a unit you feel you could burst with pride and satisfaction when everyone shows up and does what they need to do on the day it matters. But standing in that warm-up room, echoes of happiness coming from the changing room next door as the players chatted and laughed over the noise of the showers, it felt as though my brain couldn't deal with feeling such intense joy having felt such intense sadness for so long. I was so happy, so full of pride in that moment, but it was too much. I just wasn't ready for grief and joy to co-exist in my world, it was still too early for that.

The tears fell and kept falling and I was absolutely inconsolable in that moment. Some of the management team and players found me and tried to comfort me, but the more they hugged me, the harder I cried. As they were used to seeing me only with a very professional demeanour, what they witnessed probably didn't make any sense to them, my eyes red and swollen, unable to stem the flow of tears on what was clearly a happy occasion for us, so it must have looked so odd to the lads when they saw me first. But they got it, right away they understood.

Midfield player Tom Parsons looked down at me when he hugged me and he quietly said, 'She's here with us, Dara is here with us.' I honestly felt that I would break in two, the pain was so intense on hearing those words. In missing the concert, I had sacrificed something important to play my part in achieving an important win with this team and it had been the right thing to do, the sacrifice was worth it. I was proud of these honest, ambitious, courageous young men who that day had done all that we could have asked them and more and, in all honesty, I was proud of me too. But I would never be able to share that with Dara. She'd never tell me that she knew we could do it, that she was proud of me and that she had been roaring at the telly for Mayo even though we're from Dublin. With his words Tom had cut straight to the source of my pain: this was a joyful moment for me with this team and Dara was not alive to share it. He brought comfort in his kind words with the idea that even though Dara was not alive, she was somehow there with us all. Given that she had died in Mayo and that the people of that county minded us as a family so well since, something felt right about thinking of Dara here with us that day and somehow that soothed me.

Even though there was a link to Dara and the Mayo job was so much more than work to me, I was in Croke Park that day as a professional, with responsibility for the psychological preparation of a squad of players, so this wasn't a time for my own personal pain. But grief didn't care one jot that this was my place of work, it just barged in and showed up, not interested in where I was or what I was doing or that I had my work hat on. At that time I had twenty-five years' experience of private practice as a psychologist and I had never lost control over my emotions like that, and I haven't since. I was lucky that at the time that I was overcome with emotion my job for the day was done, that we had achieved what we set out to do and so in some regard I was off-duty when I broke down. But grief didn't know that and even if it did know, grief wouldn't have cared, grief has absolutely no manners. It visits whenever it wants and that day it did so with a ferocity that was staggering.

I'm very grateful to the players and management of that 2017 Mayo football team for the way they handled having a grieving team member in their midst that summer. It isn't easy dealing with grief in the workplace, often people don't know what to say or do, but they got it exactly right in Mayo. They acknowledged the loss, but they didn't act as if it defined me. From the very first night I stood in front of the group I was met with respect and even though every person in the room knew what I had been through, I was still seen as a professional who was there to do a job.

And I did deliver for the team. Even though I was in the thick of grief and stumbling around in many aspects in my personal life, something kicked in when I started back at work. I found that grief made me better. I couldn't concentrate at home, but I was sharp as a tack each time I stood in front of those players or sat with an individual client in my practice. Perhaps my brain was relieved at being immersed in something other than utter sadness. When working, I felt focused, energised, alert and inspired, pretty much the opposite to what I was feeling at other times. I see this as a survival strategy and I think that while I was ready to return to my job and help people, work also saved me, as it meant that I had neither the time nor the environment to allow me sink into the depths.

Going back to work after loss, or indeed back to any group to which we belong, can be challenging for the person who has experienced the loss and also for the colleagues around them. My experience from the perspective of the person who is grieving is that it's important to be prepared, to consider that re-entry and have a plan for your return. Have you been in contact with any of your work crowd since your loss? If not, is there a colleague who would be good to talk to beforehand, who might smooth the way and act as a supportive presence for the first while back? Maybe they could subtly let the wider group know if you're okay with people asking how you're doing or if you would rather just get into work and not have it mentioned, whichever is the case. Would it be useful to talk to your boss before you return, to have a quick chat about expectations so that you know whether you will be needing to hit the ground running or if you will be given a little space to adjust? Does your workplace have any programmes that address grief in the workplace and could they prove a useful support for you? We *can* grieve and work at the same time, that is entirely possible, but by giving a bit of time to planning that return to work, we can help ourselves take that step back into the real world when the time comes.

It's important to be gentle and give yourself a break if, despite taking time to plan your return, you still find yourself crying at work, as I did that day in Croke Park. It's also important to forgive yourself for behaving out of character in those first days back. I was so used to being hugged whenever anyone met me over the weeks when I was off work after Dara died that at my first corporate meeting when I was back at work, instead of a handshake, I greeted one of the senior managers with a hug. He got a fright, I got a fright, it looked odd to those present, but we all survived it and I had to park that as 'understandable in the circumstances' in my head.

From the perspective of the employer, it is important as part of your mental health and well-being initiatives to have conversations around bereavement and grief in the workplace, talking about what loss is really like, the impact of it on us physically, cognitively, emotionally, socially, behaviourally, what it's like returning to work after bereavement, expectations from a performance perspective and what people might need from those around them when they do return. Also talking about those secret, private losses that people may carry without anyone knowing, just having an awareness of their existence. It's important to realise from an employer's perspective that although we may be grieving, with support and a bit of time employees can be both effective and productive again. It's about finding that balance between acknowledging their loss and supporting them to be able to deliver when they are settled back in to work.

Rest is important after bereavement, but so too is occupation, having something to do, somewhere to go, something to achieve. This all has to be at a pace we're ready for, of course, and how we achieve it will be different for everyone, but I found that having thirty-five footballers to think about was the best thing that could have happened and it came at exactly the right time. I thrived on pushing myself to be better so that I could help them be better, and that proved to be a powerful antidote to the tentacles of grief that threatened to pull me under. The 2017 Mayo squad and backroom team were a joy to work with and it really did feel like family that summer. Although we fell short at the final hurdle and didn't come away with the Sam Maguire, the work we did together remains one of the pieces of work that I am most proud of in my entire career, despite, or maybe even because of, the presence of grief.

CHAPTER FOURTEEN

ALL THE FIRSTS AND ALL THE LASTS

The grief of the first weeks after a loss has a particular sharpness. When we have survived that, we then face into living with the loss and adapting our lives to fit around it. One of the difficulties in that regard are all the 'firsts' and 'lasts' that we have to get through, particularly during the first twelve months. This is why grief isn't a linear process because we have to navigate days when the memories are so strong and the sadness is so raw, we are thrown back into that sharp grief of the early weeks. We might be feeling like we are doing well, getting through 'normal' life and feeling relatively okay, but then a family occasion or a birthday comes along and those waves of grief rear up again and overwhelm us. It's understandable that special days cause an upsurge of grief and we have to be kind to ourselves about that.

In line with the nature of the loss, some of the firsts we experience are private firsts, such as a personal acknowledgment of a significant date in relation to the loss, while others are more public, like the month's mind, so it feels okay to acknowledge them with others. In the former, the grief it brings can be a solitary experience, with no one around us knowing the significance of the date or the pain of its arrival. When someone experiences a loss through miscarriage, for example, the approach of what would have been the due date for the pregnancy can bring a woman or a couple back into surviving those towering waves of grief. They must go to work, attend meetings, deal with emails and phone calls and piles of tasks, all the while silently crying inside at the loss of their baby. In this instance, the milestone date is usually a private one, with no one but those directly affected marking the date, a silent prayer or a single candle the only mark in the world that day to acknowledge a loss that may not be spoken.

With regard to my own situation and to the loss of motherhood, I might have assumed that Mother's Day was the day when I would have felt that sharpness of loss again most strongly. At the end of the journey to become parents, that became a day that I knew for sure would never relate to me, except of course with regard to wishing my own mother a happy Mother's Day. For the first couple of years there was a pang of sadness around that day, but then those feelings faded into grey, until now, six years later, I am unaffected by it. I see it as it relates to my own mother and I feel joy at the day and at having her in our lives, rather than sadness for my own lack of being a mother. That only came with acceptance of the loss and also of the new life that I had not foreseen, a life without children. For me, the firsts that brought the knife-edge of grief back again at the end of that parenthood journey were the firsts around when I began attending christenings and children's birthday parties again and congratulating friends and family on their pregnancy or birth announcements. Those were challenging times and on each occasion I felt the life I had built around the loss reduce down once more while grief took centre-stage for a moment. But before long, I returned to living that life again, to living with the loss and enjoying life even though I was not a parent, as I had wanted to be.

When a marriage ends and there is the loss of that special relationship, the wedding anniversary date can bring with it a wave of grief, memories flooding back of happier days, times of hope and possibility and the promise of togetherness for ever. I found the first wedding anniversary after we separated the hardest. It seemed incomprehensible that once, on that very day, we had stood at the altar and promised to love one another until parted by death, yet here we were, parted not by death but by our own hands signing those separation papers. I felt the loss physically that first year after we separated, a palpable sadness in my chest all day. Since then the day feels strange and there is a sense of sadness around it, but it is more bearable. While I'm very much aware of the date each year, I am not in any way overwhelmed by it at this point and when I think of my marriage and of my wedding day, I can honestly say that I think of the love and the happy times and of the fun and adventure of a long time spent together.

The firsts around bereavement are the firsts that have brought the biggest waves of grief crashing down on top of me. That is not in any way to suggest that the loss around motherhood or marriage are lesser losses, not at all, only that I felt the impact differently with the loss of my sister. I think that it's just influenced by the different nature of bereavement loss. From the day that a loved one dies, your mind is drawn to *'this time yesterday, last week, a year ago ... she was alive'*. There is a feeling of wrongness about moving into a new day, a new week, a new month, a new year without your loved one and experiencing something they never have and never will. Hearing songs she never heard, seeing news she never read, having experiences she never had, thinking of the life she never got to live. That future robbed. Grief for the moments that might have been. Life splits into two halves: before Dara died and after Dara died. Moving into the life after she died means meeting those 'firsts' while being hammered by those 'lasts', each confirming the terrible loss.

I knew there would be some difficult firsts ahead for us, but there was a first that I hadn't considered before it happened, which was seeing the replacement rescue helicopter from the Dublin base in the skies over the capital for the first time. Whether she was on shift or not, because Dara was crew we were all very aware of the red and white Irish Coast Guard helicopter as it crossed the land or sea around Dublin. If we were anywhere and we heard the heli, we'd rush outside and look up, wondering if they were heading out on a training flight or were on a callout. My mum would sometimes get a text from one of the crew to say that it was them who had flown over my parents' house that morning and that they had seen us waving. I know the sound of the Coast Guard helicopter so well that I can distinguish it from the Garda helicopter, for example. For weeks after the crash we never saw a rescue helicopter in the sky, except at Dara's funeral or other ceremonial or memorial events. When the replacement helicopter arrived and they were ready to begin flying again from the Dublin base, some of Dara's colleagues kindly let us know that we would soon see the helicopter again, so that we wouldn't be taken off-guard by the sight or sound of it in the skies over our city. They also told us about their first Rescue 116 flight back into the base at Dublin Airport, what it was like, how they marked the flight and remembered the crew who had not returned. It was emotional but also lovely to hear and very kind of them to share that with us.

The first time I saw the replacement R116 in the sky I was in my parents' house with my mother. As we sat chatting, we knew by the distinctive noise in the distance that the helicopter was approaching. We ran outside into the garden and looked across the mountains and, sure enough, the familiar shape and sound of the Sikorsky S92 came over the brow of the hill and headed towards us, flying directly over the house on its way to a training mission. It was so surreal to see it. The last time I had seen the Dublin heli in the sky, Dara was alive, life was normal, death had not visited and grief felt like it was a long way off in the distance of my life. *All the firsts and all the lasts.* This period of time, especially in the first year after a loved one dies, is about meeting those firsts and, in the same breath, being reminded of all the lasts. That can be *so* tough, in one respect keeping the wound open, in another helping us to heal as we face yet again the truth, which is that Dara is not coming back. My mother and I waved at the heli and as it swooped past we could see a wave back from the cockpit, more kindness from the crew. I didn't cry, but my throat closed over, a lump of emotion taking up the space, stifling a howl of pain. I miss Dara, we all miss Dara, and seeing the replacement helicopter fly over the skies that she used to patrol made me miss her even more.

One of the most difficult 'firsts' came in June with my brother's wedding, less than three months after Dara's death. This was a long-awaited day and we were all so happy for Johnny and Olga but as it got nearer, I wondered how I would be able to cut through the sadness on that day and find the happiness. But sometimes we just need to do what life asks of us and the most important thing that day was the joy for my brother and his wife-to-be, so along with everyone else I got up that morning and decided to make that the priority.

It was a scorching hot bank holiday weekend and the sunshine added to what turned out to be an absolutely beautiful day, filled with warmth, laughter and lots of love. During the initial moments, when I was first in the church, I found it emotional as I thought of Dara missing this, of not being with us. We were sitting in a pew in the church and she was buried in a grave only feet away. In the family we had spoken about Johnny's wedding so many times since they'd got engaged as we'd all looked forward to this day and I knew that Dara would have loved to be there. She'd have been so proud of her younger brother, so happy for him and for Olga, who we all love like a sister. I had to remind myself that being happy for Johnny didn't mean that I was being disloyal to Dara, so I gently guided my mind back to the present. The same priest who had led Dara's funeral mass performed the marriage ceremony and he did a wonderful job. It was a celebration of two people who are meant to be together and a joining of two families who both like and love each other. The reception was a festival-style party on the newlyweds' farm up on the hillside, complete with a marquee, straw bales, a bar in a shebeen and fairylights strung between the trees. Rescue 116 was on a training run that day and when we had everyone outside they flew overhead, coming roaring over the top of the hill to do a fly-past on their way back to base. It was poignant but also fitting; Dara was there with us through their kind gesture.

There was one other big emotional moment that day when our new sister-in-law Olga delivered a witty, warm and poignant speech. When she uttered that one line, *'There are people who aren't with us today',* it was as though we were on a film set and the director gave the instruction to cry, because we all wept instantaneously, as if on cue, that wave of grief washing over us and knocking us all off our feet for those ten seconds after Olga's words. But we composed ourselves instantly and we got through it and went on to have the most memorable and the happiest day. Among other things, Dara Fitz stood for courage and composure and I can't help thinking that she would have been proud of us all on that day.

As the months rolled by that first year, we came to the first birthdays, all of ours and Dara's own birthday in October. I found that those 'firsts' brought a heavy heart. Dara loved birthdays and she made a fuss of birthdays like no one I have ever known. It could be balloons outside your bedroom door, or even your front door, or little home-baked cookies wrapped up in paper and tied with a ribbon, or whatever gift she knew that you hoped for plus a little 'surprise' on the side, always a little surprise from Dara. Those first birthdays without her were *tough*, but we got through them, supported as always by the ever-present network of extended family and friends who have been like a wall of support to each of us since Dara died.

The first Christmas after Dara died is like nothing I have ever experienced. I don't tend to let my mind run on ahead, instead I work hard to stay in the present and live the life I'm living now, but as December arrived in that first year and all around me it was 'Jingle Bells', mince pies and expectations of happiness, I got a lump in my throat at the image in my mind of the empty chair at Christmas dinner. I felt I couldn't face that month of merriment culminating in a big day filled with memories.

When I think about Christmas, it brings to my mind images of childhood. The excitement of us kids as we waited for the big man in the red suit to visit on 25 December, being on our best behaviour for weeks for fear that Santa would find out that we hadn't been good and skip over our house on his rounds. Picking out the Christmas tree together and squashing both it and ourselves into the car for the journey home. Everyone helping to bring the lights and decorations down from the attic and squealing in delight as we spotted our favourite trinkets that we had forgotten about. Arguing every single year over who got to put the star on the top. By the time we finished decorating, more silver tinsel was on us than ever ended up on the tree. Going to bed on Christmas Eve nearly bursting with excitement, hoping that our letters had been received and the elves had made the gifts we had asked for. Vivid memories of that magical feeling of waking up on Christmas morning and racing each other to the sitting room to see what Santa had brought, waking up our poor parents at some ridiculous hour to show them our shiny new toys. As we grew older, different images in my head, with new hairstyles, clothes and different presents, but the same smiley faces and laughter as we enjoyed each other's company over the Christmas season. Some years the numbers might be down if one of us was travelling or if Dara was on shift, but most years we were all together, everyone moving into my parents' house for a few days to get as much time together as we could. Sitting around the table for leisurely meals together, chats around the fire, silly party games, everyone pitching in with the preparations for Christmas Day, midnight mass together. Christmas was good.

As always, that Christmas was a case of all the firsts and all the lasts, bringing back memories of our last Christmas with Dara, less than three months before she died. If life knew then that Dara was to be taken from us, it couldn't have given us a better final Christmas with her. It was brilliant because we were all there, no one travelling or working or at their in-laws', because we all moved into our parents' house for a few days and got to hang out together properly, because Fionn was two-and-a-half years old and full of fun, adding that lovely touch of toddler spirit to the proceedings, because beautiful memories were made in the ordinariness of our days together. I don't often use the word as I am not sure that it actually exists, but that last Christmas we ever had as a complete family was perfect.

I didn't want presents that first Christmas without her. All I wanted was five more minutes of Dara here with us, my family all together just one more time. Even if it wasn't for the whole day, just five more minutes, I'd have taken that. There could have been no better gift, except waking up and finding out that the past nine months had been an awful nightmare and now it was all over.

Dara loved Christmas, she always made such an effort with it, and having her family together, spending time together, was what Christmas was about for Dara. She did all she could to make Christmas warm, welcoming and fun. Her gifts were wrapped so beautifully that looking under the tree, you could easily pick out hers from the rest. No offence to anyone else, but Dara's just stood out and they always looked more inviting than the rest of ours, you'd nearly not want to open them they looked so pretty. Yet that first Christmas after her death I couldn't even get her a gift, because she wasn't bloody here. All I could do was bring flowers to her grave. How lame is that for the girl who made Christmas such a thing? I cried buckets of tears in the florist's when I asked them to make up some flowers and they asked me who they were for. I could barely get the words out as I literally howled in pain. But I reminded myself that it was okay to feel floored by this enormous wave of grief, that it was normal any day since her untimely death but especially on our first Christmas, to feel both rage and sorrow in equal measure. I allowed myself to cry and then I dried my tears and I brought the flowers up to Dara's grave and left them there for her, letting her know on the card that I was thinking of her and missing her always, even more so at Christmas. I met my twin sister and my mother up there, each with the same idea, and when we placed our flowers on Dara's grave we saw that the rest of our family had been there just before us and each had left a floral Christmas gift for Dara.

How on Earth were we going to get through Christmas without her? All of us there in the same house around the same table, with that empty chair. Christmas took place nine months after she died and if it were nine years after, I didn't think it would have been any easier. I really struggled as I just couldn't figure out how to handle the disconnect between what was supposed to be a happy time and the hollow feeling in my chest. I couldn't care less about Christmas that year, it meant nothing to me, if I'm honest about it. But we had Dara's little son to think about and we needed to make it a happy time for him. Dara would want that. In fact, that *was* a gift that we could give to her.

Ignoring Christmas wasn't an option, but neither was it realistic to expect myself to feel the joyous emotions that the Christmas songs would suggest. It *wasn't* the 'most wonderful time of the year', and that's the truth.

After wrestling with my emotions for a while, I decided one day that I would handle it by getting behind Christmas and doing what I could to make it a nice time for all of us. But I told myself that if the festivities got too much and if I wanted to scream at hearing another bloody Christmas jingle, I would remind myself that on one level, *Christmas was just a Monday and a big chicken.* It is, of course, a time of the year that is full of meaning, as well as being loaded with nostalgia and sentiment, but viewing it as simply another meal on another day allowed me to shake off the layers of painful meaning and get through it. I found this approach helpful and in the end we all got through our first Christmas without Dara; we survived what had seemed un-survivable.

After managing through Christmas, I was caught offguard by the strength of feelings I had coming towards New Year's Eve. It's often an emotional time for people anyway and the strains of 'Auld Lang Syne' bidding farewell to the year gone by is enough to bring a lump to the throat at the best of times, but New Year's Eve 2017 brought an enormous wave of grief. I just could not get away from the feeling that I was leaving Dara behind once we went into another year. She had been alive in 2017, but she would not know 2018 and all it would bring and she would be left behind, in the past, on her own. I howled at the idea, I just couldn't bear it, it felt so wrong and I didn't want to go into another year without her. There was also the fact that once we moved into 2018, I would be saying to myself and others that Dara died 'last year', indicating a chronological distance since her death. Yet for me there was no emotional distance, it didn't feel like 'last' anything, it felt like Dara had died yesterday and I couldn't marry up all that in my head. As a result, I struggled with that change of date with the arrival of the New Year and I was about as sad as it was possible to be.

I handled it by doing the only thing I felt I could do that New Year's Eve: I went to bed long before midnight and slept through the sadness. I think it is a night that many people find difficult, especially those who have experienced loss of any kind, so I imagine I am not the only person to have ever taken that approach. It's only a sundown and a move into the next twenty-four-hour period, I tried to tell myself, but that was an occasion when I couldn't focus the lens in any other direction, couldn't choose a viewpoint to help me through it, when even my psychological toolkit was unable to soothe the pain of that transition. So I made the only choice available to me and took myself out of that situation altogether. Sometimes, that's the right thing to do.

The first anniversary of the crash was 14 March 2018 and the feelings I experienced coming up to that date were similar to those I had felt coming up to Christmas and New Year. I had a lump in my throat, my chest felt hollow, I was weepy, I even felt a sense of dread, with butterflies in my stomach. If I didn't know the date, my body was telling me it was coming. I know now that this is what's known in psychology as the 'anniversary effect', which is the specific feelings or reaction we get around the time of a significant date or time in life, and the anniversary of Dara's sudden death was as significant as it got. Not confined purely to loss, the 'anniversary effect' is a temporary emotional phase that also comes into play around the anniversary of an accident or attack, a car crash or other traumatic experience.

I wasn't familiar with it prior to Dara's death, but I quickly came to know it intimately.

Coming into February that year, I began to sense these different feelings in my body – the dread taking physical form. I just couldn't believe that it was nearly a year since Dara had died, almost fifty-two weeks since I had last seen her. I hadn't gone that long in my whole life without seeing her and now I was going to live the rest of my life without ever seeing her again. I found it really hard to get my head around.

I travelled up to Blacksod, in Mayo, with everyone else for the first anniversary as there were ceremonies planned to remember the four crew. The crash happened at 12.46 am on 14 March so after midnight on 13 March we attended a vigil on a hill on the edge of Blacksod Bay, facing towards Black Rock Island, looking out to where the crash occurred. There was a huge crowd gathered and everyone lit candles and stood quietly, keeping close together to block out the cold as we waited to mark the time of the crash and remember those who died. It was a cold and blustery night and being in a remote area on the very edge of Ireland it was almost completely dark, save for the soft glow of the candles flickering in the jars that we held in our hands. It was strange being up there, knowing that Dara had been there a year before and that this was where she had spent her last moments of life. Quiet came over the crowd as it neared the time of the crash and everyone withdrew to their own private thoughts. Visibility had been clear for most of the evening but around the time of the crash a fog descended, as it had done the year before, and we lost sight of Black Rock Island. It was at the same time eerie and poignant. I found that night and that time of the night distressing, to be honest, yet at the same time I needed to be there.

The next morning there was a wreath-laying ceremony on the helipad beside the lighthouse. The weather was atrocious on the day of the ceremony, grey, cold, windy and wet, driving rain constantly stinging our faces as we huddled together on the helipad. Dara's navy woollen RNLI beanie was plastered to my head and my hair was sodden underneath. Even our wet gear was soaked through, such was the relentless force of the rain. It was as though the heavens were weeping on such a sad day.

After we placed our wreath on the helipad, we walked in procession to the end of the pier where the wreaths for the four crew were handed over to the Irish Naval Service for them to lay in the seas near Black Rock Island. There had been plans to travel out on the naval ship and lay the wreaths in person, but weather conditions meant that had to be shelved and crew members would lay the wreaths on our behalf. It was of course a dreadfully sad few days in Blacksod, but I found that it was also an important few days. I needed to acknowledge Dara's last moments on Earth and mark the loss of four people who had made a difference in this world. As Irish Coast Guard Director Chris Reynolds tweeted: 'When the wind howls and the rain drives against the windows, when ordinary people will pull closer to the fire or deeper in the duvet, we ask our teams and crews to go out into the darkness and help those they probably don't know and may never meet again.' This captures the essence of the work that rescue crews do and frames the immeasurable loss of these four crew members.

One morning, about a year after she died, my phone pinged with a notification from a WhatsApp group saying: *Dara has left the group.* This was followed by more pings that signalled her departure from all the other groups we were both part of.

I got such a fright. Intellectually, I knew this was because her phone was now cut off and she had not used WhatsApp in a year so the app was removing her from the groups, but emotionally it was like a stab, yet another way in which her presence was being slowly eroded from our lives. So many of the ways in which Dara's physical presence ebbed away happened within the first days, weeks and months that this one, a whole year later, caught me completely offguard. I think had I been aware that this would happen, I would have been prepared for it and not so rocked by it. Now, I tell others about this so that they can at least be cognisant of it and not get a shock like I did.

Alongside Christmas and the anniversary of her death, another big day for me is the date of the last time I saw Dara alive. I find that I experience feelings of the 'anniversary effect' on the anniversary of when we saw each other last. The feelings are so visceral, it takes over my body – I feel it emotionally and physically. Her loss feels part of my DNA and I feel it on a cellular level.

Surprisingly to me, after that first anniversary had passed, I found the second year much tougher than the first. Everything that second year hit harder and hurt more. I cried much more in year two than I did in the year Dara died, I could not stop crying. I think that the shock had fully worn off and in its place came the forlorn realisation that this was our new reality and I really struggled then to carry the weight of Dara's loss. I noticed that many others also appeared to feel this way, that they struggled more in that second year. It won't be the case with everyone and in every situation, but it's something to be aware of as it can take you by surprise.

The truth is that certain dates or times of the year can bring those intense and overwhelming feelings of grief roaring back with a vengeance, raw feelings that you thought you had left behind after the early days of loss. It can feel like you're back at square one or that you're not coping because you're swallowed up again by that tsunami of grief. It's important to look at it realistically and interpret all of your feelings – emotional and physical – as part of a natural and understandable reaction to loss. All that's happening is that the day, the occasion, the date serves as a stark reminder that they are not here and they aren't ever coming back. Or that the life you imagined is not here and it is never going to be realised. Each time that realisation hits, it's like another lash of the whip on your bare back, it is pure pain. It's the grief circle concept, that you have grown your life, however tentatively, around the grief, but the anniversary or the birthday or Christmas or watching your friend with her baby on the date your baby should have been born brings you right back into the raw, sharp grief.

What is helpful is to remember that information is power and understanding what is happening to us at these times helps us to cope. Now that I am aware of the existence of the 'anniversary effect', I prepare each year by being conscious that I may feel differently as 14 March approaches, by knowing what is useful for me to do (take time off work, be around family and friends, talk about it with psychologist Mark Smyth if needed, remember that it will pass, commemorate the loss), and what is not useful for me to do (have a really busy schedule planned, read news reports, expect myself to feel differently than I do). Understanding that the feelings that I experience on Dara's birthday or on the anniversary of her death or indeed those other days when I miss her with an ache, are simply a function of the 'anniversary effect' is helpful. Knowing that it is a function of the life I have grown around her loss reducing back down temporarily, so that grief takes centre-stage again and once more touches every corner of my life for a while, that just helps. It's normal. So am I. And I can get through it.

CHAPTER FIFTEEN

MAKE IT A COMMA, NOT A FULL STOP

Loss makes us a new person because it changes us fundamentally. It changes the shape of our life, our future and ourselves. The things we thought would happen are taken from us and become an impossibility. The stories we told ourselves about how our future would be are suddenly rendered null and void. The life we were supposed to live with our loved one is quite simply no more. It feels that grief has put a full stop on our life and there is no future. At least, not one we want to live. Loss forces us to become someone we never intended to be, with a life we never intended to live, and that can be very difficult to accept. But we have to work through the pain of that loss, at our own pace and in our own time, because there is a danger in getting stuck in the old stories and images, the ones of the life that we can no longer have. If we do that, we can become mired in grief and depression, anxious, unhappy – frozen in the early grief state, really.

Grief may have turned us into someone we never wanted to be, it may have given us a life we never wanted to live, but it is our reality, so how do we work with it? How do we begin again at what feels like zero and embark on a new life without a family of our own? How do we re-establish ourselves as a single person after separation when we always thought that we would grow old as part of a couple? In the face of bereavement, how do we *find the balance between remembering and living*? All three major losses that I suffered changed me, forged my life in a new shape with them at the centre of it. I can see this as awful and unliveable, or I can see it as my life. If I see it as my life, I can work to live it. If we are to avoid making it into a full stop, we have to rethink who we are, and what our life is about, which is painful but also, in truth, filled with opportunity.

When my marriage ended, and before my mortgage approval was granted and I knew for sure that I would be able to buy my ex-husband out of our home and remain living there, I spent ten months wondering where I would end up living. This wasn't idle thinking, this was a stressful and deeply upsetting thought. I love my home – the house itself, the location, my neighbours, it feels like where I'm meant to be. I've lived in different houses, counties and countries, and I have loved other houses, most especially my childhood home, but this home feels like the one I will grow old in. It's also the house where I spent many happy times with Dara. I can see her sitting in my kitchen or chilling in the back garden or curled up with her feet underneath her on an oversized armchair while we have a chat and a catch-up. I don't want to live somewhere that she has never known, somewhere that I can't see her in my mind. I need to be where she had been.

Captain Cathal Oakes came across a poem that resonated with him, so he sent it to me. The first three stanzas capture perfectly what I am trying to say about why I needed to remain living there:

> I heard your voice in the wind today
> and I turned to see your face;
> The warmth of the wind caressed me
> as I stood silently in place.
>
> I felt your touch in the sun today
> as its warmth filled the sky;
> I closed my eyes for your embrace
> and my spirit soared high.
>
> I saw your eyes in the window pane
> as I watched the falling rain;
> It seemed as each raindrop fell
> it quietly said your name.
> (Author unknown)

Naturally, the idea of leaving my home felt like a huge threat hanging over me. I felt I couldn't cope with the idea of it, never mind the potential reality. The huge reason for wanting to remain there was to be close to Emer and Fionn. As one of Fionn's guardians, I need to be able to support Emer as she raises him and step in quickly when needed, and our set-up as near neighbours makes that very easy. And even if I was forced to move, it wouldn't be as if I could put my home behind me. I'd have to return several times a week to be with Fionn and Emer, for we are in each other's lives almost every day. It would be horribly difficult to see another family in my house, their car parked outside instead of mine, their things where my things used to be, it would really rub salt in the wound. For a long time I was distraught by thoughts of that scenario, it was like a fly buzzing around my head, tormenting me with its sound.

Sometimes we act without thinking, and sometimes we think without acting. In my psychology work, I refer to both thinking and taking action as much as I do to feelings. One day it struck me that if I took some action, it might just swat that fly out of the way. I arranged to look at some houses, just to try on the idea of moving and see if I could start to process the possibility of handling the worst-case scenario, should it come to pass. I suppose that I was checking out my Option B, looking it in the eye to see what I was up against. I arranged to view a beautiful house in a lovely area about twenty minutes from my own home. As I walked around the house and stood in each room and tried to imagine myself living there, I knew that although it was genuinely a beautiful place to live, I *really* didn't want to live there. It was a stunning house that was comfortable and conveniently located, but it felt like someone else's house. My heart was back at my own home.

As I walked around with that thought buzzing around my head, I had an in-my-head chat with myself and quite simply told myself that even though I did not want to live there, I must face the truth that I might have to move to a new house and make it my home. I found that saying those words of truth to myself and occupying the actual space of a potential Option B for my life clarified that I knew what was best for me, which was to remain in my own house, but at the same time it also clarified for me that if I did have to move, I could do it. Standing in this house, I was getting some idea of what that move would look like, seeing what I would be dealing with, and I felt I would be able to cope with it. As that realisation began to sink in, I remember standing in one of the bedrooms and looking out on the lovely garden below and making a decision. I decided that the best way to look at this was to tell myself: *'I'll be okay. I just don't know what okay looks like yet.'* By adopting this useful perspective and taking this positive action I was acknowledging the uncertainty in my situation, but I was also reminding myself of the most important fact, that I would be okay. The details of where and how were not yet known to me, but what I did know was that I had survived outliving Dara and I had survived the end of my marriage, so whatever was ahead in terms of where I would live, I could survive that too.

This proved to be an important moment for me in reshaping the end of my marriage. So many things were out of control in my life at that time but deciding to view other houses made me feel like I was taking the reins again, and that felt good. It's easy to feel buffeted about by all the things you cannot control in a marital separation, but this small positive action made me tune back into what I could influence, which was the focus of my attention and thus my emotional state. I have found that controlling the controllables is a very effective method for coping in the face of stress and grief.

Sometimes things are within our control, but we *don't* take action and exert our influence over them. This was the case for me with my physical health. While I was focusing on my mental and emotional state and receiving help in the form of psychological sessions, I let my body slide into ill-health. As I described before, I was beset by infections and viruses, unable to fight them off, which ended in a bad bout of pneumonia. I was taking more steroids and antibiotics than I ever had in my life before. I was exhausted all the time. I wasn't exercising. My hormones were all over the place and causing mischief. I was surviving on tea and toast, a will of iron and not much else. I was still sharing the house with my ex-husband, which was stressful even though we were on friendly terms. I really felt at that time that whatever length my tether was, I was millimetres away from the end of it from a physical perspective, my body running on fumes as I couldn't get a foothold on the ladder when it came to my health.

At the time, I was angry at myself for not working harder on my physical health, but looking back on it now I can see that my body just wasn't ready or able. It was wholly depleted. So were my head and my heart. I wanted to control the controllables, but I couldn't manage all of them at the one time. I prioritised mental and emotional health, and that's how I fell down on the physical side. It's important to be honest about what is controllable when we are grieving. Yes, it's perfectly possible to exercise regularly and eat well, and I have begun to do those things now, but I didn't have the resources at that time to manage it, and I had to forgive myself for that.

It's possible to exert influence in ways that seem very minor but can actually have a big impact on us. While my husband and I were still sharing the house, I was trying to mentally prepare for the moment when he would leave. I married a lovely man, he is kind and warm and funny, and even though our marriage didn't last until the 'death do us part' bit, I was going to miss him. I dreaded that final goodbye when our life together was dissolved and we went our separate ways. It was like waiting for the axe to fall.

In order to take positive action about this, I had lined up painters, tilers, gardeners and an electrician to come in and renovate the house once it was mine. I felt it was necessary to quickly make it feel like my own home rather than the space that we had shared in our marriage. I couldn't do anything to expedite the legal process, the delays and reams of documentation, the insurance process or the separation process, so this was my bid to take the reins on the situation in the only way I could. But before the house sale went through and these renovations could start, I needed to make some change, no matter how small. My mind settled on the garden shed: I wanted to paint it. There would be no harm in doing this as even if the house sale fell through for any reason, the shed wouldn't have any impact on the value. The old shed colour was a standard brown, the garden version of magnolia. I decided that I wanted a big change, so I chose blue, a light, soft cornflower blue. I was short on cheeriness in my actual life, so I figured that I could inject some cheer into my garden instead.

It was a hot summer that year, with scorching temperatures for weeks on end, and given that I'm a shade person rather than a sun person I got up at 6.00 am for three days and I painted my shed. I remember standing up on a step-ladder to do the apex of the roof – the sky was blue, the sun warm already but thankfully not yet hot, the birds were singing and the world was otherwise quiet, and I was painting my shed blue. It was a tiny dent in all the enormous things that were happening in my life at that time, but it was my dent, one that I instigated. I thoroughly enjoyed those early mornings, dipping my brush into the happy blue paint and getting that second coat onto the shed.

When it was finished, I loved it. It was a beautiful splash of colour in place of the mundane brown and I noticed in the days and weeks afterwards that each time I looked out of my kitchen window into my garden and saw my lovely blue shed with its little white accents on the apex and the windows, I smiled. Even on the days when yet another week had rolled over and the house sale had not gone through or when I was ill with yet another chest infection, that blue shed made me smile, even if for just a moment. I realised then that even a few moments' break from feeling worn out with life was a help and that those blue-shed smiles punctuated those tough days and encouraged me to keep going. I decided then to remember to *find the blue shed* whenever I'm in situations where it's hard going. It might not be a big thing or an important thing or even a lasting thing, but the point is that it's something which will give me a small sense of control in situations where I may have very little. What I mean is that there is always some way of making a dent, of effecting a change that's your choice, of finding one thing that makes you smile in a day of frowns or tears.

After a spring and summer of legal and financial admin, the marriage separation documentation and the house sale documents all eventually went through and so began the start of the end of our lives together. It was a trying and testing time getting to the point of it all being signed and it was a relief when that aspect got over the line. We could each move on with our own lives, which was sad in one way, but also a relief in another. What was our house became my house. I'm very grateful to have my home, my safe place, beside my sister, my nephew, my best friend Tara and my wonderful neighbours. My blue shed is no longer in my garden, but it remains in my head as that important lesson to 'find the blue shed', to find the thing that will help me smile for even a moment, because that will give momentary respite and will be enough to get me through each day and on to the next.

I had to work out the blue shed for myself because I didn't have the rituals that exist around death to help me work out how to live through the separation. When someone dies, everyone starts following the social script of wake, support, funeral. Those rituals don't really exist when you lose your marriage or when you learn that you can't conceive. They are lonelier losses and there's so much you have to figure out on your own. For me, taking control of small, manageable elements – like painting a shed – was an important way of feeling that I did still have some say in what was happening to me, it was a way of pointing my life in the direction of a comma rather than a full stop when my marriage ended.

In response to loss and pain, I think it's important that we don't come to view ourselves as something broken that needs to be 'fixed'. There's nothing we can do that will end the grief or stop the feelings of anger and hurt and despair. These are natural reactions to loss, so we benefit from accepting them and allowing ourselves to feel them. They won't stay for ever but they are part of the process. We are broken, but we should not look to fix it. We have to live around the cracks, the fissures, the gaps. They are now part of us. This might sound like an awful thing, but I think it's a comfort to realise that you don't ever have to be 'better', you just have to be good enough to carry on.

One of the most impactful pieces I have ever read in a psychology book is in *The Body Keeps the Score* by Bessel van der Kolk. In a chapter entitled 'Healing from Trauma: Owning Your Self', he says this:

Nobody can 'treat' a war, or abuse, rape, molestation, or any other horrendous event, for that matter; what has happened cannot be undone. But what can be dealt with are the imprints of the trauma on body, mind and soul: the crushing sensations in your chest that you may label as anxiety or depression; the self-loathing; the nightmares and flashbacks; the fog that keeps you from staying on task and from engaging fully in what you are doing; being unable to fully open your heart to another human being.

Trauma robs you of the feeling that you are in charge of yourself ... The challenge of recovery is to re-establish ownership of your body and your mind – of yourself. This means feeling free to know what you know and to feel what you feel without becoming over-whelmed, enraged, ashamed, or collapsed ...

Trauma is much more than a story about something that happened a long time ago. The emotional and physical sensations that were imprinted during the trauma are experienced not as memories but as disruptive physical reactions in the present.

I have reached for this book many times over the past few years just to re-read those lines because they resonate so much with me in the context of traumatic loss. Dara's death was a traumatic loss, it was shock, trauma and distress layered on top of grief. For me, I welcome the understanding that there is no help I could ever get that would undo what happened. This refocuses my goal as being to regain ownership of my body, mind and spirit so that the capacity of grief to imprint on my life becomes manageable.

By this I don't mean that I want to stem the feelings of grief in any way, not at all. I believe that grief is a natural process and that I need to lean in to it rather than avoid it. What I mean is that as time goes on, I realise that I want to be able to remember Dara and mourn her loss and that I also want to be able to live my life. I'm at a place where I want both.

I feel that if grief had a goal, it wouldn't be for me to feel better or to feel like myself again or even to get back to normal, because the truth is that I'm for ever changed and I'll never feel like myself again, that old self is gone. There is a new normal now. It's not about either of those. Instead, I think that the goal of grief would be to *find the balance between remembering and living*, to get to a place where I can carry the loss of Dara and at the same time live life, really live, not just exist in the shadow of her loss.

I never want to not grieve for Dara, that feels all kinds of wrong to me. She may not be here any more but Dara *is* my sister, not *was* my sister, she's a part of me, the same blood running through our veins, the same memories threaded through our lives since childhood. When Dara died a part of me died too and it feels since that a part of me is missing, that a part of us as a family is missing, so respecting that loss matters to me and I welcome grief in that regard. But as well as respecting Dara's loss I also want to honour her in how I live my life, that matters too and it means that I don't want to be stuck in grief, with the imprint of traumatic loss so great that it prevents me from living the life that I am lucky enough to have.

Dara fought *so* hard to get back to her child and to her family after the crash. Given that Dara's body was found that night and her helmet washed up in the days following, it would seem fair to suggest that underwater, in the deep darkness of the Atlantic Ocean, she managed to remove her seat-belt and her helmet and get herself out of the helicopter and she inflated her life jacket before she tried to make it to the surface of the water. But sadly, we aren't owed anything in life and even her heroic efforts didn't mean that she got to live. Fighting until her very last breath didn't grant her the gift of staying alive. She died before she reached the surface. If I put my hand on my chest right now, I can feel my heart beating, a slow and steady thrum against my fingers, and I'm acutely aware that I'm lucky to have a heart that beats. Knowing how far Dara got in trying to keep her own heart pumping, I know that I cannot waste the life that I have, and I want to live it ... and *find the balance between remembering and living*.

Dara's death layered on top of the loss of my marriage and the loss around not being a mother could be a full stop in my life, easily so. There's enough pain within to keep me stuck in anger and grief for ever, if I let it. But I think that the loss in my life can also be a comma, or a semi-colon, or a dash, anything but a full stop, because that's just not an option. What would it achieve if I stepped out of life and stopped living, just existing until the day I died, marking time because I couldn't carry the hand that life dealt? If I were consumed with rage and a sense of injustice at the ways in which life laughed in my face and dismissed my hopes with a flick of the hand, not even big, wild, outlandish hopes but normal ones, such as being a parent, or knowing the joy of a lasting loving relationship, or having my siblings with me until we are all old? If I gave myself permission for the end of life as I knew it to in fact be the end of my living, that would only bring pain to my family and friends because it would be as though I died while I'm alive. It would also bring intense pain to me. I can't think of anything that would disrespect Dara's memory more.

In my experience, grief could be likened to a set of scars after a fall from a height. Raw, open wounds after the impact, areas of skin ripped off my back, limbs smashed and bent at angles they shouldn't be, bloodied and broken, not life-threatening but life-changing impacts from the fall. The wounds painful beyond measure, excruciating in those early days, halting me in my tracks as my body wouldn't work because of the damage done to it. Over time and with rehab the wounds not so much healed as evolved to be scars, marks left for ever on my body, not visible to others but very much there. Although they no longer prevent my body from working as it should, I can always see the scars, feel them, touch them and though they may not bleed like they did in the beginning, they do hurt badly sometimes, a powerful reminder of the horrifying fall.

It didn't kill me, though. It changed me, but I survived to live another day. That's what grief feels like to me, I feel that the scars of loss are very much part of me now, but they don't have to stop me from living. In fact, the scars of loss serve as a daily reminder that I *must* carry on living, that a life that is both full and rich in experiences and feelings is not only possible but also desirable, even after loss. As I write that sentence a flicker of guilt flashes across my consciousness, but the truth is that there *is* life after death, as unpalatable as that may sound, and being some version of okay and living life doesn't mean that I am unaffected by Dara's death, just that I have learned to carry her loss.

There is great comfort in knowing that Dara would want that, I know she would. She was a cheerleader in my life when she was alive and she would want me to remember her but also to experience life, not to just exist. She'd want that for me but also for her, because she fought so hard to live and would give literally anything to have her life back and she would be *so* angry with me if I wasted the life that I have, that would be such a disrespect to the life that she has lost. When life goes on and good things happen it won't balance out the bad, nothing will ever make it okay that Dara's gone, but me failing to live won't bring her back and will instead bring a whole other world of pain to our door. We've known ten lifetimes of pain in the past three years and I'm not knowingly inviting any more into our lives. My focus now is to see what's there after the comma, to recognise that while recent times have brought me to my knees and have left me feeling broken in so many ways, it's not a full stop. Whether I feel like it or not, I need to pick myself up and keep going.

CHAPTER SIXTEEN

GRIEF IS THE GATE-CRASHER WHO BROUGHT GIFTS TO THE PARTY

oss brings clarity, perspective and freedom like nothing else I've ever experienced. Trailing in the wake of death like a sort of peace offering for all the suffering, surviving loss is like wiping the smudges off our glasses because as we slowly find our way through the fog, things become clearer and we see life in a way that we never did before. When someone we love dies, we learn first-hand about life and how fragile it is. We learn about love and what it *truly* means to love someone, not the movie-scene 'hearts and flowers' love but the 'my life has a hole in it without you' love. We learn about value, because of all the things that vie for our attention and time, loss teaches us what truly matters and what truly doesn't. We learn about ourselves and we find out just what we're made of deep inside. Finally, we learn about humankind, that humans have a huge capacity for kindness and an inherent need to help. Kindness is a powerful force in the face of adversity and the ones who care will come and they will show us kindness when we need it. With this new-found clarity and perspective comes freedom, because we no longer feel constrained by many of the incessant demands of life. We see now what really matters and we see things for how they really are, and this combination serves to give release from the chains of expectation and a sense of freedom to live life in our own way.

Before Dara died I would have said that I had a fairly good perspective on life and that I was reasonably good when it came to cutting through the chaff to get to the kernel of the wheat, but now I know that I was in the ha'penny place. It's only now that, after her death, I can cut through the noise in life and get straight to what really matters, or at least what matters to me. I know, for example, that being perfect doesn't matter, that people liking me doesn't matter and that pleasing everyone doesn't matter. I would have never got too caught up with the first two, but the third one would have tripped me up a bit and I'd often have ended up saying said yes to things that I didn't want to do solely to keep others happy.

Naturally, there's a balance needed. I haven't turned into some horrible selfish shrew who never does anything for others, but these days when I'm asked to do something, either personally or professionally, I stop and have a quick check with myself to see if it's something I really want to do. I have no interest in wasting time any more. I want to do things that matter to me or to those I care about. If I feel something doesn't fulfil these criteria, I'll say no – and it will be a guilt-free, unhesitant no. Sometimes I may not particularly want to do something, but I know that it would make a difference to people I care about if I did it, so

I'll say yes for that reason. I feel more content in my life now because my values and my behaviours are more aligned than they have ever been. I feel as though I am living my best life, personally and professionally. There's more change to come in both spheres, I expect, but there's a huge solidity and steadiness in knowing that I have no regrets now in how I am living my life, nor will I have regrets as I move into my future life.

I know, too, that the current global obsession with image doesn't matter one bit, not to me anyway. I care how things are, not how they look like they are. I value real, flaws and all. We live in a world where the highest value is placed on a notion of perfection dreamt up by somebody else and it's all about 'Likes' and the approval of others and fitting into a norm. We are told online and in magazines what the perfect body looks like and what the perfect life needs to have in it in order to be a 'success'. Such nonsense. We're all going to die one day. Every single person who reads this book, and indeed every person who doesn't, will one day die, along with everyone they know and love. That's a sobering thought, but it's not just a thought, it's a truth. I think that we are fooling ourselves if we think that we are getting ahead of others in life. There *is* no ahead, we are all going the same way because we all end in death. I don't say that in a frightening way, just in a perspective way. Now, if someone cuts in front of me in a queue or tries to pull the wool over my eyes or even, as happened recently, scams me out of money, I simply let it go. I'm no longer affected by the rat race of life and the people who try to clamber over others. They haven't 'won', nobody wins, because we all end up in the same place. There's huge freedom in that realisation and real peace of mind.

There's no one on Earth who shares the unique combination of our gene pool combined with our specific experiences in life, which means we are all one of a kind. Who, then, could possibly do a better job of being us than we can ourselves? So why would I waste any time chasing someone else's view of 'perfection' or 'success'? That makes even less sense to me now than it ever did, in fact it makes no sense whatsoever. Loss has brought a definite clarity to the table in that regard. Unlike those with hordes of 'friends' on some social media platforms, my life would get no Likes on Instagram and it wouldn't get any followers on YouTube, where image reigns supreme. It's a life that has been messy, complicated and layered with sorrow of late and there's no prettiness, perfection or desirability in that picture. But grief has brought freedom in being able to like what I like, value what I value and live how I want to live. I simply don't care one jot about adhering to an arbitrary idea from some random stranger of what is a worthwhile life. It may be short or it may be long, because it's different for everyone, but life is finite, that's a given, and now, with the perspective of loss, I choose to live whatever time I have my own way, without the need to conform to the standards of others. This feels liberating and empowering.

Grief also brought a useful perspective on my weight gain over the past few years because no matter what state of fitness I've been in and how far I've travelled from my optimum in that regard, the way I see it is that this is still the body that allows me to do the important things in life. Fionn and I do this thing where he starts at the end of the hallway and runs full tilt towards me, with his head down and his little arms pumping, while I'm kneeling, waiting for the impact, then he takes off and hurls himself into my arms, somehow we miss clashing our heads and we squeeze each other tightly and have 'the best hug ever'. It's great fun and we both fall about laughing each time we do it. Well, my body may be currently out of shape, but it's the body that enables me to have that moment with Fionn, to cheer him on at his first day at school when his mama wasn't there, to read to him, listen to his stories of how his day went, hear him tell me that he loves me and tell him that I love him back. This body enables me to listen to clients and hear their stories and help them through the therapy process. It lets me spend time with my family and friends doing the everyday things that connect us and make us happy.

Even if it's not perfect, there's perfection in a body that allows us to do things like put our arms around a loved one, hear the worries of a friend, tell someone we care, smile thanks to a stranger. These are things that really matter, and I can do them. So even if I am unfit at the moment, I am still grateful for all that this body allows me to do. After all, 'failure is a bruise, not a tattoo' (Jon Sinclair) and in life we all fall down at times. Mentally, emotionally, physically. Little falls, big falls, huge falls. That's being human, not being weak, and when we fall we need to be kind to ourselves and give ourselves a break, let ourselves get back on track when we're ready. When you carry excess weight, like me, you are wearing your struggles on the outside. If this is also you, be kind to yourself. Trust that you'll find your way when you're able to because hope will get you places that criticism won't. I know that some will look at me and say, 'Hasn't she put on a few pounds?' But I've faced the fact that my sister died not in a warm bed with her family around her at the end of a long life, but in the cold, dark waters of the sea on her own when she had many years left to live. I can therefore handle someone saying that my arse is bigger than it should be. And anyway, I'm well aware of the size of my arse, so someone pointing it out isn't any surprise to me. That's a welcome perspective and I've got grief to thank for it.

For me, surviving loss and living with loss have clarified that love, honesty, integrity and peace of mind matter to me. Being authentic matters. Being kind matters. Being real matters. Gratitude for the good in my life matters. Saying 'thank you' matters, as does sending thank-you notes. Holding doors open matters and letting cars out of side roads. Paying attention when someone else is speaking matters, not busying myself in my head preparing my own reply. Eye contact matters, a smile matters, human touch matters, a hand on the arm when appropriate, or on the shoulder, supporting, guiding, comforting, or a big warm, long, strong hug. Listening matters, and hearing matters, really hearing what someone is saying or not saying, spotting the clues that someone I love is perhaps struggling. Remembering what matters to those I care about matters to me, being tuned in as a sister, daughter, cousin or friend. Not taking myself – or life – too seriously matters. Being able to laugh at myself and see the funny side when I mess up matters to me, as does being able to learn from my mistakes and get better at getting better. Being brave matters immensely to me, facing challenges with courage no matter how scared I am and never, ever being afraid to fail. Ambition matters to me, pushing myself out of my comfort zone and asking big things of myself, being willing to take the risk. Spontaneous three-hour cups of tea chatting around a table matter to me and noisy dinners with everyone chattering, laughing and passing the potatoes. Bracing walks on the beach in winter with my pals matter to me, sharing each other's stories and putting the world to rights as we walk and talk. Belly-aching, rib-tickling laughs matter to me, when I'm in a room full of people I feel safe with and the conversation flows and the laughs follow. Above all, love matters to me, spending time with those I like and love, soaking it all in, imprinting them onto my mind because I never know when that's all I'll have of them. Loss has taught me that feeling loved is not about being in a relationship, it's about people being there in your life, showing up, being in your corner and believing in you, even when you're making a bit of a mess of something. It's about having people in your life who just get you and who like and love the essence of who you are as a person. I am blessed to have such people in my life and even though I'm single, I don't feel lonely. I love and I feel loved.

In surviving loss I have learned that there is more in me than I might ever have thought. I think our capacity for growth is like the depths of the ocean, there's always more, and that perspective allows me to ask more of myself in my life. I work with clients from all walks of life, helping them move emotionally, and subsequently in other ways, from where they are now to where they want to go, and I've also done lots of moving and growing in my own life. Given the work I do, it will not be surprising that I'm a believer in the concept of a growth mindset, as opposed to that of a fixed mindset. Someone who has a growth mindset believes that their basic qualities, talents and abilities can be developed through learning, work and commitment. A person with a fixed mindset tends to see their qualities and abilities as traits that cannot change. I believe that in terms of development, we are not static, we can grow and change. However, even I had no real idea of the potential extent of that growth. In the wake of Dara's death and the end of my marriage, as a person I have been pushed and moulded and developed in ways that I didn't know I could. I've learned that as a human being I'm not *either/or*. All the times I have been or am sad, stumbling, falling down, for ever changed by loss, I am at the same time also learning, growing, healing, whole. I'm not written off because I struggle, that is part of me and part of my growth as a person.

I see growth as something we need to actively choose, to be open to, to decide to explore, as this kind of development is not something that will necessarily happen naturally over time. Helped by that mindset of openness and development, I find myself now, with a few years' distance from my journey to become a mum, in a very different place than when I began travelling that road. I spent my late thirties to early forties on the assisted fertility path, and my early to mid-forties on the adoption route, giving my all to every appointment, every test, every procedure, every task set in front of me along the way. But life decided that motherhood was not part of the plan, and in time I was able to first accept and then embrace this 'comma'. It feels to me now that I have grown and developed exponentially as a result of that experience. I had faced other challenges over the years prior to this, but infertility was the first really big loss in my life, and although it took the deeper thinking after Dara's death to actually recognise it as a loss, and it remained an unnamed grief until recent years, I nonetheless still had to develop, adjust and grow in order to adapt after the experience.

When I was growing up, except in the case of a parental bereavement, all the children in my class in Junior Infants had two parents, all of whom were married, with the men working outside the home and the women working within the home, raising the children. Despite such uniformity in the roles I saw in front of me, I never believed that what was modelled for me was the only path in life: to grow up, find a man, get married and have children. I was always of a mindset that life could be wonderful via different routes. Going through that journey of assisted fertility and adoption has gifted me that belief from an experiential perspective, and I know now from my own lived experience that I was right when I was young, there truly is not just one way to live life. Nor is there only one way to be contented in life. Or fulfilled. There are many highways, byways and boreens along which we can travel on our personal journey through life and there is beauty to be found on all. There is *such* freedom and such peace in that understanding, as well as such a sense of contentment. Living through and surviving that first big loss in my life has helped me to become even more open-minded, more relaxed around options in life, less defined in terms of expectations and more accepting of possibilities that I cannot yet see. I enjoy my life. I feel free, yet connected. And loved. I have discovered that while continuing our bloodline, or giving our parents a grandchild, or experiencing that mother–child love are all undoubtedly wonderful experiences, they are not the only experiences that are wonderful, nor are they even the experiences that are the most wonderful in life. Because: *there is no one way to live life!*

We can find contentment, joy, peace, fulfilment and love on any of those roads we may find ourselves on; motherhood is but one of those roads. I may not know the joy and purpose of motherhood, but I have a great life. I find a real sense of fulfilment from my work helping others, it is rich and rewarding and it feels like I'm making a difference in the world by making a difference in people's lives. I find contentment in my freedom, enjoying the luxury of space in my daily life, with time to think and time to catch my breath. I find joy in those unique opportunities that life has sent my way, particularly the role of psychologist to the Irish team at the Olympic Games and having been a contributor to weekly radio shows on the national airwaves. In this life that I love, one of the things that really makes it great is the love I find in my family and in my friendships. There I find connection, companionship and care. I find loyalty and friendship, mutual respect and kindness. I find encouragement and support and people who believe in me. That's love. I don't need to be a mother to know what love is like, I can love and feel loved just as I am. Surviving this loss has proved this to be true.

Emerging the other side of a marriage separation has also stretched my understanding about love and has taught me, once again, that love is love and that it's possible to feel loved without having romantic love in your life. Being married is wonderful and having a spouse can be a beautiful adventure on so many levels, but similar to what I learned with the mother–child love, romantic love isn't the only love that matters, nor is it the best love (because there's isn't one). We're encouraged to think of it as the Holy Grail of love, but it's just one type of love. I've learned to truly value the love that comes from my family and friends and in doing so I have found real contentment in life, surrounded by my tribe, a band of people who know me, get me and love me for who I am. I've learned that love isn't necessarily about having a partner in your life, it's about having people in your life.

I've noticed that coming through a marriage breakdown and separation has also stretched me on a practical level. My parents brought us all up to be self-sufficient and I have always been independent and capable of getting things done myself, but when you're married you tend to fall into roles within the home and each of you ends up doing certain jobs. After our separation, when I settled a bit and got used to my ex-husband not being there, I adjusted to being the person who had to do all the jobs that needed doing. I catch spiders on tissue paper and gently relocate them outside. I unblock plugholes. I even managed to pull the fridge freezer out of its place after I punctured it while defrosting it recently. It took me three days to figure out how to fix a problem with a tap that my ex-husband would have fixed in half an hour, but I still did it. There are some jobs that I do need to get some help with, but there's a lovely sense of satisfaction in being self-sufficient in these little things and that feeling is very welcome after the rigours of the separation process.

Undoubtedly the loss that has stretched and grown me most is the sudden loss of my sister. Since Dara died I feel that I have become more compassionate, accepting, patient and capable and I feel more grounded, more solid, more secure in myself because of this growth. In ways I have become a better person, a nicer, more rounded version of myself. Upgraded, if you like. It sounds odd for me to say that of myself, but I think you know how I mean it. I don't say it in an arrogant way, just in an honest way. I've also become more fearless, because there's something about surviving the hardest of times in your life that strengthens your armour. It's as though the harder the times I have faced, the more I feel able to face hard times. That, in turn, brings a fearlessness that I never had before. I'm not afraid of dying and I'm not afraid of living either. Whatever life brings, I'll face it.

My experiences over the last few years have taught me that life doesn't owe us anything, life isn't always fair and sometimes bad things happen to good people. But it has also taught me that human beings can handle a *lot* and be okay. I have grown into that space of feeling battered and bruised by life, but also feeling like I'm handling it.

Things can change in a heartbeat and everything you knew about life as you're living it now can end with one knock on the door or one phone call. But A.A. Milne got it right in *Winnie the Pooh* when Christopher Robin says, 'You are braver than you believe, stronger than you seem and smarter than you think,' because even in the most difficult times, when loss brings you to your knees, you can survive. And when you do survive, you find layers and depths to yourself and to life that were never there before. Grief is a gate-crasher, it smashes down the front door and barges into your life uninvited and living with it is the most awful thing that you'll ever go through. But the truth is that it also brings gifts, because it is also the most enlightening thing and the most powerful teacher I've ever known. If we open our minds and be brave, we can learn lessons from loss that can enrich our lives and if I can't bring Dara back, if I can't undo the loss of motherhood and the loss of my marriage, then I'll take that with gratitude.

So, what now? Now that I have survived the first days, weeks, months and the first three years since Dara's death. Now that I understand grief and what it has been doing to my body, mind and emotions while I learn to live with her loss. Now that I can see that grief brought gifts when it came to stay without invitation. What next? What's life like when you come out the other side of that awful?

I will grieve the loss of Dara for the rest of my days, so when I talk about being out the other side of awful, I'm not talking about grief. As long as I breathe, I will mourn the loss of my brave and beautiful sister who died when she was only halfway through her life. What I mean by *the other side of awful* is that I have survived hearing that Dara had died. I survived accepting that she is not ever coming back. I survived the early days of learning to live with her loss. At the same time, I emotionally processed the loss of my marriage. I have coped with the savagely difficult legal, financial and practical processes of ending a marriage and I've also survived the horrifying fallout of wondering if I was going to have to leave my home as a result of separation. I endured the re-opening of old wounds around not being a parent, I processed the loss of any children that I might have had, and I found my contentment around being a guardian to my nephew. The intense stress of it all was horrendous, a cumulative distress that nearly finished me. But I survived. Now, I've lived through those first huge and terrifying waves of bereavement and have adapted to a new normal of life without Dara. I have become used to the fact that I am no longer someone's wife, neither am I somebody's mother, I'm just me, and I'm okay with that. I'm living in my lovely home, safe in the knowledge that I remain nearby to support my sister and nephew. It feels as though I am now 'only' dealing with grief for Dara, there are no added layers on top and that's what I mean about being out the other side of awful.

The gifts that grief brought in its wake have shaped my life and in this life after awful my newfound sense of clarity, perspective and freedom have given me the ability to live a much more rewarding life. If I take the fact that Dara is dead out of the equation for a moment, I'm probably happier than I have ever been in my life. This is not to say that I didn't know great happiness in my life and indeed in my marriage, because I absolutely did. But having lived through the past couple of years I now truly know myself. I know what I'm really made of and I'm happy with what I've discovered. It has added a layer of contentment that I've never known before. I know that I can step up to handle whatever needs to be handled, that I can face my fears, that I can endure immense stress and distress and that I can survive the toughest and darkest of times. I feel strong and capable, able to bounce back from broken. I don't feel invincible, I'm not stupid and I know that I have limits, but I also know that those limits are much further out than I had ever imagined. It's a pretty powerful feeling. It feels like I've finally arrived in my life, that I'm ready to shift up a gear and live life with an extra dimension, with layers of fearlessness, contentment, peace and gratitude that I've never known before. I find myself looking at life after death and thinking about living that life, feeling like I'm ready to give it a try and see how I get on.

Acceptance of what happened to Dara and getting to this place of feeling ready to live again didn't happen quickly. Just like the grass growing or the sun rising, it occurred gradually, so that things which felt unbearable in year one after Dara's death felt more bearable by year three. My emotions have evolved and changed over time. This holds true for life in general. Indeed, this summer I watched golfer Shane Lowry talking about this very thing after winning the Open Championship in July 2019. Speaking about his experience the previous year at the 2018 Open, he said 'I sat in the car park in Carnoustie and I cried. Golf wasn't my friend at the time. It was something that was becoming very stressful and it was weighing on me and I just didn't like doing it. What a difference a year makes.' He summed up a truth with those words, which is that our feelings can change, perspective can change, life can change and that remembering this at our lowest ebb can bring enough hope to keep us going. Given the changes in me over this time, it feels right that, moving towards the third anniversary of Dara's death, I find that I want to live again. I suppose it's that I want to *feel* again, to be present and really experience life once more.

Let me be clear, however – there are some days when I don't want to do anything other than stay in bed and cry because I am just so sad for Dara and for the loss of her life, sad for how much I miss her and the life we all shared. That's understandable. But now those days are interspersed with days where I want to live, not just exist but *live*. After all I have witnessed and experienced of late, I'm acutely aware of the fragility of life. All we have is now, so wasting time is not an option for me any more. It turns out that this vantage point makes for a better life. There's a fullness to what I experience in life now, a richness to it and a sense of appreciation for being alive that I didn't have before, that I couldn't have had before, in fact, because my perspective had to evolve through experience before I could see things as I do now. Life feels more vibrant in the aftermath of loss, a bit like Dorothy experiencing the world in colour when she arrives in the Land of Oz. There's an awe to life now. I would even go so far as to say that I have probably never felt more alive. I'm so sad to say that when Dara is dead, it feels wrong to voice such a thought, but the truth is that her death changed my perspective and brought me to this place. There's a Japanese practice called Kintsugi that involves using gold to repair broken pottery so that the break or crack in the ceramic becomes a beautiful part of the whole piece and it doesn't have to be discarded just because it was broken. I feel like a piece of that pottery; the scars and traces of the breaks in my life are evident, but not in an ugly way. Instead, it feels that they are there in a beautiful way because I feel as though I've woken up and I am living fully, happily in myself as a person, perhaps for the first time in my life.

I'm aware that this might sound like an extraordinary statement – perhaps an unbelievable one – when I've lost so much. I'm not in any way living the life I thought I'd be living now, nor will I get to live the life I thought would be my future. Here I am, separated, not a parent like I thought I would be, one of five siblings, with the fourth sibling ever present, ever missing. It's nothing like how I planned things to be. And yet, here I am, also saying that there is joy in my life, happiness, vibrancy. I know it seems odd that both statements can be true, but it is true nonetheless. I lost the life I wanted to live and I'm living a 'lesser' life in its place, because Dara's not in it, but even so I can say with honesty that I have adapted and am finding a new version of contentment. I never wanted this life, but seeing as it's mine, the best thing I can do is accept it, embrace it and live it. Yes, there have been horrible changes, but from them has come good changes as well.

I enjoyed life before, but there's an added dimension now in that I really do find pleasure in the simplest of moments. I know that the little things are really the big things in life and there's satisfaction in not needing x, y or z in order to feel content but feeling that all is okay in the world in those little everyday moments. Sitting in my garden for ten minutes in the early morning, sipping a cup of peppermint tea as I enjoy the beauty of my Red Robin (photinia) tree and my tree fern while I listen to the birds chattering is something I love doing. It's my little oasis in the suburbs of Dublin and it sets me up for the day to have a few minutes out there. Or if I see a little bird on a fence or a butterfly landing on a flower, I stop and watch. The same with a rich pink sunset or a bright full moon or snow falling. I just stop and watch, taking a moment to see what's in front of me. My phone has been welded to my hand since that call from Emer on 14 March 2017, but I've begun to leave it upstairs for a while when I'm at home at the weekend, getting a break from the sixty-four WhatsApp messages that usually pop up each time I check in. I sit on the Luas and I look out the window at my city as we pass. I don't sit with my head bent towards a screen, rather I sit with my head up, looking out. I also more often watch TV without my phone now, paying attention to what I'm watching without simultaneously scrolling through Twitter to see what's going on in the world. I tend to have a busy diary, but now I also consciously leave space in my life to be able to say yes to spontaneous invitations to do random good stuff. With this approach I feel content, not rushed or hurried, but relaxed and at ease. Life feels peaceful, I suppose.

I also make time now to do some of the things that I always meant to do but never got round to doing, like calling friends I don't get to see too often for a big old catch-up, or looking through the photos I've taken over the years but never make time to enjoy. Actually, I got lucky with this recently – poring over old albums, there, stuck in the pages, I found some photos from twenty-something years ago when I was on a flight with Dara and the crew. The opportunity had arisen to go up in the heli and I'd jumped at it, as we all did any time there was a chance to see Dara at work. Actually, when she died it was a comfort to have been in the heli with her several times over the years because in my head I can still hear her over the headset, talking to air traffic control in preparation for take-off or discussing aspects of the flight with the crew as we flew over the countryside, and it's comforting to have those memories in my head. On that particular day, back in the 1990s, we flew over Galway Bay and as the crew wanted to do some training, they winched me down onto a vessel for a bit and I got a trip on the boat before they winched me back up again. The winch operator took a couple of lovely photos from the heli, one of me on the boat with some of the crew and another as I was being winched back up towards the helicopter. That one is my favourite. I'm on the end of the winch, my hands holding on to the line, helmet on, looking up at the winch op as he hung out the door high above me with his camera, trying to capture a good shot of me with the white-capped waves in the background below. He got his shot and I have a big smile on my face because I absolutely loved it. What an incredible experience to have had; I felt very lucky. Now, of course, that photo is about as precious as it gets and when I found those pics again, it made me so happy. It was pure joy to find this link to Dara given that so many links ended when she died.

The other change on the other side of awful is that I don't take either myself or life too seriously. I find that I laugh at things which before now might not have seemed too funny. It's only in the past few months that I've definitely got my sense of humour back, and I'm glad of it. I found myself in a pickle one morning that demonstrates this beautifully, if ever so slightly embarrassingly. I had picked up a prescription for HRT but had a question about the instructions on one of the two boxes of medication. I put both boxes into the side pocket of my car door and headed down to Dundrum Town Centre to do an errand, planning to stop off at the pharmacy on my way home. When I arrived at the pharmacy I could find only one box of the tablets, in spite of a thorough search under seats and floor mats. I figured that the box of HRT patches had fallen out when I opened my car to leave Dundrum Town Centre, so I jumped back into the car and drove back there. I drove straight to where I had parked my car, only to find another car in that spot. I parked up and walked around the other car, to check the ground near where my door would have been. I ended up on my knees in the middle of the car park, searching for a box of hormone tablets with my name on it. When I think of it now, I want to cover my eyes … what must I have looked like?!

There was nothing underneath the car so in one last-ditch attempt to find it, I went to the ticket machine and pressed the Help button. Yes, I did ask the anonymous man whose voice echoed through the speakers, and who had in all probability seen me on the CCTV cameras in the car park on my hands and knees looking under cars, if anyone had left in a box of medication with my name on it. Needless to say, they hadn't. I had to leave empty-handed and scratching my head as to where the damn box of HRT had got to. When I recounted the tale to my friends, they laughed out loud at the image of me on my knees in the car park, bent over, my face pressed to the concrete as I furtively searched underneath a random car for a box of tablets meant to keep me on an even keel. Oh, the irony! I laughed myself as I told the story, one of those belly-aching laughs where your cheeks hurt afterwards. I laughed like that all over again when, eight weeks later, I reached into the side pocket of my car door for my sunglasses and my fingers wrapped around the offending box of tablets!

I find now that, even in little ways, I feel a freedom to do what I want without a need to conform. I was in a department store one day, for example, and a sales assistant asked me if I would like to smell a new scent for men. It was Christian Dior's *Sauvage* and it was gorgeous, very fresh and clean. As I stood there sniffing it, I thought to myself that it could be a long time (if ever) before I might be close enough to a man to smell his aftershave, so I bought the scent for myself and I wear it. I wear my perfumes too, of course, but some days I wear *Sauvage* and I smile at doing things my way. I don't need to have a man in my life to enjoy this scent, I like it, so I wear it. Simple.

What's also great about life now is that I have found my tribe. I know that the people who are in my life are real connections, that they are in my corner and I'm in theirs. If I could choose from everyone in the world, I would pick my family again in a heartbeat. We are just ordinary people who have lived through extraordinary times, but who knew they were such amazing examples of the best of the human spirit? The way they have handled this tragedy is powerful, such dignity, courage and mutual support throughout, it has been inspiring to witness. There was no instruction booklet, yet my siblings, parents and extended family stepped up and did what life asked of them and got through it, minding each other along the way. My friends showed up too and were incredible, propping me up when my own two legs wouldn't hold me. It's amazing how perfectly they gauged their support given that they could have had no idea of the tragedy that would visit our lives when they got involved with me way back when we first met. Some of Dara's work colleagues from the search and rescue bases also form part of my tribe. They have been right there beside us on this journey and we get regular messages, visits and invitations from several people who were pals of Dara's. A few of the lads feel like brothers to me now and the two female pilots too have become confidantes and a great support. I'm in touch with these few regularly since the crash. We don't particularly talk about the crash itself, but more about how we're all doing. They all just want us to know that they're there if we need them. Even recently, on what he knew was a tough day for us, one of the crew said to me, 'Remember, we walk with you.' The kindness of that statement on a difficult day was a powerful support. I feel that through recent times I now have friends for life, the challenges we faced strengthening the friendships I already had and forging new connections along the way. In a tragedy of this scale you're all laid bare in many ways, so you see people for who they really are. Knowing who I can count on and who I really care for is a lovely part in my life now.

Honesty definitely has a presence when we come out the other side of awful, and I find that I am able to be properly honest with myself and with others. It's not that I was dishonest before, but both at work and in my personal life I've been able to have some tough conversations that others wanted to have but didn't feel able, out of a concern for upsetting people. Clarity has shown me that honesty, combined with a big dollop of good intent and a tablespoon of kindness, can oil the path for even the most difficult of conversations. Another facet of this honesty with myself is that I am aware that it's important not to blame everything on grief. I've noticed sometimes that others will say things to suggest that I get a pass of some sort because I'm grieving. I think that does hold true in the early days after a death, when we really do need to be cut some slack, but now, three years after Dara died, I can see that if I am less considerate than I could have been sometimes, that's not grief, I'm just being an idiot and I need to ask more of myself than that.

In essence, what's out the other side of awful for me is a simple life, unfettered by clutter and noise, filled with the people I like and love, doing the ordinary, everyday things that bring joy and contentment, mixed in with ambition when it comes to my work and an openness to the adventures that life may bring. There's a piece from the Bible that I would have heard many times at mass growing up, but it only properly resonates with me now. These words always come to mind when I think of my life after death and loss.

> To everything there is a season, and a time to every purpose under the heaven:
> A time to be born, a time to die;
> a time to plant, and a time to pluck up that which is planted;
> A time to kill, and a time to heal;
> a time to break down, and a time to build up;
> A time to weep, and a time to laugh;
> a time to mourn, and a time to dance;
> A time to cast away stones, and a time to gather stones together;
> a time to embrace, and a time to refrain from embracing;
> A time to get, and a time to lose;
> a time to keep, and a time to cast away;
> A time to rend, and a time to sew;
> a time to keep silence, and a time to speak;

A time to love, and a time to hate;
A time of war, and a time of peace.
Ecclesiastes 3:1-8

This now feels like my time to live. I'm fifty-one years of age, soon to be divorced, with no children, and a big hole in my heart after losing Dara, so it's a new life, one that I'm not really sure how to live, but I do know that I'll figure it out. I want to figure it out. I want to live well for myself and I want to live well for Dara, honouring this kind, funny and courageous girl who was so full of love and life in the years that she lived. I know that she would want that for me.

When I think about how I feel about losing my sister and my marriage and my dream of motherhood, like Garth Brooks I'm glad I didn't know the way it all would end. The pain of losing my sister has been like nothing I've ever known before, my world ended, and that her loss went on to have such significant impact on my physical health just added to the agony, but if I was offered the chance to avoid that pain, I wouldn't take it. Because I would have had to miss having Dara in my life and I just cannot contemplate not having known her as my sister and my friend. It has been a privilege to have her as my sibling. She brought warmth, laughter, kindness and support and loving her has always been easy. I would rather know that love and have to face the pain at her death than to have never known that love. It was a love that was about always-in-your-corner encouraging chats, laughing until our sides hurt, being there for one another when life got sticky, an honest and balanced perspective when decisions had to be made. A love that was about going to concerts and musical theatre, trips to London, Paris and New

York, finding the fun and the joy in the little things in life as well as the big. A love that goes back five decades, encompassing childhood and teenage years as well as all our adult lives, a constant and unwavering presence throughout everything we both faced in life. I have a lifetime of memories of that love and I will remember those times with greater emphasis on the joy and gratitude for having had them than on the sadness for having lost them.

Whenever we planned to meet up to go somewhere and Dara got delayed, she would phone and say that she was on her way, and when I'd say that I'd wait for her at home, she'd say, 'No, I'll meet you there, you crack on.' I can almost hear her whispering that to me now, her soft, gentle voice … 'Niamh, you crack on.' Telling me to live my life, to get out and do things again, to see people and go places and experience something other than the gut-wrenching sorrow of the past thirty-six months. Urging me to grab life with my two hands and to commit to living fully, without fear or constraint. Wanting and maybe even needing me to crack on.

So that's what I'm going to do. I'm going to bring Dara with me in my heart and in my head wherever I go and in whatever I do. I'm going to speak her name and share her values of courage, hard work and tenacity, spreading the message that we can do what we set our minds to, we can be whatever we want to be, even if the path is neither obvious nor easy. I'm going to bring into my own life her sense of kindness, her sense of adventure and her fierce loyalty to those she loved. I'm going to champion the underdog as Dara did all her life. And eat Chef tomato ketchup instead of Heinz, because that's a bit of Dara too. I'll wrap my presents with extra prettiness so that they look lovely on the outside as well as on the inside. I'll wear her RNLI beanie hat and her Chanel pearls (not at the same time) because they're the only things that fit me and I will think of her when I do. I'll push myself to exercise and look after my body because Dara was a champion at that. And no matter how busy life gets, I will always make time to connect with those I love and I'll remember and honour Dara each time I share those precious times with the people who matter to me. She may not be sitting at the table with us, but she is most definitely sitting in our hearts.

The truth about loss is that I have found the balance between remembering and living. The gifts of clarity, perspective and freedom have turned me into a better version of myself. I would give anything, anything, to be as I was and to have Dara back, but that is not an option. I'll take the gifts and do the best I can, honouring Dara and her memory in the process.

I'm going to crack on and live. I think Dara Fitz would approve of that.

AFTERWORD

DARA'S LEGACY – FINDING MEANING IN THE WRECKAGE

have mentioned Dara so many times in this book, but I haven't really talked about what kind of person she was, this girl whose loss we all feel so hard. Here, I'd like to share some of the memories and thoughts that have surfaced over the past three years and you'll get an idea of what kind of person Dara Fitz was from a sister's perspective.

My first memory in life is the day that Dara was born. My twin sister Orla and I are the eldest in the family and one day, when we were three years old, two of our uncles brought us to Herbert Park in Dublin to feed the ducks while our mother was in hospital, giving birth to Dara. Apparently, the ducks didn't get the memo that we wanted to see them and they showed no signs of wanting to come over to see us, so I decided to jump into the pond to go and pay them a visit. I was quickly hauled out of the pond by the scruff of my neck by one of the shocked uncles. Even now I can vividly remember that squelch of wet clothes, sodden garments hanging off my cold body as we walked home. I can even remember the strange feeling when they put my grandfather's dry socks on my not-completely-dry feet. Of course, I had no idea what I had done nor did I have any idea how much trouble my uncles would be in when my mother heard about what I had done! I only knew that I was disgusted at not being able to see those ducks up close. Somehow, this event became inextricably linked in my mind to the new baby who came into the house soon after my close encounter with the pond. A cherubic, bald-headed baby who smiled from the moment she arrived.

Thinking of Dara as a child, I think of a little imp. Looks-wise she was petite, like a little doll, and she had a smiley, cheeky face with freckles and dimples and big blue eyes and a head of lovely auburn hair. She had a roguish look about her and when she flashed her smile with that twinkle in her eye, you'd know that she was up to something. As a child Dara had an innocent look about her, too, a butter-wouldn't-melt sort of vibe, but we knew not to be fooled by that as she had a wicked sense of fun and got up to all sorts. When she was very young, for example, and they realised that there hadn't been a peep out of her for a while, my parents would go looking and find Dara in the bathroom, sitting on the top of the closed toilet seat, sucking the contents out of the tube of toothpaste while she ran all the taps, bringing the sink and the bath to the point of overflowing. I can remember hearing the exasperated sighs from my parents each time they realised that they had been caught out once more and that Dara had done it yet again and flooded the bathroom. Having a sense of fairness even from a young age, Dara didn't save this behaviour for our own house and she was even found in other people's houses indulging in her favourite pasttime of sucking toothpaste and flooding bathrooms. She grew out of it, of course, but now when I look back and think of our childhood, that's one of the memories that stands out and it speaks to that roguish side of Dara and makes me smile every time.

When we were growing up, Dara could never understand how it was that Orla and I were twins but she didn't have a twin. She knew that in some way we had an extra connection to one another and it bothered her that she didn't have a connection like that. When she was very small, she would often ask my mother, 'But who's my twin?' and my mother would kindly say that she would be her twin. Dara took great comfort from this and loved that she wasn't left out in the twin thing. She and my Mum developed a close bond early on and remained very close throughout Dara's life, becoming great friends when Dara went into adulthood. Dara's love for her family and her desire to be connected to those she loved was a trait that I saw from childhood right the way through to the days before she died. Above all else, she valued love and friendship and family. Indeed, looking back at Dara's last days of life, she spent time with her family, her friends and her pals from work on each of those days, chatting, laughing, doing ordinary things with the people who mattered most to her. I'm so glad for her, and for us, that those last days were filled with love and friendship.

Dara was also very much connected to living creatures other than humans and throughout our childhood a succession of goldfish, budgies and guinea pig-type animals came through our home. Dara loved these pets with a passion and when they inevitably shuffled off to the petting zoo in the sky, she would make us all traipse down to a nearby field and participate in a funeral for the much-loved animal. Woe betide anyone who sniggered, looked bored or in any way seemed like they were not taking this ceremony seriously. Dara would be on your case right away and she had a scathing look that she reserved for such offenders. Donkeys were the animal that held the most special place in Dara's heart. She had an affection for these gentle and stubborn creatures and by adopting a donkey (called Lorcan) she supported the Donkey Sanctuary in Cork and did her bit to help with the rescue of animals in need.

I paint a nice picture as we had a lovely childhood and I remember Dara being a happy child. We have a set of double cousins, by which I mean that my father and his brother married my mother and her sister, making the children of those marriages double cousins. Complicated but cool! We spent much of our childhood with them, the eight children pretty much raised together so that we feel more like siblings than cousins. Whenever we weren't at school, we all went on adventures down to the river at the bottom of the garden or trekking up the fields in the farm, a bit like Enid Blyton's *Famous Five*. Those were such innocent days we spent together, seeing ourselves as great adventurers as we headed off each morning to explore another part of the river or far-off corner of the field, eating jam sandwiches that were squashed from being in our pockets, arriving home hot, sweaty and exhausted, muddy from head to toe. When we were a little older, we helped out on the farm and creosoted fences, whitewashed walls, picked stones from the land and stacked hay bales. Those times spent alongside one another, playing and working, forged lifelong bonds. We could never have known as children that decades later these friendships would help all of us through the trauma that life would bring when Dara was ripped from our lives overnight. I see it as part of Dara's legacy that we have strengthened those connections even further.

As children we played many sports and Dara showed her kind side even when she was supposed to be competing. One day she won a rosette in a competition, but her friend didn't win anything. When she discovered that her pal was upset at not having won a prize, Dara gave her rosette to her friend so that she could have one for her wall. This was typical Dara, soft as butter and always wanting to make sure that no one was sad or lonely.

Her career brought out her steelier traits, such as ambition, determination, persistence and courage. She had always been interested in business and economics, so after school she signed up to study in this area but soon realised it was not for her. She really wanted to work with an airline, but failed to get into Aer Lingus because she, in her own words, 'hadn't worked hard enough at school'. When she was about eighteen, Dara heard an ad on the radio for a helicopter lesson. She went off to do it and after one half-hour trip, she had fallen in love with aviation. She called a halt to the business course and followed her dream of becoming a pilot, signing up for a flight training course in Knocksedan Airport in Dublin. In the days after her death, one of the men who had trained Dara in those early days told me that she drove through the passenger gates of Knocksedan, somehow getting her car in through the tiny space not meant for cars. She walked into the office and said, 'I'd like to learn about flying a helicopter', to which he replied, 'Well, you've made good start with that entrance'. She laughed and had her first helicopter lesson and that was it, she loved it. Dara Fitz was born to fly.

After much hard work and persistence, Dara qualified as the first female commercial helicopter pilot in Ireland. She set about working in the field of aviation, a striking sight hopping into her first employer's privately owned Enstrom helicopter with her long red hair and her brown leather flying jacket. In 1994 Dara began her career as a Search and Rescue pilot with the Irish Coast Guard and it's a testament to her determination, resilience and professionalism that she became the success that she did. It's a testament to her character that she also made great friends in this field. Based first in Shannon with Rescue 115, then in Waterford with Rescue 117, where she was Chief Pilot for ten years, and finally in Dublin with Rescue 116, Dara loved to fly and she loved to rescue people. The combination of the physical skill of flying and saving lives was what gave her the buzz from her job. She participated in the RTÉ fly-on-the-wall documentary entitled *Rescue 117*, when cameras followed the rescue crew as they went about their work, capturing rescues on film. In any of those interviews with Dara shown on the programme you can see in her face and hear in her voice that she absolutely loved what she did. Many people are alive today because of Dara and her colleagues and that is an incredible legacy.

Dara had no background in aviation and no contacts in the industry, but having started from zero and working her way up to being a search and rescue pilot she also had to navigate the challenging factor of being a female in a male-dominated field. In 2013 Dara and Captain Carmel Kirby, her colleague and great friend, made history when they became the first all-female flight crew to fly a rescue mission for the Irish Coast Guard, piloting the Shannon-based helicopter Rescue 115 together on shift. It's incredible to think that in the twenty-first century it is still somewhat unusual for a flight crew to be all female, but that's how it is. Indeed, I remember being at an emergency services day at Dún Laoghaire harbour, in Dublin, one summer only a few years ago when Rescue 116 landed on the pier so that the crew could show the helicopter to the public and answer questions about sea safety and talk about the work they do. Dara was one of the pilots that day, along with her colleague and friend Captain Anne Brogan. Standing in the crowd after the helicopter landed on the pier, as the crew disembarked I could hear people saying with a mixture of surprise and awe in their voices, 'The pilots are women!' When everyone walked up to the helicopter to see it and meet the crew, lots of people were fascinated with Dara and Anne.

These three women, Carmel, Dara and Anne, are ground-breaking pioneers in this industry and I'm so proud that Dara is in those ranks of people in life who push boundaries and challenge stereotypes along the way. She didn't do so because of any need to prove a point, but simply because there was a job that she wanted to do and she went out and made that happen despite it not being a common job for a woman. She didn't see an obstacle, only a challenge, and she rose to it.

Dara's legacy through her work was important and inspiring and fundraising in her name is one way that our family has sought to build on that legacy and find meaning in the tragic loss of her life cut short. The RNLI is a charity that we have nominated on many occasions when asked to choose a worthy beneficiary for funds donated for different events. The RNLI saves lives, their lifeboat crews are made up mostly of volunteers and when they get a callout these volunteers drop everything in their own lives and take to sea in all weathers and at all hours of the day and night and go to the aid of someone in trouble on the waters in or around Ireland and the UK. Even though Dara was dead when they recovered her from the water, the work of the RNLI's Achill Island Lifeboat crew meant that her body was brought back to us. Giving the bereaved a body to bury saves lives in a different way. This is why my family feel a strong connection to the RNLI and sometimes fundraise for them. If we can facilitate them helping other families as they have helped us, it does something for us too, and that's another layer of Dara's legacy.

Six months after Dara died four of her Waterford friends, including two colleagues from Rescue 117, organised a 5k charity memorial run on the runway at Waterford Airport. Winner of the runninginireland.com Short Distance Race 2017 and 2019, the Dara Fitzpatrick Memorial run has been so popular that it has been held each September since Dara died and has sold out each time. I'm biased, I know, but it's a very special run and it has a unique atmosphere, poignant but also warm and friendly. Dara was held in high regard and people come from all over the country and further afield to honour this woman they respected.

With the family's blessing, British Search and Rescue contractor Heli Operations named one of their Sea King helicopters *Dara* and they have also proposed setting up a scholarship in her name to provide Private Pilot's Licence (PPL) training for Irish women seeking to get into aviation. We will be working with them to implement this wonderful proposal. Dara was often contacted by young girls and young women who wanted to be pilots on either fixed wing aircraft or helicopters, and Dara always gave her time to talk to them about the industry and to help them wherever she could. To think that one day women who may otherwise not have been able to afford to take flying lessons will be able to do so in Dara's name feels wonderful. It's an exciting legacy.

Over her lifetime Dara did many charity events, including the New York marathon on behalf of Crumlin Children's Hospital, the Four Peaks Challenge on behalf of Focus Ireland and the Barretstown 42k walk for children living with serious illness. She used to dress up as an elf when Rescue 117 brought Santa Claus to Faithlegg Castle in Waterford to give children with special needs a memorable Christmas experience. She volunteered at the Dogs Trust for a time and adopted Lorcan the donkey from the Donkey Sanctuary. Dara wasn't a do-gooder, she just liked to do things with her time to help benefit others. It feels right that we, her family, can continue her work now that she is not here to do it herself.

Dara was one of those special people in life who never saw her own specialness. Surprisingly shy, she was big of heart and full of love for those most important people in her life. Living her life the only way she knew how, what Dara saw as normal was actually an extraordinary level of selflessness and generosity of spirit. As a sister, she was a giver, both of her time and of her advice; she was just there, no matter what. She was well able to have a good sisterly disagreement with you, but she was also well able to make up straight after and forget about it. She never held a grudge or let the sun go down on an argument. For ever in your corner, she could be a cheerleader when you needed encouragement, a drill-sergeant when you needed straight-talking and a mama when you needed consoling. Kind from the cradle to the grave, Dara couldn't pass someone who was in trouble. She was just one of life's good people. Authentic. Honest. Real. She had a wicked sense of humour and she loved to laugh, she would find the fun wherever it was, and if she couldn't find the fun, she'd make it. She worked hard and tackled anything she did with dedication, discipline and attention to detail. Accomplished in surprising pursuits, Dara could play the violin and ride a horse side-saddle. She could also feed a table of ten at a moment's notice, without breaking a sweat, and no matter where she lived her home was always a welcoming place, where you would be well fed, well watered and well looked after. For all that and for so much more, I love her.

When Dara lost her life on the night of 14 March 2017, all our lives changed for ever as we lost this beautiful girl who we had lived with, laughed with, cried with, shared with for forty-five years. I think that the best way to honour Dara is for each of us to live our best life. To have the courage to dream and to believe that it's possible to achieve that dream. To find ways around obstacles. To persist in the face of setbacks. To support and back ourselves and to support and back others. To never let perceived barriers stand in our way. During the eulogy I referred to this as 'Do a Dara', and it's about bringing some of her characteristics into our own lives to help us live our best life, remembering and honouring Dara in the process. We may never be able to speak to Dara in person again, or hug her, or share adventures with her like we always did, but this way we can keep her memory and her values alive and that is *so* important. We have to live our lives and we cannot and should not remain stuck in the past, but equally we cannot let this brave and beautiful woman fade into nothingness. She was too bright a star and she had too much left to give to let the values she stood for go to waste.

My cousin Stephen Fitzpatrick captured some of the essence of Dara's story, both professional and personal, in a poem he wrote for her month's mind. He was out of the country at the time and couldn't get back to be with us all, so on the morning of the mass he sent me a poem that he had written the day before, while he sat far from home, thinking about us all mourning for this lovely girl who had been alive and well just four weeks previously. The moment I read it, I knew this poem was special. There was heart and soul in the words. The fact that Stephen was the author made it all the more touching because he was one of the double cousins who had spent their childhood with us, having adventures at the river at the bottom of the garden. Dara was like a sister to him, which is why when he wrote about her there was admiration, respect and love threaded throughout. I read out the poem at the end of mass and it touched the hearts of everyone present.

> Banríon Na Spéire, Queen of the Sky
> A call, a calling,
> A mission, *a mercy,*
> Top cover needed, Rescue 116 heeded,
> A tragedy, a search,
> Brief hope and a prayer,
> Despair.
> A church, a piper,
> A song, a word,
> A whirl, a sound, Rescue 117 abound,
> A nod, a hover, *top cover.*
> A rest on the hill of R116,
> A mum, a daughter, a sister, a cousin, a friend,
> No matter which, it isn't the end.
> Brave to the core, her spirit will soar,
> For the Queen of the Sky was destined to fly.

After Dara died, we discovered that a few years prior to the crash the Irish Coast Guard had involved the public in the process of naming their helicopters. The name chosen by the people of Ireland for the Dublin-based helicopter, callsign Rescue 116, was *Banríon Na Spéire/Queen of the Sky*. Dara's career in aviation spanned over four decades of her life, she flew from her late teens through to her mid-forties, and twenty-three of those years she spent as a Search and Rescue pilot, flying the skies of Ireland with her colleagues as they went to the aid of those in trouble on land or sea. How fitting for Dara Fitz that the final aircraft she ever flew happened to be named *Queen of the Sky*. That was the inspiration for Stephen's poem, which was also a perfect tribute.

Dara Fitz left this world too soon, but as well as an inspiring professional legacy she left a powerful personal legacy for her family. Thanks to Dara we have a little boy who is the light of our lives and we are the light of his. It's a beautiful love between us all and Fionn, threaded with loss and sadness but filled with warmth and laughter and joy. Dara gave Fionn a loving and solid foundation in life, shaping and guiding him in his formative years, preparing him to grow into the kind, warm, sensitive, fun-loving, family-oriented child that he is now. Thanks to her generous approach to mothering, Fionn's aunties, his uncle and his grandparents have been a daily presence in his life from the start because she welcomed us all into the little family unit that she and he became. As a result, when Dara died, Fionn had a village around him to step in and raise him. Despite such loss early in his life, there's no pressure on Fionn to be anything other than whatever he wants to be. He has nothing to live up to nor does he have anyone to make proud. We know that all Dara would want for him is that he is a kind and decent human being, true to himself and considerate towards others, and at only five years of age he is already becoming those things in so many ways. I think that Dara would be very proud of the little boy that her little baby has become, and I hope that she would also be proud of herself for the legacy that she has left behind in his presence in our world.

Our own lives have been enriched beyond measure by having Dara in our world. We are a big, warm, noisy, close family, people who like each other as well as love each other and who happily spend time together. Any time spent with her son, parents, siblings and extended family was vital to Dara. When she wasn't working, the majority of her time was spent with her family, just chatting, laughing and enjoying those simple shared activities loved by us all. This was normal life for Dara, family and friends were truly valued, appreciated and precious to her. She didn't just say that, she lived that. She was always a huge driver of that strong sense of family between us, always one to suggest family nights out, weekend breaks away, or meals around the table together. She remembered birthdays and big days in our lives, was our cheerleader when we did something great and our encourager when we failed. Always and ever in our corner. Dara was fiercely loyal and as a member of her family you knew that Dara always had your back. Even in the times when you might not agree on something, you knew that she loved you with her whole heart.

Looking back at the photos from our lives together, the joy in Dara's face jumps out from the images captured when she was around her family. I can see it, for example, as she looks on with love at Fionn when he was a teeny baby, sitting on the couch propped up beside our dad while he read him a story, or as he hugged our mum 'just one more time' before he and Dara left for home after a Sunday dinner in my parents' house. That joy is there too when I see her in photos with her arms wrapped around Emer at the end of the night at a family wedding, or when she and Orla laughed at themselves dressed up as elves at Christmas with Rescue 117. Or when I see her standing tucked in beside our brother, Johnny, with her arm linked through his as they get ready for a night out, she looks so happy. I see that joy when I look at photos of her among our extended family of our double cousins and their children, singing along to one of the many *Happy Birthday* moments that we all shared. I see it too when I called her name and captured her beautiful smile with my camera when she turned back to look at me when the two of us were on a trip of a lifetime to New Zealand.

Dara loved her family and I think she would be heart-warmed to see how the members of her family have turned towards one another in the face of tragedy, supporting one another, allowing for differences in how we grieve and appreciating the role we each take as we navigate this new family life without her. The bond we've had throughout our lives has been strengthened immeasurably in the wake of Dara's death, as we pulled together to get everyone through all we've had to face since the night she disappeared from our lives, surviving the horror of that night and of the days, weeks, months and years since. It's fair to say that Dara's presence is threaded throughout both our family connection when she was alive and our family unity after she died. She leaves a powerful legacy in that regard.

The people we have become since Dara's death is also part of her legacy, we seem to be calmer, more patient, more fearless. In how she lived her life but also in how she conducted herself in her final moments of life, Dara role-modelled courage better than anyone I know and I think that as her family we have subconsciously honoured her by being brave on the occasions when fear has shown up. We have become more composed in the face of fear. How could we not face down our own fears and keep going when we know what Dara went through that night? She lived through what was surely her worst fear and she may not have survived, but she did not flinch. She fought, she kept going, she gave it her all. By her courage and her actions she gave herself an incredible chance and to me her bravery and effort feel like they are the standard now, so I ask more of myself in those big moments in life and I see others in my family and extended family doing the same thing.

Losing Dara means we all have a true appreciation for the moment that we're in right now. I notice that none of us seems to look too far into the future, nor do we need anything else other than the people who matter in our lives and spending time with them. Things mean nothing. People mean everything. Life has become quite simple in many ways and there's a gift in discovering this sense of appreciation for life while you still have time left to live. The world is so fast-paced, so busy, so full, and it's wonderful to feel that you are a step removed from that, largely unaffected by the expectations to read everything, watch everything, keep up to date with everything. Instead, part of Dara's legacy to us is that we are able to live peacefully, enjoying the ordinariness of the present moment, a gift that many may not ever unwrap.

We also have a model of a life lived to the full, because there were no half measures for Dara Fitz. She took the life that she had and she lived it completely, with all of her heart and all of her head. Never afraid to think for herself or to do things that scared her, she lived not in the safe confines of comfort but in the rich reward of vision, ambition and hard work. Managing somehow to be as beautiful on the inside as she was on the outside, Dara lit up a room with her warmth and kindness even more than with her beauty. She is the girl I would have wanted as my friend if she had not been my sister.

When I think of Dara now, I think of the girl who laughed so fully that her nose would crinkle and the laughter reached her eyes. I think of the girl who said birthday as 'bert-day' and we, her siblings, teased her mercilessly for it. I think of a girl who loved her home family and her work family and for whom her friends were the family that she chose for herself. I think of a big heart and a big smile. I think of adventures from childhood all the way through to adulthood, the little days and the big days shared. I think of a world that is a better place for her having been in it. And I feel grateful.

My hope now is that Dara is resting in peace, safe in the knowledge that she made a significant impact on the world both personally and professionally. I hope that wherever she is, she knows that in our hearts and actions we carry her with us every single day, that her values live on through all of us who love her, and that as long as even one of her family is alive, so will her memory and her legacy be kept alive.

I hope that as Dara rests in peace we can all live in peace, that we can carry the pain of her loss with courage and dignity, finding that balance between remembering and living. My heart is full as I observe how my family have stepped up and handled all that life has asked of us in the wake of Dara's death, no instruction book, no teacher, just finding our foothold as we walk this rocky path of grief, moving from loss and pain towards healing and hope. And despite all the pain, I imagine that my family share my conviction that I would rather love Dara as fully as I do and feel this pain as I grieve after her death than to not have loved her with such heart when she lived and feel less pain now.

Dara Fitz, loving you has been and continues to be a privilege and I feel sure that, over time, the joy of remembering the ways in which we have loved one another all through our life together will continue to be a welcome comfort in the pain of your absence.

Sleep well, my sister, my friend.

ACKNOWLEDGEMENTS

Commissioning Editor, Deirdre Nolan: Deirdre, you saw something in me that I never knew was there. I knew it was you I wanted to trust with my personal story of loss. You have been kind, patient, helpful and encouraging throughout this process, always understanding when grief robbed my capacity to write. We never managed a meeting over two years without both shedding tears, and knowing that this book matters as much to you as it does to me has been so important. I hope that the finished book is all that you wanted it to be. Thank you is not enough.

Managing Editor, Catherine Gough: Catherine, you oversaw the editorial process with a calm head, a clear vision and a firm hold on our deadlines. With kindness and gentleness you pushed me all the way through the editing stage, not batting an eyelid when my initial efforts at meeting deadlines were what we eventually termed 'a bad dress rehearsal'! Your unwavering belief powered me on to dig deep and find my best to get the job done. Thank you for everything.

Editor, Rachel Pierce, Verba Editing House: Rachel, at the time of writing this, you and I have not met, yet I feel I know you so well. We've worked together intensely, emails back and forth from early in the morning to the early hours of the morning. It was you who showed me how to bring the reader into my story, how to get my message across. You brought out the best in me, a best that I never knew was there and I flourished under your warm, clear, inspiring tutelage. Thank you for taking such good care of my story and for helping me do justice for Dara in the telling of hers.

The Gill Family: to **Teresa Daly**, Marketing & Communications Manager, **Ellen Monnelly**, Senior Publicist and **Paul Neilan**, Sales Manager, thank you all for your support, guidance and preparation in bringing this book to the reader. Also, Teresa, for your beautiful vision which provided the basis for the cover design. I also know that there is a large team working for my book in Gill and I'm grateful to each and every person, even if we haven't met yet.

Graham Thew Design: Graham, I only had to view one potential book cover because yours was the first one shown to me and I knew immediately that it was my cover. Your beautiful image captures the essence of grief with the aloneness of that difficult journey and the rays of hope shining through the dark days. I am proud to have it as the visual image of my story of loss.

Jane Russell, Outlaw Management: Jane, for being beside me from the start of this process and for knowing as soon as I did that Gill Books was the right fit and for your advice and support always.

My family, the Fitzpatricks: to my father John, mother Mary, twin sister Orla, sister Emer, brother Johnny and nephew Fionn. I struggle to find the words for you lot. Since Dara died and our lives changed for ever, each of you has handled all that has been thrown at us with dignity and courage. We have stuck together and weathered the hurricane, even though we had neither equipment nor experience. If I could walk the world over and choose my family, I would choose you guys. I love you all and I'm proud to call you my family.

My close family, the Fitz Clan: to my cousins Stephen and Rosemary Fitzpatrick and their respective spouses, Orla Murphy and Daragh Clarke; my cousin Andrew Fitzpatrick; my aunt and uncle Gay and Peter Fitzpatrick. You all feel like siblings to me and together with my family we make up the big, noisy, lively, fun-loving Fitz Clan. The way in which you have tightened in around us as we learn to live with the loss of Dara has been heart-warming and life-affirming, you walk beside us every step of the way. I know that you love and miss Dara as we do, yet you mind us despite your own grief. Thank you.

Thanks also to my sister-in-law, Olga Harrington, and the Harrington clan: Barry, Bernice, David, Amy, Aileen and Jo. Your constant love and support have served to cement our mutual affection, respect and friendship.

My extended family: my cousins Fiona and Eoin Fitzpatrick; the Duggans from Kilkenny and the Fitzpatricks from Dublin and Cavan; Alan and Michael Murphy. Thanks to you all for your love and friendship.

My friends: grievers make awful friends. For a long time, I wasn't present as a friend. But my friends have waited, without pressure or judgement. They have seen me at my worst and they love me anyway, and me them. In this group I include: Nichola Forrest, Dr Giles Warrington, Dr Eleanor Galvin, Dr Ciara Losty, Sarah Dunphy, Cáit O'Neill†, Dr Kate Kirby, Triona Coughlan, Bill O'Shea, Ciara and Margo O'Driscoll, Liz McDonagh, Michelle Pearson, Regina Quinn, Jean Hughes, Derek Mulvey, Patricia Murphy, Ciaran Hickey, Maureen Brennan, Pamela Blake and the Today FM crew, Liam Griffin, Fergal O'Donnell and Stephen Rochford.

I also received invaluable professional support from Clinical Psychologist Dr Eddie Murphy, Chartered Clinical Psychologist Mark Smyth, Dr Mary O'Kane, Dr Ray O'Neill and Margaret Dunne. I will be for ever grateful for your support and guidance.

My best pal Tara O'Shea: from day one, you dropped your own life and stepped into our life to help. In the days leading up to Dara's funeral, you were rarely seen without a pot of tea in one hand and a pot of coffee in the other – earning yourself the nickname 'Tara Two Kettles' – ensuring all visitors were looked after. Since then you have been a constant support to me. In the early days, sneaking in to put food in my fridge, or driving me to appointments and doing my errands while you waited for me to be finished. As time went on, dragging me round the block for a walk or wordlessly passing the tissues when I cried silently at both the sad and the happy scenes at the cinema. You are the best 'best pal' I could ask for and I can never thank you enough.

Neil Delamere: Neil, from the first day we sat opposite each other in the studio in Today FM, it was clear that you are sincere, kind, compassionate and insightful, so when the day came for me to return to work on your show after Dara's death, I knew that I was in safe hands. It was an important moment on my grief journey. My warm and sincere thank you for that and for everything.

Blacksod Lighthouse Keeper, Vincent Sweeney: Vincent, you listened to your instinct and experience and raised the alarm early and were the first link in the chain that brought Dara back home to us. Thank you seems so inadequate; my family is indebted to you.

Crew of Rescue 118 (Sligo): Captain Mike Scott, Co-Pilot Paraic Slattery, Winch Operator John McShane, Winchman Conal McCarron. You had to make that awful journey back from far out at sea to search for four of your own. In that search, you located Dara in the water. You became the second link in the chain of people who brought Dara back to us. Thank you.

Crew of RNLI's Achill Island Lifeboat: Dave Curtis (Coxswain), Michael O'Hara (Mechanic), Sean Ginnelly (Navigator), Declan Corrigan (Crewman), Patrick Kilbane (Crewman), Joe Casey (Crewman). Called in by R118, in changing seas with significant swell and in the dark of night, you worked under appalling conditions to recover Dara from the water. You then minded Dara with a gentleness that was above and beyond duty. In addition, you met with me and shared details of the night, having to relive your own experience in the process. For that and for everything, thank you.

Crew of RNLI's Ballyglass Lifeboat: John Walshe (Coxswain), Allen Murray (Mechanic), James Mangan (Navigator), Matthew Togher (Crew), Frankie Geraghty (Crew), John Heston (Crew) and Paul Carlin (Crew). Like your colleagues on board the Achill Island Lifeboat, you got out of your beds in the dead of night to join the search. For that and for all you do, thank you.

Crew of Rescue 115 (Shannon): Captain Mick Meally, Co-Pilot Captain Carmel Kirby, Winch Operator Eamonn Ó Broin, Winchman Phil Wrenn. You airlifted your colleague and friend from the guardianship of the lifeboat to lay her down in the helicopter she had previously flown in your presence. Then you brushed aside offers of help and carried Dara into the hospital yourselves, staying with her afterwards so that she was not alone. I am eternally grateful. You also took the time to speak to me about that night and, in doing so, you filled the gaps in my mind. You are brave and kind and I hope that life repays that to you in spades.

Captain Mark Donnelly and Aircraft Engineer Eoin Murphy: you could have declined that job of delivering the news that would change our lives for ever; instead you stepped up for a colleague and friend with a courage, kindness and selflessness that as long as I live, I will *never* forget. Thank you both. Mark, as liaison with my family, you continue to be there for us and with us. You wait patiently and kindly until I stop crying the choking tears that halt our conversation each time you explain the phrases and terms in official reports and you respond on our behalf to ensure we are well represented in all decisions. I know that Dara valued your friendship over the years and I have no doubt that she would value your contribution to our family as a continuation of that friendship. I can never thank you enough, but I do thank you, always.

Garda Paul Flood (FLO), Dublin: Paul, you were one of the lifelines for our family as we navigated our way through those early hours, days and weeks after Dara's death. To step in and be by the side of strangers while they go through the darkest times of their life takes a special kind of person, with a particular skillset, and you have both. Calm, knowledgeable and full of practical advice, you were a great fit for our family and your presence and input has been of immense help. Thank you.

Garda Sinéad Barrett (FLO), Mayo: Sinéad, you were my first port of call for information coming from the authorities to my family, and whatever information you had to deliver, you did it with clarity, composure and compassion. My gratitude will last a lifetime.

Devine's Chauffeur Service: tasked with transporting my family to Mayo to see Dara for the first time, John, Clive and Paul arrived to bring us on that difficult journey. You all approached us that day with sensitivity and kindness. We could not have been more fortunate in the company we got. Sincerely, thank you.

The team at Mayo University Hospital, Castlebar: after a long journey from Dublin, we arrived at the mortuary, exhausted, nervous and shocked. Duty Manager Fran Power and Chaplain

Fr Sean Cunningham helped us navigate those difficult moments of seeing Dara for the first time. Sincere thanks to you both and to the wider hospital team for how we were looked after at that time.

Captain Cathal Oakes and Captain Ciarán Ferguson: you drove to be with Dara in the mortuary, minding her until we got there. Then you stayed with us, sharing memories, helping us absorb the shock of that most awful day. Thank you both immensely. Cathal, you also delivered a eulogy at Dara's funeral, you were with me on that first trip to Blacksod, and you were with me when I experienced the initial sight of Black Rock Island. You were a great friend to Dara during her life and you have extended that to support her family after her death. Thank you.

Captain Tony O'Mahony: Tony, I never knew you properly beforehand, but you were also with me on that first trip to Blacksod. You came with me to those first official meetings with authorities in Mayo, so that I wouldn't be alone. You stood with me on the beach where Dara's helmet was found. You accompanied my family on the trip to the crash site and helped us make sense of the information we received while there. You may not always talk as loudly or as much as others, but when you do, it is always worth listening and I have learned a lot from your wise words and insightful perspectives. Thank you.

Captain Brian Fitzgerald, Commander of Irish Naval Ship the LÉ _Eithne_: Brian, you gave families an opportunity to visit the crash site and, from a personal perspective, it helped to see close-up the seas in which Dara died. Your crew were welcoming, kind and helpful. Thank you all.

Search crews: significant thank you to all parties who participated in the search, one of the largest ever in the history of the State: members of An Garda Síochána, the Irish Air Corps, the RNLI, the Army, the Navy, Civil Defence, the Irish Coast Guard, the Marine Institute, the Commissioners of Irish Lights, who worked alongside fishermen, volunteer divers and locals in combing the region surrounding the crash site from the air, sea and land. Thanks to the on-scene co-ordinator of the shoreline searches, Michael Hurst, Officer-in-Charge of the Ballyglass Coast Guard Unit, and his counterparts in the other agencies for their work in co-ordinating the search.

Crews at the National Maritime College of Ireland (NMCI): you took Dara through her dunker training less than two weeks before the crash of R116. In our final conversation she spoke about that dunker experience, so I know that it was in her mind and I suspect it played a big part in her getting out of the helicopter, which led to her being brought home to us. For all that you taught her, thank you.

Irish Coast Guard crews: after so many journeys in the helicopter with her over the years, it was fitting that it was you who carried Dara on her final journey into the church and crematorium. Thank you to all who were part of the celebration of Dara's life in different ways that day.

Those who work in search and rescue are the bravest of the brave, you run towards danger while the rest of us run away from it. You are human beings before you are engineers, winch crew or pilots. You are sons, daughters, brothers, sisters, fathers, mothers, friends. You are people first. To support my family in the face of your own devastating loss is a measure of the kind of people you men and women are. Thank you. You and your families are always in my thoughts. Particular mention to: Captain Mark Donnelly, Captain Carmel Kirby, Winch Operator Neville Murphy, Captain Cathal Oakes, Captain Ciarán Ferguson, Captain Tony O'Mahony, Winch Operator John Manning, Captain Anne Brogan, Captain Lee Bennett, Captain Barry O'Connor, Winchman Conal McCarron, Winch Operator Neil McAdam, Winch Operator Adrian O'Hara, Captain Jim Kirwan, Avionics Engineer Liam Hannon, Aircraft Engineer Eoin Murphy and Winch Operator Eamonn Ó Broin.

Dunmore East RNLI: thank you to the RNLI's Dunmore East Lifeboat crews for organising the beautiful wreath-laying ceremony and to Neville Murphy for inviting me to lay Dara's wreath myself. That day stands out in my mind even now; there was healing in those hours. Thank you to the crew of Rescue 117 for the flypast: Captain Martyn Rayner, Captain Lee Bennett, Winch Operator Dermot Molloy and Winchman Sean Jennings.

Fr Andrew O'Sullivan, PP Sandyford, Kilternan and Glencullen, and Colliers Funeral Directors: thank you to Fr Andrew O'Sullivan and to Stephen Collier and team for your kindness and professionalism when helping us to arrange Dara's funeral. We did Dara justice. Thank you.

Authorities: thanks to those who carried out the necessary and difficult investigations with sensitivity and care after the crash of Rescue 116. I include the Air Accident Investigation Unit (AAIU) team and the coroner for North Mayo, Dr Eleanor Fitzgerald.

Contributors: thanks also to the priests who concelebrated Dara's funeral mass; Olive Treacy and Claire Fitzgerald in the parish office; piper Sergeant Anthony Byrne; the Glencullen Choir, led by Renee Roe; singer Rebecca Murphy; the church sacristan of St Patrick's Mary Mahon; the stewards organised by the Glencullen Graveyard Committee; and the gardaí on duty. To these and to all others for the work behind the scenes, thank you for your contribution to that most important day.

The crew of Rescue 117: Captain Ronan O'Flanagan, Co-pilot Jason O'Flynn, Winch Operator Ken Skelly, Winchman Sean Jennings. You would not have heard it, but there was a collective gasp from the crowd when Dara's colleagues and the aircraft that she had flown showed their respect with a bow towards her coffin. It was beautiful, poignant and very much appreciated. Thank you.

Organisers of the Dara Fitzpatrick Memorial Run: a warm thank you to Waterford brothers Ray Leahy and Kim Leahy and Captain Barry O'Connor and Winch Operator Neville Murphy. When Dara died you lost a friend and you channelled your grief into organising a charity run in her name. For the time, effort, detail and love you four put into this run, I say a heartfelt thank you from my family and from me.

Community support: thank you to the community of friends and neighbours belonging to each member of my family. You bravely came to our door when you heard the awful news, you hugged us, stayed with us, took care of the practical jobs such as making tea, minding Fionn and running errands. Food was supplied, refreshments were delivered, ovens were heated up, glasses were polished, napkins were folded. You had families to take care of, businesses to run, employers to answer to, yet you were there for us. None of us will ever forget the kindness shown to us then and since. We are fortunate to call you our friends and neighbours. Thank you.

Thank you to all who sent letters, cards, emails, text messages or who made phone calls to offer condolence or support. Your efforts were greatly appreciated.

Thank you to the aviation community – pilots, cabin crew, air traffic control. Your respect for Dara as a pilot and a professional in your own field has been a source of comfort. Also to the wider emergency services family; we have felt minded by you in so many ways since Dara died.

Thank you to Sandra Mongan, Declan Geoghegan and Keith Devaney for all the support after Dara's death. You were kind, compassionate and helpful in equal measure.

Thank you to the people in the community of Eachléim, who set up their community centre as a meeting place, a place for searchers to rest or eat in the aftermath of the crash. Approximately seventy local women staffed the centre seven days a week, with an estimated 10,000 meals served over the six-week period of the search. Quite rightly, the community of Eachléim received a People of the Year Award in 2018 for their outstanding contribution to the search operation. The old Irish term *meitheal* describes a community coming together to respond to a need in the locality; thanks to John Gallagher and Máire Ní Ruadhain and to all who contributed to the meitheal.

Since Dara died, we have been surrounded by a wall of compassion and kindness. As my mother says, it's been like a hug from the whole of Ireland. Thank you to each and every person who has shown kindness and concern to my family in the wake of Dara's death and to those who remember Dara as time marches on. *Go raibh míle maith agaibh go léir.*